School Choice and Student Well-Being

Other books by Anthony Kelly

BENCHMARKING FOR SCHOOL IMPROVEMENT

DECISION MAKING USING GAME THEORY

THE INTELLECTUAL CAPITAL OF SCHOOLS

School Choice and Student Well-Being

Opportunity and Capability in Education

Anthony Kelly

First published 2007 by
PALGRAVE MACMILLAN
Houndmills, Basingstoke, Hampshire RG21 6XS and
175 Fifth Avenue, New York, N.Y. 10010
Companies and representatives throughout the world

PALGRAVE MACMILLAN is the global academic imprint of the Palgrave
Macmillan division of St. Martin's Press, LLC and of Palgrave Macmillan Ltd.
Macmillan® is a registered trademark in the United States,
United Kingdom and other countries. Palgrave is a registered trademark in
the European Union and other countries.

ISBN-13: 978–0–230–54926–5   hardback
ISBN-10: 0–230–54926–8   hardback

This book is printed on paper suitable for recycling and made from fully
managed and sustained forest sources. Logging, pulping and manufacturing
processes are expected to conform to the environmental regulations of the
country of origin.

A catalogue record for this book is available from the British Library.

Library of Congress Cataloging-in-Publication Data

Kelly, Anthony, 1957–
  School choice and student well-being: opportunity and capability in
    education/Anthony Kelly.
      p. cm.
  Includes bibliographical references and index.
  ISBN 0-230-54926-8 (alk. paper)
  1. School choice. 2. Education–Social aspects. I. Title.

LB1027.9.K45 2007
  379.1'11—dc22   2007022488

10   9   8   7   6   5   4   3   2   1
16 15 14 13 12 11 10 09 08 07

Printed and bound in Great Britain by
Antony Rowe Ltd, Chippenham and Eastbourne

To Ann, Jane & Colum

Contents

List of Tables and Figures   x

Preface   xi

Acknowledgements   xv

**Part I School Choice, Globalisation and the
Commodification of Education: Choosers and Losers**

1 School Choice: An Overview   **3**

Neo-liberalism and the political debate   3
Advantages and disadvantages to school choice   8
Private and faith schooling   13
Choice, effectiveness and motivation   17
Social class and risk   23
Choice and geographical location   26
Choice and segregation   28

2 School Choice and Transition   **33**

School admissions policies   33
Factors which influence individual and
group parental choice   36
Choice and the psychodynamic of moving
from primary to secondary school   45
Gender and the transition to secondary school   49

3 School Choice and Globalisation   **53**

Global trade agreements and their effect on education   53
The changing agency of the state in education   56
The rise of 'performativity' in the United Kingdom   65
Between regulation and the free market:
demarchical control   68
Between regulation and the free market:
mobility and the leisure curriculum   70
Globalisation and school improvement   71
Globalisation, managing change and
teacher professionalism   73

4   School Choice and Marketisation   79

The General Agreement on Trade in Services   79
The emergence of state-market partnerships   82
The calculus of choice and risk   85
Hierarchies and local markets in schooling   93
Voter support for marketisation and
competition in education   95

5   School Choice, Competition and Performance   100

Quasi-markets in education: competition
and cooperation   100
The impact of marketisation on student
attainment   105
The dynamics of local competition   111
Headteachers' perceptions of competition
and student attainment   112
Competition and curriculum diversity   114

6   Actualising Choice in Schools and Communities   118

Assumptions about choice and school
organisations   118
Education triage and school markets   122
School choice and school closure   124
The practice of school headship in the
education marketplace   125
School choice and the role of headteachers   128
Local education authorities and regulation   129
The self-selection of pupils between schools   132
Schools and employers under marketisation   134

**Part II   Adapting Sen's Theory of Capability to
School Choice**

7   Well-Being and Capability   141

Social choice   143
The meaning of utility   146
Well-being and advantage   147
Commodity and capability   148

8 **Utility and Functionings**   152

   Approaches to utility   152
   Functionings   155
   Valuation   158
   The measurement of well-being   159

9 **Aggregation and Evaluation**   163

   The aggregation of well-being   163
   The Impossibility problem   164
   The problem of using the same valuation function   166
   The evaluation of advantage   167

10 **Asset-Mapping**   170

   Freedom and agency in school communities   172
   Deficiency and empowering assessments   175

Notes   179

References and Further Reading   192

Index   233

List of Tables and Figures

Tables

Table 1.1   Percentage of African-American pupils in
United States Catholic and public schools   10

Table 2.1   Most frequently used admissions criteria   34

Table 2.2   Percentage of secondary schools in England and
Wales selecting a proportion of pupils by ability   35

Table 2.3   Reasons for school choice   38

Table 2.4   Parental satisfaction with schools in Alberta, Canada   42

Table 2.5   Reasons given by parents for rejecting schools   43

Table 5.1   Comparison of results by sector   109

Figures

Figure 5.1   Low levels of attainment: the percentage
attaining one or more GCSE grade G or better   107

Figure 5.2   High levels of attainment: the percentage
attaining five or more GCSE grade C or better   108

Preface

Amartya Sen, Nobel prize-winning economist, constructs the following scenario to demonstrate the absurdity of public choice theory. A stranger in a town asks a bystander, *'Can you direct me to the railway station?'* *'Certainly'*, answers the native, pointing in the opposite direction, towards the post office, *'and would you post this letter for me on your way?'* *'No problem'* says the stranger, resolving to open it and steal its contents! The story is quoted by Linda McQuaig in her book *All You Can Eat* (2001). The idea that selfishness by individuals in a marketplace necessarily results in the public good being served is false: the letter is never posted; the railway station never found; there is nothing of value in the letter.

So it is with schooling, says the Left. The state must purge the education marketplace of choice because choice is not about freedom but selfishness, which serves ill the common good. In the United Kingdom, the near monopoly of state-funded schooling is traditionally seen as the last stand of collective welfarism, despite an emerging centre-Left consensus that is moving public service provision towards a mixed economy; from initial abhorrence, via indifference, to advocacy. In the United States, in the collective psyche at least, public schooling is similarly viewed as a counterbalance to unfettered individualism. It is a vestige of the pilgrim conscience perhaps, but ironically research there suggests that individuals for whom public education is a necessity are also those best served by its alternatives. Thus is a tension emerging in developed countries between the rhetoric of the public good and the actualité of everyday personal disadvantage, or as Chomsky would say, between 'doctrine and reality'.

The Right also proclaims its dissent, positing that new mixed economies in schooling are destined to failure because choice programmes do not go far enough. A mixed economy defers to historical passions on the Left, they say, whereby failing state schools continue to be supported by the public purse without any realistic expectation of improvement. For disadvantaged communities, such half-hearted policies are absurd. Having a choice between a poor school and a good school, whereas previously there was only a good school, does not increase well-being; neither does having a choice between three poorly performing schools as opposed to two. And what use is the freedom to attend a school away from home for those without the wherewithal to organise family life around travel?

Fundamentally, school choice is about freedom, which is a complex notion, unlike marketisation, which is merely instrumental. Some freedoms can be surrendered in order to enjoy greater ones, and some can be surrendered for the common good. The difficulty for both advocates and opponents of school choice is that the debate about freedom has not been had in the rush to action by concerned governments facing the prospect of societal and economic decline as a result of inadequate public schooling. Most education policy reforms in developed countries over the last 15 years have involved efforts to establish an education market because (it is claimed) the exigencies of competition naturally make public school systems more responsive to the needs of students, parents and communities:

> Since 1997, there have been two stages of reform. In the first, we corrected the underinvestment ... In the second stage, essentially begun in 2001, we added another dimension. We started to open the system up to new influences and introduced the beginnings of choice and contestability ... We are now at the crucial point where the reforms can be taken to their final stage ... In both the NHS and in education, there will in one sense be a market. The patient and the parent will have much greater choice.
>
> (Tony Blair, speech at 10 Downing Street,
> 24 October 2005)

The theoretical assumption here is that a free market can more effectively provide the range and quality of education demanded by parents and needed by students, and lead to upward pressure on standards. Public schools are thus forced to operate on Darwinian principles: those that attract 'customers' and best utilise resources thrive; the weak and the unpopular go to the wall. To opponents of school choice programmes, the notion that education can be treated as a commodity that is tradable using commercial rubrics is unacceptable. While understanding that there might be some benefit to be derived from a degree of competition, opponents are concerned that access and equity across the social divide is necessarily jeopardised by market forces. Schools are not supermarkets, they say, and education is not a commercial product but a basic human right.

The doctrinal arguments for and against greater school choice translate well between cultures and across oceans. Whether tacitly accepted or formally proscribed, school choice is everywhere understood in the political shibboleths of both Left and Right. The Right says choice is of itself good; the Left says it disadvantages the already disadvantaged. The subtleties are a nice mixture of erudition and hypocrisy: to paraphrase Chesterton, it is the function of Progressives to make mistakes and the function of Conservatives to prevent those mistakes being rectified.

There are those, of course, who take neither committed view and who support an *argumentum ad temperantiam* – a 'third way', if you will – though it seems wrong somehow to benefit from public education and yet remain undecided or indifferent to its plight. Some have always had the facility to choose schools; what is new today is the desire among parents and policymakers to extend to the public sector what has long been available in the private sector. Yet even that putative dichotomy is an over-simplification. England's fee-paying schools, for example, are full of students who cannot afford to be there; and many middle-class families cannot avail of 'free' public education because they cannot play the 'postcode lottery' that would enable their children to attend good schools.

Irrespective of the political debate, it can reasonably be claimed that our understanding of school choice and its impact on student well-being is under-theorised. Research is inconclusive in respect of the theoretical complexities involved in the way choice is offered, understood and actualised within families, and the way society and students are thought to benefit from it. In part, this has led not to more debate, but to less contestation. Adapting the ancient Greek concept of *parrhesia* (παρρησίαν) as a desirable model for the academic as critic means speaking truthfully and unflatteringly to policymakers and powerful interest groups out of a sense of duty, rather than persuasively and from self-interest, even if that means abandoning the quest for consensus. In keeping with that spirit, this book attempts to develop a more open and complex theoretical framework for understanding school choice and its relationship to student well-being. It comes in two parts. The first part is an exegesis of research on choice, globalisation and the commodification of education. More than a thousand research papers, books and monographs were reviewed, and about half have found their way into the finished text. Chapter 1 is an overview of school choice and its associated political debate; chapter 2 concentrates on secondary school admissions and transition; chapters 3 and 4 focus on globalisation and marketisation, respectively; chapter 5 considers the dynamics of competition and cooperation in a quasi-market; and chapter 6 reports on research on actualising and leading choice in schools and communities. The second part of the book adapts Sen's theory of capability to choice in schooling: chapter 7 describes the notions of well-being, advantage and capability; chapter 8 describes various approaches to utility and the measurement of well-being; chapter 9 focuses on the aggregation of well-being and the evaluation of advantage; and chapter 10 describes asset-mapping, freedom and agency in school communities.

The provenance of Sen's capability approach in economics is rooted in its attempt to understand poverty, but even in that paradigm Sen included educational attainment as one of his three indicators of capability. In every sense – economically, politically and socially – education impacts on the ability of people to participate in society, and one of the outcomes of Sen's work was to shift the emphasis away from material well-being to the broader concepts of freedom and choice, without which a person cannot have a good quality of life. Of course, there is no claim here that adapting Sen's approach to school choice of itself offers a simple answer to the all-important question of how best to run schools so that no one is disadvantaged, but it does make more realistic our theoretical framework and hopefully adds a little to our understanding.

Acknowledgements

Thanks to Michael Erben, Nick Foskett and my colleagues at Southampton. Thanks also to my friends in ICSEI for their support and camaraderie: Mel Ainscow, Panayiotis Angeleides, Maggie Balshaw, Chris Chapman, Paul Clarke, Bert Creemers, Stephan Huber, John MacBeath and Mel West. Thanks to Prof. Des Carney, Dublin, and to Amartya Sen, of course, whose unique insights have both inspired and informed this endeavour.

Part I School Choice, Globalisation and the Commodification of Education: Choosers and Losers

1
School Choice: An Overview

Neo-liberalism and the political debate

The facility for parents and pupils to choose their secondary schools free from government constraint appears to make manifest, in some as yet ill-defined way, the spirit of twenty-first century socio-economic freedom. This *zeitgeist* is increasingly popular in a growing number of developed countries, though it has not been proved beyond doubt to raise pupil achievement (OECD, 1994; Glenn & De Groof, 2002; Holmes *et al.*, 2003). In the United States, the growing number of Charter Schools being founded by socially advantaged parents is creating a public school system *ipso facto* more responsive to parental demands (Wells *et al.*, 1999; Gill *et al.*, 2001), and in the United Kingdom, most education legislation enacted since 1988 has been similarly geared.

Charter Schools are public, non-faith schools created by contract between an 'operator', such as a group of parents or a private school acting *pro bono*, and a sponsor, such as a local school authority. United States federal and state law allows various education stakeholders – parents, teachers, private schools and public organisations – to set up Charter Schools. They receive public funds but operate outside the normal regulatory system, thus offering operators more freedom in how money received from the public purse is spent (Molnar, 2006). Some aim specifically to accommodate socially disadvantaged students or those with special educational needs; others aim to develop specialist curricula. The public purse funds students *per capita* to attend Charter Schools in the same way it does students attending ordinary public schools, and additionally maintains the public buildings in which these schools are usually housed if they are not maintained by local universities or

3

commercial companies. In Stambach's (2001: 200) view, Charter Schools, as alternatives within the public school system,

> condense a range of views about parental involvement in public education. On the one hand, they represent some parents' desires to have more control over their children's education . . . On the other hand, [they] reflect the logical extension of an education system that is dedicated to reaching every student individually.

Most research on Charter Schools has focused on organisational structures; little work has been done on their impact on schooling and society generally. The neo-liberal view of education, underpinned by the desire of middle-class parents to have the freedom to use their resources to choose a school for their children, has contributed both to the emergence of market-responsive schools and to the paucity of research on their wider societal impact. Advocates of choice claim that competition both improves the quality of education provision and increases parental involvement, though some studies have shown that it may lead to increased social segregation (Karsten, 1994; McArthur *et al.*, 1995; Bagley, 1996; Goldhaber, 2000). Competition between schools creates winning and losing institutions, and aspirant parents naturally seek out the former (Whitty & Edwards, 1998; Gorard, 1999). Poor schools are shut down – which is the whole point – and informed parents transfer their children to better schools, perhaps at a cost to the underprivileged in society and to society's fabric. In such circumstances, rather than seeing local schools as places where a variety of curricula and abilities coexist, parents send their children to institutions that have successful track records, which further isolates those children who have to (or choose to) 'go local'. More insidiously, say critics, pro-choice government policies and financing are intended to force low-income children to become compliant.

Thus political philosophy enters the education debate over school choice. Choosing a school is something more than mere pragmatism. Many commentators (Ball, 1990; Ranson, 1990; Bush *et al.*, 1993; Bridges & McLaughlin, 1994) see it as a political struggle between social democratic liberalism, represented traditionally in the United States by the Democratic Left and in the United Kingdom by the Labour Party, and neo-liberalism, represented in the United States by the Republican Right and in the United Kingdom by the Conservative Party (and some would say New Labour). Others (Jeynes, 2000) see this Left-Right bipolarity as a contrived over-simplification; that the debate is as much between the vested interests of those who work in public education, like teachers and academics, and those who depend on it to reach their material goals or realise their social ambitions, like employers, pupils and parents. Certainly it is the case in the United Kingdom that many of the reforms relating to school choice intro- duced by the neo-liberal Conservative governments of 1979–97 were con- tinued and extended by successive New Labour governments.

The claim that school choice harms principally the underprivileged and lays bare the fabric of society is not without dispute either. Those in favour of it claim that choice offers the best way of escaping the poverty trap for those in it, generating opportunities for marginalised families and creating better schools for everyone as a result of competition. Without freedom of choice in schooling, the argument goes, there would be 'cul- tural ossification' (Kirkpatrick, 1990). Others, like Finn (1999), argue that school-choice programmes provide working-class families only with enough education to perpetuate their 'domesticity and powerlessness', and that such programmes serve to keep working-class children trapped in working-class jobs. Choice advocates, in response, suggest that such recusant, left-wing orthodoxy is what makes reform of public schooling both necessary and difficult (Boulding, 1973), and is in any case incon- sistent with the Left's support for pluralism and choice in other aspects of life. Critics rejoin by saying that pro-choice policies promote 'the few over the many' and a culture of subservience among the weak:

> The rule of the day in too many US schools is . . . merely to comply, to accept, to do as told. . . . The arguments for school choice . . . are just the most recent attempts to dress the indoctrination of low- income students in the language of reform. In essence, US school choice proponents argue for a system of education that will . . . con- tinue to privilege the lucky and/or connected, will foster a mindless acceptance of social inequities, and will continue to graduate pro- ductive citizens in spite of, rather than because of, its efforts.
>
> (Fecho, 2001: 622)

Treading a middle path is a phalanx of policymakers and commentators (Glazer, 1983; James & Levin, 1983; Goldring, 1991) who see Charter Schools, and similar pro-choice public school initiatives in the Netherlands and the United Kingdom, as a marriage of the best in state and private edu- cation, which at worst introduces an increased sense of ownership among parents (Bush *et al.*, 1993). These third-way policymakers, who enable the actualisation of choice by allowing *per capita* funding to follow pupils going to pro-choice options, have led the drive for greater school choice. Their basic *credo* is that every child deserves an opportunity to access a quality education and the state has an obligation to support that aspiration even if it means going outside the traditional public system:

> We believe that parents should be in charge of their child's education. If parents are not in charge of the school that their child attends, nor the subjects he is taught, nor who teaches him, then they are not really in charge of anything.
>
> (Califano & Bennett, 2000: G1)

However, according to critics of school choice, this places public schools in the United States, Finland, the United Kingdom, New Zealand and elsewhere (Ahonen, 2000) under an intolerable and unsustainable burden. Creating a market in education does not necessarily grant parents more autonomy nor does it *ipso facto* improve school performance or broaden the curriculum (Lauder *et al.*, 1999). Rather it pressurises schools that are successful in market terms to focus on short-termism and examination results and, it is suggested, indoctrinate rather than liberate working-class students who are thereby no longer offered opportunities to critique their own educational experience (Finn, 1999). Fecho is of the opinion that

> [Those] schools most frequently pointed to by school choice advocates as the kinds of schools parents will select for their children too often provide curriculum and pedagogy that domesticates rather than liberates, alienates rather than includes, and encourages complacency rather than fosters engagement. The way toward true reform and equity is not to heap blame on schools that have struggled under adverse conditions, remove even more of their resources, and leave them for dead.
>
> (Fecho, 2001: 629)

Why this working-class powerlessness should be regarded as a feature of school choice *per se*, as is suggested, and not of capitalism generally, is not made clear by opponents of choice. Nor do they explain why schools away from a neighbourhood are necessarily more perpetuating of domesticity and encouraging of compliance among working-class students than local schools, although Finn (1999) does argue that working-class parents who opt for schools away from their neighbourhoods are more likely, almost by definition, to be improving their lot in terms of resources and material environment, if not necessarily in terms of curriculum. However, nothwithstanding arguments about the efficacy of school choice, greater resources do not necessarily make for more independent thinking students (Gee, 1996). The curriculum in all schools, irrespective of choice programmes, largely remains one of compliance (Anyon, 1997); and what working-class students need in order to advance academically, socially and economically is a school staffed by teachers for whom social justice is of primary importance (Finn, 1999: 206).

In practical terms, the legal basis for school-choice programmes in the United States is the Supreme Court decision (June 2002) in the case of Zelman *v.* Simmons-Harris, which upheld the constitutionality of voucher programmes funded by the public purse,[1] including those in private and denominational faith schools. Four years prior to that, the Wisconsin Supreme Court had ruled that publicly funded vouchers could be used at faith schools, and as a consequence, the Milwaukee Parental Choice Programme had expanded almost four-fold in one year (Witte, 1999; Geske, 2003; McElwee, 2005).[2] During the 1990s, the exponential growth in school-choice programmes in the United States also saw voucher experiments in Cleveland (Ohio)[3] and Florida (Woodhead, 2002), and several voucher programmes sponsored by private organisations in New York, Washington DC and North Carolina. In fact, several states enacted legislation specifically enabling Charter Schools to be set up (Bulkley, 2005) and by the end of the decade, there were over 2000 Charter Schools in 35 states with half a million pupils (Geske, 2003).

In the United States, parental demand for choice programmes designed for low-income urban families[4] remains greater than the supply of scholarships (Geske, 2003). The voucher programme in New York, for example, was more than 15:1 oversubscribed in its first year of operation;[5] this pattern was common across other states and programmes. Despite the evident popularity of such schemes among parents, according to James and Levin (1983), there are growing legal concerns among opponents that such programmes threaten the separation of church and state, which although not something actually specified in the American Constitution, is cherished in the national psyche (Barton, 1995). At least one noted legal opinion suggests that including non-religious private schools in choice programmes to the exclusion of religious private schools is discriminatory (Scalia, 1989) and discourages diversity (Ravitch, 1992), but this view is not widely accepted (Jenson, 1983).

In the United Kingdom, where teachers are more opposed to school choice than in the United States (Hatcher, 1994), the legal basis is the 1988 Education Reform Act, which brought a market ethic to schools (Herbert, 2000), and the earlier 1980 Education Reform Act, which introduced the Assisted Places Scheme to schools. Specifically, the 1988 act introduced open enrolment in local catchment areas and school league tables based on examination performance.[6] It set out to improve the standard of education in schools by allowing children from disadvantaged areas the opportunity to attend better schools in other areas. It was hoped that bad schools would close due to unpopularity (because funding was tied to enrolment) and good schools would grow in popularity (Whitty *et al.*, 1998). However, research (Conway, 1997; Levacic & Hardman, 1998; Reay, 1998; Hook, 1999) found that, under the act, families already advantaged were more likely to gain places at desirable schools than disadvantaged families, to the extent that schools became more socially polarised:

> Families with knowledge of the system, confidence, leisure time and, above all, the ability to transport children to non-adjacent schools [were] more likely to look for places in popular schools. Popular schools [were] over-subscribed and in the allocation of contested places, at least inadvertently, [showed] preference to pupils likely to boost their raw-scores.
>
> (Gorard *et al.*, 2002: 368)

The Parents' Charter introduced in 1991 and the subsequent 1993 Education Reform Act further enabled school choice and strengthened market forces (Herbert, 2000). Headteachers thereafter came under increased pressure to satisfy parents and attract pupils in a competitive market, though to date there is no unambiguous evidence that under circumstances of competition, parents make rational informed choices about alternatives (Echols & Willms, 1995). There are signs that education markets may contain a 'constrained majority' who do not or cannot exercise choice (Herbert, 2000), informed or otherwise.

Advantages and disadvantages to school choice

It is suggested that school choice is attractive to parents and pupils in the United Kingdom and the United States because it appeals to the 'cherished desires' and cultural liberties enjoyed in those countries: the primacy of the family and the consequent freedom for parents to choose a school for their children; the consumer expectation of being able to choose a particular kind of curriculum; and the cultural experience that suggests that choice and quality are intrinsically related:

> The fact that greater school choice means, by definition, enhanced liberty attracts many Britons and Americans to the concept of school choice. . . . On the one hand, opponents of choice warn against the excesses of privatisation and especially church-sponsored privatisation.

On the other hand, supporters of choice warn against the price of cultural uniformity.

(Jeynes, 2000: 232)

Gorard (1997) has suggested that any beneficial effect of introducing choice may be minimised by the fact that parents do not have complete information when choosing; for one, they do not actively consider many schools when making decisions. In addition, as schools become more customer-focused and more market-oriented, they become more similar (Pardey, 1991; Saltman & Von Otter, 1992) in that they shy away from being and appearing to be 'too distinctive' (Gewirtz *et al.*, 1995; Jeynes, 2000). Simply put, greater choice in a market does not necessarily produce greater variety, which is one of the purposes of introducing choice in the first place. There are also concerns that introducing greater choice in schooling exacerbates the gap between rich and poor and inhibits social mobility (Woods *et al.*, 1998), that choice favours the wealthy and the better informed to the disadvantage of others, particularly the underprivileged, because a disproportionate amount of resources are directed towards choice programmes and away from traditional non-choice provision. Some commentators additionally suggest that the more a government supports selfish non-societal interest by privatising health care and education provision, the more public schools are likely to become places of last resort for those who, for whatever reason, cannot take advantage of the privatised option (James & Levin, 1983). Disadvantaged sections of society rarely have the right information at the right time to enable them to make the right choices (Hardy & Vieler-Porter, 1990; Martin & Burke, 1990; Edwards & Whitty, 1992; Willms & Echols, 1992; V. Lee, 1993; Wells, 1993). Increased school choice may be linked to increased educational differentiation that has negative effects on already disadvantaged groups (Bagley, 1996; Ball *et al.*, 1996; Woods, 1996; Gillborn, 1997; Tomlinson, 1997; Goldhaber & Eide, 2002). It can contribute to and reinforce educational and social inequality (Bourdieu, 1986a) – in fact, the mere possibility of having school choice without compensatory safeguards may be enough (Bernal, 2005) – though as Ball *et al.* (1996) point out, most research on differentiation has concentrated on the selection of pupils rather than on the selection of schools. It is not axiomatic that introducing markets into education and turning parents from partners into customers (Bridges, 1994) is in the wider public interest (Willms & Echols, 1992; Bottery, 1994; Wringe, 1994; Gewirtz *et al.*, 1995). For example, in the United Kingdom, ethnic composition is a major factor in parental choice of school (Bagley, 1996), as it is in Spain (Bernal, 2005), though it is not such a significant factor in other countries like the Netherlands, where it appears only to play a minor role in school choice.

Opponents of school choice suggest that since social class and race largely determine access to and benefit from school choice (Hardy & Vieler-Porter, 1990; Murphy, 1990; Gewirtz *et al.*, 1995), greater choice must accentuate differences in educational attainment along socio-economic and racial lines:

> Those who have superior economic resources can exercise choice not just between schools, but between schools and the private market.
>
> (Lynch & Moran, 2006: 232)

Contrary to what critics suggest, the pro-choice lobby argues that school choice actually *reduces* social inequality (Moore & Davenport, 1989a), citing evidence from Germany and France that suggests that choice is of greatest benefit to the most disadvantaged – minority and working-class students (Glenn, 1989). Furthermore, there is evidence that the Darwinian self-selection of students going to private and faith schools, much dreaded and derided by opponents of school choice, does not in fact disadvantage minorities. For example, Table 1.1 shows the percentage of African-American pupils in Catholic and public schools in the United States (Moynihan, 1989). Levels of segregation are almost the same, though this may be explained by the fact that faith schools generally have an ethical mission to help the disadvantaged in society and not merely to serve specific ethnicities or faiths.

There is also evidence from the United States that African-American families favour school choice programmes more than white or other race families (Kirkpatrick, 1990). It appears that school choice in an education market, which encourages parents and pupils to behave like consumers, provides greater opportunity (or the perception of greater opportunity) for racially disadvantaged groups to advance socially and economically.

Table 1.1   Percentage of African-American pupils in United States Catholic and public schools (from Moynihan, 1989, cited in Jeynes, 2000: 231)

	Catholic schools (%)	Public schools (%)
Few blacks	30	29
Half black	31	28
Mostly black	22	24
All black	17	19
Mostly or all black	39	43

Added to these sometimes-contradictory conclusions from research is a lack of agreement among policymakers and community leaders regarding the role of choice programmes in the context of public education (Bosetti, 2004). In Alberta, Canada, for example, school-choice legislation regulates both public and accredited private schools on issues related to funding, governance and the curriculum. So school-choice programmes there are not actually operating in a free market and are constrained by factors such as legal decisions about racial balance and the cost of transportation for transferring pupils, but they do serve as

> a mechanism to leverage change in public education. . . . In this context, schools are forced to be more responsive to the needs and values of parents by providing programmes of choice that accommodate their preferences, and to be more accountable to the public by demonstrating improvement in student achievement scores.
>
> (Ibid.: 400)

Supporters of choice and neutral observers recommend that policymakers put measures in place to develop the capacity of poorer parents to maximise available choice options, including better access to appropriate information about choice programmes and their suitability. Parents and students in public schools and from poorer socio-economic backgrounds tend not to exercise choice in an optimal way due to inadequate information and a lack of awareness about how best to use it. Typically, they are satisfied with their schools even when they are not being well served. The *exercise* of choice is different from the *existence* of choice.

However, the differences *within* poor socio-economic groupings in how choice is realised is conceivably no greater than the differences *between* socio-economic groupings. Research suggests that better-educated parents in the public school sector are more choice-active, whether they are in lower or higher socio-economic groupings (Bosetti, 2004; Eccles & Davis-Kean, 2005). Their decision-making patterns and goals are generally similar to private school parents, though income constraints naturally limit their access to fee-paying alternatives. Without financial help such as tuition vouchers and bursaries, parents are obviously confined to alternatives within the public school system, but the fact that there is differentiation even within the groups who cannot afford private schools demonstrates that cultural capital and educational *nous*, which comes uniquely from first-hand experience, is a significant resource in the exercise of choice, perhaps even more than money. Since school choice is driven by the cultural value placed in most Western economies on consumer freedom, rather than by concerns for social equity or the needs of local communities, the onus has been put on parents proactively to lobby for choice and take responsibility for exercising it properly, which itself takes a certain amount of social and cultural capital. Yet policymakers, rather than parents, are the stakeholders best placed, financially and politically, to enable choice, and therefore have a responsibility to see that the less fortunate in society have the means to acquire the social and cultural capital necessary to enjoy the supposed benefits.

If research has been inconclusive on the effects of greater school choice on existing stratifications in society, it is fairly clear that marketisation of education has resulted in increased stratification of schools (Bourdieu & Passeron, 1992; Willms & Echols, 1992; Blair, 1994; Bowe, Gewirtz & Ball, 1994; Gewirtz *et al.*, 1995; Waslander & Thrupp, 1995; Ambler, 1997, Glatter *et al.*, 1997; Woods *et al.*, 1997; Lauder *et al.*, 1999). This is due, in part at least, to families avoiding schools on the basis of race and religion (Bagley & Woods, 1998), and to poorer-performing schools having a higher proportion of transient students (Berki, 1999) who congregate there because aspirant families use better schools further away:[7]

> The recent media stories of high-profile government ministers, and even radical left-wing politicians, seeking to avoid their local Comprehensive and using more distant Grant-Maintained/Foundation schools can be seen as illustrations of [this] trend.
>
> (Gorard *et al.*, 2002: 369)

This is a long way from claiming that great school choice *per se* increases the stratification of individuals and families within society. Some commentators do indeed suggest that in the United Kingdom, the market in education has exaggerated the existing divide between socio-economic classes (Gipps, 1993; Waslander & Thrupp, 1995) and that in the United States, school choice simply means providing places at private schools for bright pupils who could not otherwise afford to go there (Powers & Cookson, 1999). Others see little evidence of change over time as a result of pro-choice policies, firstly because of the importance to schooling of community and geographical catchment (Herbert, 2000), and secondly because the research lacks comparison since no data are available from before the introduction of choice. In the United Kingdom, as elsewhere, social classes are typically grouped by postcode anyway (Taylor & Gorard, 2001), so that local Comprehensive schools are not actually comprehensive in terms of their social mix (Dore & Flowerdew, 1981), a segregation that is reinforced by the fact that property prices in the catchments of good schools rise faster (Gorard *et al.*, 2002).

Parents in the United States[8] traditionally rely on teachers' inherent sense of responsibility for accountability and quality-assurance purposes, but recent trends have challenged this arrangement. Between 1980 and 1994, average reading proficiency for pupils aged nine fell by more than 3 per cent (National Center for Educational Statistics, 1997) while spending on education rose by nearly 300 per cent (National Center for Educational Statistics, 1996). Parental perception of public schools thus became increasingly unfavourable (Elam *et al.*, 1996) and today there is widespread acceptance that private schools can be at least part-funded in certain circumstances from the public purse. In 1993, just 24 per cent of parents supported pupils attending private schools being supported at the public's expense. This had risen to 36 per cent within three years, and voucher-type programmes were generally welcomed as a measure to ensure that a school's enrolment became a function of its performance:

> Under competitive school systems, parents can choose to respond to unsatisfactory teaching by using either exit (transferring their child to a new school or district) or voice (demanding greater effort by teachers). Without school choice, parents have only one option, voice, and might thus be more 'vocal' consumers of education.
>
> (Rapp, 2000: 59)

Today, there is some evidence from experiments with school choice in the United States that greater choice is linked to gains in student attainment, but the research is not conclusive. For example, a correlation has been found between school choice and improvement in reading and numeracy scores (Powers & Cookson, 1999), but an evaluation of a small-scale choice programme in New York did *not* find any significant differences in reading and mathematics attainment when compared with public school attainment, except for African-American students, who fare better in private and choice schools. Gill *et al.* (2001) report similar findings in three other cities: Dayton, Ohio; Washington DC; and Charlotte, North Carolina.[9] While choice may be claimed to be particularly effective for ethnic minority students, who typically need the most help and show the greatest improvement as a result (Jeynes, 2000), one needs to be cautious. Just as it is difficult for opponents of school choice to claim that choice *per se* increases social segregation, it is equally difficult for advocates of choice to claim that its introduction, especially when accompanied by other reforms, has a causal relationship with improvement in pupil attainment.

Private and faith schooling

Chubb and Moe (1990) and others (Doerr & Menendez, 1991) have suggested that school choice policies must involve private schools in order to succeed, but in the United Kingdom, policymakers are unsettled as to the extent to which school-choice programmes should express selfish as opposed to societal preferences (Adler *et al.*, 1989; Kogan, 1990). Armey and Jefferson (1991) suggest that school-choice programmes that include private schools means an end to quality public schooling, but this is disputed by Jeynes (2000) and others (Glenn, 1989), who point out that countries that have included private schools in their choice programmes still maintain thriving public systems. In support, Brimelow (1985), Kirkpatrick (1990), Naismith (1994) and others argue that any lack of personal incentives in a social-service system such as education means that the system is inherently resistant to market forces, even if and when those forces increase efficiency and choice. Jeynes (2000) quotes Sherman (1983) in summarising the tensions:

> Most people are either strong supporters or strong opponents [of choice] . . . with their views based on diverse value premises. Proponents base their arguments on several grounds, including the value of choice. . . . They argue that . . . forms of financial support, such as vouchers . . . significantly broaden the opportunity for people to choose the kind of education they want for their children, especially people who are currently constrained by limited financial resources. Opponents . . . cite concerns about equality, arguing that . . . [state] aid to private education promotes . . . economic and racial stratification and will result in the demise of the public school.
>
> (Jeynes, 2000: 233)

Greater school choice carries with it the accompanying promise of better quality education: choice produces competition and competition enhances quality. This assertion appears to be supported by the fact that private schools and faith schools (which make up a significant proportion of private schools) outperform public schools, in the United Kingdom and elsewhere, in terms of examination results (Coleman *et al.*, 1982; Lee & Bryk, 1993). It is suggested that the success of private schools is, in part at least, due to better discipline, an emphasis on old-fashioned 'basics', higher expectations and the self-selection of ambitious and affluent clients (Hoffer *et al.*, 1985; Chubb & Moe, 1992). Jeynes (2000) makes an interesting point in this respect: if policymakers do not attribute the success of private schools to choice *per se*, why make choice a key ingredient in public school reform (Roseberg, 1989)? Where private school choice exists, critics suggest, the system benefits those who make a choice and disadvantages those who do not (Glenn, 1989).

Supporters, on the other hand, believe that choice forces the worst schools to close down and thereby improves the lot of all students (Finch, 1989; Chubb & Moe, 1992), which is a stance that appears to unnerve academics and practitioners more than it does parents and pupils (Honig, 1993).

In the United States, school choice and religious commitment have become entwined; in fact, it seems that school choice has become a battleground for the wider struggle between religion and secularism in American life. It is suggested that this is the result of the widespread perception – at least partially justified – among religious-minded parents in the United States that public schools are intolerant of religious expression (Barton, 1995; Case, 1996; Wilson, 1996). In many areas of the United States, the choice for parents is often between fundamentalist private religious schools and completely secular state schools whose values are akin to 'those of the shopping mall' (Brighouse, cited in Cush, 2005: 438). The problem can be traced to a series of Supreme Court cases in the early 1960s, which removed prayer and Bible-reading from public schools (Jeynes, 2000). Religious-minded parents suggest that as a consequence, the values taught in public schools are not just intolerant of religion, but actively anti-religious (Olasky, 1988; Doerr & Menendez, 1991), a situation exacerbated by the fact that in response, parents committed to their religious beliefs have largely abandoned the public school system for private schools or home schooling,[10] leaving an irreligious remnant behind to justify the (now self-fulfilling) allegation of bias. In the United Kingdom, with the publication of guidelines requiring public schools to timetable the study of atheism, a similar trend towards secularisation is emerging (Gokulsing, 2006). As a consequence, the parents, teachers and students who remain in the state system tend to be less religiously committed than would otherwise be the case, which in turn, of course, means that the secularised public school system begets a secularised curriculum to match.

Matters seem less fraught in Canada. In Edmonton, Alberta, Catholic schools, which together constitute more than a quarter of all the schools in the city, have been in the vanguard of the school-choice movement (A. Taylor, 2001a). Public school students have the choice of a variety of programmes, including ones in technology, sports and fine arts, generated by consultation, and the (re)introduction of Christian programmes to the public school sector has brought pupils back from the Catholic system (Taylor & Woollard, 2003).

Of course, faith schools – insofar as the debate about secularism and school choice is concerned, the term refers to schools with a religious character that exist *within the state sector* – are not always chosen for religious reasons, as research from the Netherlands proves (Denessen *et al.*, 2005). School religious affiliation is only rated highest by parents with that particular (or a similar) religious background, and group-specific reasons for school choice are found mainly to exist with respect to these religious groups. In the Netherlands, religion is an important factor in segregation within the educational system (Dronkers, 1995), particularly for Muslim and orthodox Protestant parents (Driessen & Van der Slik, 2001); in other words, parents who have chosen an Islamic or Protestant school have more often selected that school for religious reasons than parents of other religious persuasions (Denessen *et al.*, 2005).

In the United Kingdom, faith schools have existed since the advent of state education in the nineteenth century (Gardner *et al.*, 2005) and they continue to enjoy government support (DfES, 2001). Schools in the established Anglican tradition make up the bulk of the state-funded 'Voluntary Controlled' sector, in which 'Local (Education) Authorities' or 'Children's Services' provide full funding in return for control over religious education and school governance (Jackson, 2003). Schools in the Catholic tradition, historically having reason to suspect Protestant proselytisation by the state, make up the bulk of the 'Voluntary Aided' sector, wherein the church provides a percentage of the capital budget in return for retaining control over religious education and governance.[11] The ideological decision by the two main churches to go with faith schools – particularly that by the Catholic Church to fund its own schools in the (for it, more expensive) voluntary aided sector – appears in retrospect to have been a better one (in terms of self-interest) than the pragmatic decision made by the Dissenting churches to engage exclusively in the secular system (Gates, 2005). In Britain, as in other countries with high immigrant populations, for example New Zealand (Collins, 2005), the church's dual mission to 'protect the faith' while accommodating a growing prosperity among its members and facilitating their participation in society was well served by the system of faith schools.

The faith schools controversy goes to the heart of the debate about school choice and the fundamental purpose of education. According to Cush (2005), it is a debate that 'cuts across traditional clusters of allegiances'. Advocates of faith schooling suggest that religious schools value more than just children's academic potential and performance; that although they separate children (as other schools do on the basis of gender, age, wealth and ability), this leads to respectfulness of difference and not to inequality; that they give children a sense of their own identity (Leblond & Trincaz, 1999); and that despite serving marginalised communities as part of their moral mission – for example, Roman Catholic schools in England admit twice as many black African and Afro-Caribbean children as non-faith schools (McElwee, 2005: 32) – they achieve better academic results than secular schools (Garrod, 2003). Opponents challenge the assertion that faith schools achieve better examination results when other variables[12] are factored into the equation (Schagen *et al.*, 2002; Pring, 2005a). They also maintain that faith schools are socially divisive and hinder racial equality (Gokulsing, 2006); that their admission policies are unfair (Garrod, 2003); and that they do not provide an education that allows pupils to understand their own beliefs while simultaneously preparing them to tolerate the pluralities of a society that depends for its existence on such an appreciation.

Generally, whether for faith schools or secular ones, research shows that parents who *actively choose* schools are better educated and wealthier than those who *passively accept* schools (Gewirtz *et al.*, 1995; Goldthorpe, 1996; Bosetti, 1998; Hatcher, 1998; Whitty *et al.*, 1998; Smrekar & Goldring, 1999), so some commentators have suggested that introducing school choice for everyone is a way of counteracting the effects of wealth and privilege on educational opportunity (Bosetti, 2004). It offers opportunity to low-income families who would not normally have it. In Canada, for example, children from both extremes of the income spectrum attend private schools: approximately one quarter are from families with incomes below $50,000 and one quarter are from families with at least twice that (ibid.). However, there is a marked difference between religious and non-religious private schools in this respect. The proportion of poorer families in non-religious private schools is very small compared with the proportion of poorer families in religious private schools. According to Bosetti (2004), this suggests a two-tier system even within the private school sector. Religious private schools attract pupils from families with lower socio-economic status, most likely because the fees tend to be lower there than at non-religious private schools, and religious schools tend to have a schedule of tuition concessions for families with more than one child or who face hardship of one sort or another.[13] The 'moral mission' of religious schools – to serve their faith communities irrespective of socio-economic considerations – appears to be alive and well.

Choice, effectiveness and motivation

There is some evidence to suggest that greater school choice results in an increase in student attainment (Meier, 1992a; Peterson *et al.*, 1996; Witte & Thorn, 1996), but perhaps not immediately, as changing schools can be upsetting for some students (McLanahan & Sandefur, 1994) and 'failing' students tend increasingly to drop out of school as time goes on so that there is always some improvement in school-wide attainment in the later stages. Either way, choice is coming to be regarded as a necessary, though not a sufficient, condition for improvement (Chubb & Moe, 1992; Meier, 1992b; Tooley, 1993, 1994), though as has been mentioned already, this is occasionally balanced by a concern that markets ignore the needs of the most disadvantaged (Chubb & Hill, 1991; Morris, 1994). There are additional concerns in the United Kingdom that there is an inherent contradiction in the way policymakers concurrently establish a compulsory national curriculum and introduce greater school choice to promote diversity (Whitty, 1990). Nevertheless, reports from students involved in choice programmes are 'very good', especially those from disadvantaged backgrounds (Colopy & Tarr, 1994). For example, a much higher percentage of students from choice programmes are more ambitious to continue their education than students confined without choice, even allowing for the fact that students who opt into choice programmes are likely to be more ambition-friendly anyway. It has been suggested that the reason for such success is that many parents are frustrated by the lack of school improvement resulting from government reforms (Jeynes, 2000), and that this drives and reinforces success in choice schemes. More affluent and better-educated parents are 'more particular' about the schools they choose, especially when governments do not extend choice programmes to include the private sector or provide the necessary transport assistance to increase participation rates (Gewirtz *et al.*, 1995; Eccles & Davis-Kean, 2005), and this generates resentment.

However, not all is sweetness and light in school-choice programmes. The few cities in the United States that have implemented choice programmes in public schooling and which are held to be models of successful practice (Nathan, 1990), like Minnesota and Massachusetts, have very low participation rates (Colopy & Tarr, 1994; Nathan & Ysseldyke, 1994), which some have suggested might eventually stop choice programmes from becoming the solution to the crisis of attainment in schools:

> It appears unlikely . . . that school choice will emerge as the grand source of reform that its advocates promise. The primary reason for this is that in all the areas where a considerable choice programme exists, the participation rate is low. As a result, few children will benefit from the programme and few schools will possess the incentive to change significantly.
>
> (Jeynes, 2000: 236)

Gewirtz *et al.* (1995) suggest that empirical research on school choice and its effect on student attainment has generally been 'inadequate'. While some research in the United Kingdom, like that of Bowe, Gewirtz & Ball (1994) and Woods *et al.* (1998), has focused on how choice affects the distribution of pupils among schools and what parents consider when making their choices, there is a generic difficulty in researching how choice impacts on student attainment and in fairly selecting cohorts to supply the data (Jeynes, 2000). For one thing, socio-economic status is not usually accurately accommodated in social research because surveys are returned by self-selecting participants (Bosetti, 2004). For example, rural children almost by definition do not have the same level of school choice as urban children but are less likely than urban children to be poor or from minority backgrounds, so assessing the effects of choice by comparing the academic attainment of students who had it versus those who did not is vulnerable to bias (Schulz, 1993). Similarly, research that focuses on whether students who attend private/choice schools show higher levels of attainment than those who attend public/non-choice schools (Levin, 2000) will always be affected by the fact that there are various factors impacting on school choice and effectiveness that might account for any differences in attainment (Greene, 2001): social class, ethnicity (Gewirtz, 2002; Ball, 2003a), level of education of parents (Duckworth & Sabates, 2005),[14] family income (Davis-Kean, 2005), parental involvement in learning, time spent in school-related activities, home values and beliefs about education (Bosetti, 2004) and family circumstance (Milne *et al.*, 1986). For example, pupils living with two parents do better at school than pupils living with one parent or step-parents (Cherlin *et al.*, 1991; Kiernan, 1992; Downey, 1994), and this might be a factor,[15] though research from Hong Kong suggests that even this might be bound in culture: the negative effects of single parenthood are not as prevalent in non-Western societies because of the ameliorating effects of extended families (Chiu & Ho, 2006).

In short, there will always be an unassessable element in the differential between choice and non-choice groups that may not be due to choice. At best, research on school choice and student outcomes must be inconclusive, and some commentators have alleged that advocates of greater choice therefore base their claims of success on 'contrived data' (Finch, 1989). Yet there appear to be hard data from projects like the one in Alum Rock, California, which suggests a positive link between greater school choice and higher attainment: students who had school choice subsequently demonstrated lower absenteeism rates and a greater enthusiasm for learning (Jenkins, 1973).[16]

There is also some research from the United States on the relationship between school choice and school-level effects. Gill *et al.* (2001), for example, comparing the characteristics of Charter Schools and public schools in the United States, found that the former tend to be smaller, have lower pupil-teacher ratios, offer more diverse academic programmes – though with less expansive programmes for children with Special Educational Needs – and have less experienced teachers paid substantially lower salaries. Assessing achievement in the three states with the largest number of Charter Schools – Michigan, Texas and Arizona – they found only a small significant difference in student attainment between Charter Schools and comparable public schools. Conversely, other research (Hoxby, 1994, 1995; Peltzman, 1992; Rapp, 2000) suggests that choice programmes not only benefit students,[17] but also result in teachers working more diligently. Rapp's (2000) research, for example, presents a 'positive impression of the effect of school choice' on teacher work, irrespective of whether or not competition is confined to a local education district, though when teachers become more concerned with how their efforts are perceived in the marketplace they tend to concentrate on activities that are more likely to be noticed by parents, and not on tasks like classroom preparation. The research also found that teacher effort is lower where household income is lower, where the percentage of minority students is higher and where collective bargaining with teacher unions predominates.[18] Neither open enrolment policies nor private school competition has a significant effect on how much time teachers spend on their tasks, though there is a tendency for teachers to work longer hours in areas where there is a high participation rate in choice programmes and greater parental involvement.[19]

Rapp (2000: 38) also suggests that where there is sufficient engagement by parents, choice in a free market can reduce the principal-agent problem between (on the one hand) parents and taxpayers as principals, and (on the other) teachers and schools as agents.[20] The principal-agent problem, which is essentially a problem of motivation and control in trying to align the interests of an agent with those of a principal, occurs when a principal delegates authority to an agent, when conditions of incomplete and asymmetric information prevail (Pratt & Zeckhauser, 1984), when an agent's actions are not completely observable and when the outcome is affected (but not determined) by the agent's actions (Arrow, 1984). The work effort of the agent is hidden, but extensive monitoring by the principal is costly, and explicit contracts are not the solution because risk-averse agents like teachers naturally balk at payments based on outcomes beyond their control. In these circumstances, according to Rapp (2000), greater school choice can resolve the principal-agent problem in schools, firstly because the threat of losing funding encourages headteachers to be more proactive in pushing teachers to greater performance, and secondly because greater school choice entices parents to become more involved in schools and thereby provide some external monitoring of performance.

At the core of principal-agency tension and motivation generally is the provision of incentives. In schools, heads oversee teachers but cannot monitor them completely, and student attainment is only partially determined by teacher effort anyway. So performance-related pay for teachers is based on risky outcomes not under their control. Pratt and Zeckhauser (1984) suggest a number of possible solutions to this problem. One is a performance pay scheme under which teachers' pay is linked to success at serving the *school's* goals, whatever they may be, which can be designed to measure either individual or whole-staff performance. Unfortunately, performance pay schemes are difficult to implement in schools because there is no universally accepted measure of educational worth, the cost of extensive individual monitoring is very high and there is no way of properly controlling for the fact that some teachers work with students from less supportive backgrounds (Rapp, 2000).[21]

Rapp (2000) describes a useful mathematical exercise to illustrate the way greater school choice can incentivise teachers.

The *utility of parents* at school, 'i', is a function of the work effort, 'w_i', of teachers at that school and the transfer expense, 'e', associated with moving children from one school to another. Parental utility increases with teacher effort and decreases with transfer expense because harder-working teachers mean better-educated students and low transfer expense means more money for other things (ibid.: 41).

Assuming two equally popular schools, 'i' and 'j', in a neighbourhood, the number of students at school 'i' is 'n_i':

$$n_i \text{ is proportional to } \varepsilon(w_i - w_j) \qquad (1.1)$$

where 'w_i' and 'w_j' are the work efforts of teachers at the two schools 'i' and 'j', and 'ε' is the degree of choice parents have between schools, defined as the reciprocal of transfer expense. The number of students in a school is therefore held to be positively related to the work effort of teachers in the school 'i' and negatively related to the work effort of teachers in competing school 'j'.

The *utility of the headteacher* at school 'i' is a function of the number of students at the school, 'n_i'. Headteacher utility 'H_i' increases with student number because more students mean more teachers, more money and perhaps greater prestige.

$$H_i \text{ is proportional to } n_i$$

Substituting from (1.1) yields:

$$H_i \text{ is proportional to } \varepsilon(w_i - w_j) \qquad (1.2)$$

The *utility of teachers* 'T_i' at school 'i' is a function of both headteacher utility 'H_i' and teacher effort 'w_i'. Teacher utility increases with head-teacher utility and decreases with teacher effort.[22]

And assuming that teacher utility 'T_i' decreases[23] quadratically with teacher effort 'w_i' as:

$$T_i \text{ is proportional to } -w^2_i + T(H_i) \qquad (1.3)$$

Substituting from (1.2) yields:

$$T_i \text{ is proportional to } -w^2_i + T\varepsilon(w_i - w_j) \qquad (1.4)$$

Differentiating (1.4) with respect to 'w_i' represents teachers choosing their level of work effort:

$$\delta T_i/\delta w_i \text{ is proportional to } -w_i + \delta T_i/\delta H_i \cdot \delta H_i/\delta w_i$$

Differentiating (1.2) and substituting gives:

$$\delta T_i/\delta w_i \text{ is proportional to } -w_i + \delta T_i/\delta H_i \cdot \varepsilon \qquad (1.5)$$

And the *optimal* level of teacher work effort 'w_i^0' is got by putting (1.5) equal to zero:

$$w_i^0 \text{ is proportional to } \delta T_i/\delta H_i \cdot \varepsilon \qquad (1.6)$$

Thus, according to Rapp's model, optimal teacher effort depends positively on the degree of choice parents have between schools, 'ε', which is by definition inversely related to the cost of moving students between competing schools:

> The implications for [school choice are] clear: the more choice parents have over the school their child attends, the harder teachers should theoretically work.

> (Ibid.: 44)

Rapp points to a necessary caveat in considering the model: the assumption that teachers in school 'i' act independently of (and not strategically with) those in school 'j'. What Rapp does *not* explain is why teacher utility should decrease *quadratically* with teacher effort. Certainly, it is reasonable to assume that teacher utility should generally decrease with teacher effort, but it is not clear why it should be to that order, though in fairness, even were the order of the polynomial in equation (1.4) higher, teacher effort would still depend positively on degree of choice, so the model's conclusion is still reasonable.

Social class and risk

Education policy in most developed countries emphasises the role of parents in school choice and educational decision-making (Tomlinson, 1991; Fine, 1993; Vincent, 1996, 2000; Whitty *et al.*, 1998; Crozier, 2000; Martin *et al.*, 2000), partly as a means of encouraging active citizenship (Blunkett, 1999) and partly as a means of building social, cultural and financial capital. However, there are differences between socio-economic classes in terms of access to choice and how they deployed it. This is not unique to schooling, of course, but parental engagement in education is an important activity in class formation and reproduction, particularly for the middle classes, who, as Giddens (1991) put it, are more capable of 'challenging expert systems':

> There are common sense assumptions concerning the interrelationship between social class and parental agency: that an individual's sense of agency . . . is heavily structured by social class; that opportunities for exercising agency are sought and taken up mostly by the professional middle-classes, secure in [their] sense of entitlement.
>
> (Vincent, 2001: 348)

Parental knowledge about (and attitude towards) 'expert' issues like school discipline, special-needs inclusion, streaming, curriculum options and the like, which research tells us are important factors in parental choice (Denessen *et al.*, 2005), is linked to social class (Vincent, 2000) and therefore to levels of parental engagement with schooling. Research by Vincent (2001) illustrates well the differences between social classes in this respect. Based largely on work by Bourdieu, it presents a scale of intervention types among parents predicated on social status; habitus; social, cultural and material capital; issues of concern; and parental agency (namely, actions and reactions in response to concerns). At the high-achieving end, the most obvious form of activated capital is cultural capital, accrued from educational experience. High-achieving parents typically feel responsibility for their children's education and act knowledgeably on their concerns. They feel the need for a connection between home and school, and are unwilling to leave education solely to the school and its teachers. They manage educational risk – in the case of home schooling, a very large risk and a huge investment of time and effort – and leave as little to chance as possible (Vincent, 2001), though this is no guarantee that problems are then always resolved to their satisfaction (Vincent & Martin, 2000). Other research supports this; parents who exercise choice in schooling are better educated and have better jobs than those who send their children to local catchment-designated schools (Willms & Echols, 1992). Some high-achieving parents, typically those who have had career success but were not themselves very academic at school, adopt a more remote approach. As Vincent (2001: 350) put it, they 'maintain a distance between themselves and the schooling process' because of their own lack of educational achievement (Vincent & Martin, 2000). They like 'to feel they can have a say', but for the most part they do not: they 'confine their interventions to non-academic issues'. This sub-group typically consists of white-collar workers who have worked their way up to positions of managerial responsibility.

At the other extreme, low-achieving parents see home and school as separate entities. Typically, they have left school early themselves and, irrespective of their present economic standing, have little by way of cultural capital. They have only superficial knowledge of the 'expert systems' that comprise education and they manifest a reluctance to get involved with (and even visit) schools. This behaviour is typical of immigrant communities especially. They have high levels of dissatisfaction, relying solely on the school to educate their children while seething with mute anger at their lack of progress. Vincent (2001: 352) terms their attitude 'risk-allowing'.

Of course, most parents come somewhere between the two extremes. They have less knowledge about educational issues than very high achievers, though they themselves are 'achievement-focused', and they feel let down by their own schooling experience and want their children to do better. Generally, they are not convinced that their own interventions as parents in school matters would improve things for their children, and so they restrict their involvement and are 'risk-balancing' (Vincent, 2001: 351).

Bourdieu's concepts of habitus and cultural capital form a basis for trying better to understand parental beliefs and engagement with schooling (Savage *et al.*, 1992). According to Bourdieu, human habitus is a socially acquired system of dispositions and predispositions that make commonsense thinking possible. Literally, it means the condition of the body – quality, style of dress, disposition, state of feeling and habit – but in the sociological sense, it refers to socially acquired embodied systems of tendencies and inclinations, and many academics have used it to link social class with culture.

As an alternative, Savage *et al.* (1992) suggest an asset-based approach to understanding class, which according to Vincent (2001) and others emerges from dissatisfaction with the concept of a single 'service class' (Butler, 1995). They argue that different sections of the middle class rely on the accumulation of different assets, some of which (like property and cultural assets) are relatively easily transferred, while others (like organisational assets) are not. Dunleavy (1980) and Perkin (1989) take an opposite stance to Savage *et al.* (1992), arguing that the greatest divide among the middle classes is between public and private sectors of employment, rather than between asset bases, while Featherstone (1991), M. J. Lee (1993), Massey (1995), Wynne (1998) and others have explored divisions between socio-economic sub-groups based on mobility.

Whatever the basis for exploring and explaining social class, all agree that socio-economic class affects *attitude* to education and schooling. Some groups are more liberal than others. For example, the highly educated professional classes do not lay great emphasis on regulation and strictness (Vincent, 2001); instead of control, they emphasise friendliness and seek out caring teacher-pupil relationships.

Social class also affects *involvement*. Less educated parents, or those who have 'worked their way up', give greater support to clear hierarchical systems and defer to 'professional autonomy' and 'expertise' (ibid.: 358). They trust the hierarchies of expertise in schools more than high-achieving parents, who are ready and willing to act as advocates for their children in educational matters. Less educated parents do not have the predisposition or will to engage fully in the educational marketplace; they lack an awareness and understanding of choice and alternatives and, typically, do not have the social and cultural capital necessary to navigate their options. Generally, they do not see sufficient advantage in their children participating in school-choice schemes and instead prefer the familiarity and reliability of neighbourhood schools.

Most families, whether working class or professional class, want to guard against their children moving down the social pecking order (Bosetti, 2004), but what differentiates the professional classes from others is that simultaneously they have higher levels of aspiration for their children (Hatcher, 1998). Working-class students can maintain their social positions and 'even achieve some upward mobility' simply by completing their compulsory schooling in public schools. Professional families, on the other hand, feel a tension between the benefit of obtaining higher qualifications at university and the risk of 'social demotion' by trying and failing, and this management of risk among middle-class families makes them more favourably disposed to engage in the education market.

Some commentators have suggested that if greater school choice is to extend meaningful opportunity to economically disadvantaged families, there must be greater financial incentives for private schools actively to recruit pupils from low-income families (Bosetti, 2004), and that the state should discriminate positively in favour of such schools since they enhance the social and cultural capital of working-class children, which is to the state's long-term benefit. Schemes such as the (recently abolished) Targeted Individual Entitlement scheme in New Zealand, the (recently abolished) Assisted Places Scheme in the United Kingdom and Charter Schools in the United States were all designed to provide financial support for low-income pupils to gain admission to the top private schools (Gaffney & Smith, 2001), even if some choice schemes – like the one in Alberta, Canada – may benefit middle-class families more (Bosetti, 1998; O'Reilly & Bosetti, 2000). In the United States, voucher programmes for low-income families are used predominantly by non-white families whose children are doing poorly in the public school system, and which are frequently headed by better-educated single mothers who understand the benefits of education as a means of escaping the poverty trap (Standing, 1997; Geske, 2003; Duckworth & Sabates, 2005).[24]

Choice and geographical location

The efficacy of school-choice policy depends in part on the number of accessible schools within a geographical catchment area. In fact, C. Taylor (2002) and others have found that the marketisation of education in the United Kingdom has failed to impact significantly on social structure because the geographical area from which parents choose schools is generally too small to offer real choice.

Pupils living in urban areas generally enjoy greater choice of schools than those living in rural areas, where parents have greater concerns about the availability and cost of transport to and from school, especially when and if the school of choice is not the nearest one. Some school improvement policies are actually inherently biased against rural schools. For example, certain provisions in the *No Child Left Behind* programme in the United States, signed into federal law in 2001, are such that small and rural schools[25] are unsympathetically treated, are more likely to be 'incorrectly labelled as failing' and, as a result of the programme, find it more difficult to attract and retain competent teachers (Jimerson, 2005). However, the problematic effect of geographical location is not confined to rural communities. It also features in urban areas where in addition to cost and inconvenience, parents have concerns about the safety of children travelling to and from school on public transport, sometimes in dark and inclement weather.

Poorer families trying to avail of the benefits of greater school choice are obviously harder hit, as research and experience in public school choice schemes in New York show (Moore & Davenport, 1989b, 1989c; Levin, 1991; Barbanel, 1992; M. J.Lee, 1993). The poorest students generally tend to stay in the community in which they grow up (Vincent, 2001; Mickelson & Southworth, 2005). In some choice programmes, like the one in Minnesota, USA, the state pays for associated transport and childcare costs because experience has shown these to be barriers to participation for poorer children. In Massachusetts, USA, the schools themselves pay for transport and there is an information centre in every school to help parents make better-informed decisions (Bamber, 1990). In the United Kingdom, free school transport is not provided for parents rejecting their allocated local school – families are entitled to free travel if they live more than a certain distance (usually three miles) away – but if parents choose religious schools, and generally parents so choosing are better off, free school transport is available. Obviously, if a large number of pupils avail of school choice, the cost *per capita* of transport and the provision of information to parents falls as economies of scale kick in, but the overall cost rises considerably (Jeynes, 2000).

Hunter (1991), Morgan *et al.* (1993) and Hughes *et al.* (1994) found that geographical convenience and the extent to which a school is viewed as part of a local community are prominent reasons for choosing schools in the United Kingdom. Research in the Netherlands has similarly found that geographical convenience is one of the most frequently cited reasons for parental preference, though many immigrant parents find that they cannot choose the school type they want – Islamic schools, for example – because of lack of availability.[26] Conversely, parents frequently cite distance to travel to school as a negative factor in *not* choosing a school (Bagley, Woods & Glatter, 2001): typically, schools in neighbouring towns are rejected because of lack (or cost) of adequate public transport. When parents reflect on the difficulties associated with getting children to and from schools, they are simply weighing the perceived inconvenience against the potential benefit other schools might offer (Bagley, Woods and Glatter, 2001), and sometimes inconvenience comes out on top.

Quasi-markets in education can erode communities and lead to social polarisation (Taylor & Woollard, 2003), but most parents still believe that they should be able to exercise a preference regarding their children's schooling, even if that is at the expense of social division (C. Taylor, 2002). People make choices about where to live that are informed by the sense people have of their own identity (Butler, 1995; Massey, 1995), so geographical or spatial mobility is closely related to social mobility (Fielding, 1995). All that can (and should) be done to correct for increased segregation, advocates of choice say, is to ensure that pupil selection is fair and that the criteria are transparent. To that end, Thrupp (1999) and others suggest transferring control of pupil admissions from individual schools to local authorities as a way of reducing 'selection by mortgage', even though this would have obvious costs in terms of student transport.

Choice and segregation

Segregation describes the situation wherein children from different socio-economic, ethnic or religious backgrounds attend different types of school as a result. The principles of segregation (Coleman, 1992) change over time, but middle-class parents typically seek niches in education systems that are likely

> to foster privileged access to better examination results, higher education, the exercise of power within the division of labour, higher incomes and social standing.
>
> (Fitz, Taylor & Gorard, 2002: 127)

That niche might be a private school or an academically selective public school; either way it 'differentially confers' educational and social advantage:

> The ability and willingness to pay is the stratifying principle . . . Since 1944 [in the UK] this has worked alongside another, namely academic selection, where, on the basis of tests at [age eleven], children were divided by ability. However, . . . this system of allocation [is] also stratified by social class, insofar as the middle classes were over-represented

in the [selective] grammar schools . . . and there were many more places for boys than for girls.

(Ibid.: 127)

In the United Kingdom, the switch to Comprehensive schools in the 1960s and 1970s was accompanied by admissions policies that emphasised neighbourhood catchment areas, which in turn gave rise to segregation by postcode, that is to say, 'residential' or 'mortgage segregation' in which the ability to buy a family home in the catchment area of a good public school reinforced the educational advantages of wealth. A similar phenomenon occurred following the expansion of New Zealand's choice policies in 1989 (Pearce & Gordon, 2005). Indeed in many areas of big cities, house prices were and still are significantly driven by the presence of good public schools.

After the 1988 Education Reform Act, open enrolment 'markets' were introduced to this system of residential segregation. There were fears that the act would solidify segregation on the basis of income and the ability of middle-class parents 'to read and respond rapidly to the opportunities afforded by' educational markets, but authoritative research has found that this did not happen (Fitz, Taylor & Gorard, 2002).[27]

Research by Denessen *et al.* (2005), which examined school choice and segregation in the Dutch educational system, using data from more than 10,000 parents, suggests that in addition to the quality of education on offer, parental reasons for school choice (and therefore causes of self-segregation) are principally religion, social status and ethnicity. In the Netherlands (and in similar countries like Denmark), support for school choice is not confined to white, middle-class families, but is also strongly supported by immigrant – especially Muslim – families. In the Netherlands, where there is total freedom of school choice (Whitty & Edwards, 1998) and where catchment areas do not exist, both public and faith schools – the latter comprises approximately 70 per cent of the total number in the primary school sector – receive equivalent funding from government,[28] and despite an increasingly secularised Dutch society, the number of faith schools has remained constant, suggesting that parents choose them primarily for non-religious reasons:

As the availability of Islamic schools in the Netherlands increases, immigrant parents may collectively opt for such schools and in this way contribute to segregation within the educational system. . . . As opposed to the expected 'white flight' or departure of native Dutch pupils from 'black' schools, a form of self-segregation is likely to occur when immigrant Muslim parents actively seek and select a 'black' school for their child. This process of self-segregation has yet to occur on a scale of marked significance due to two factors. The first is the tightening of the criteria for the establishment of new schools by the Ministry of Education (Driessen & Merry, 2004). The second is the fact that Muslim parents are not very well organized, have little experience with and are often frustrated in their efforts to establish new schools (Driessen & Bezemer, 1999).

(Denessen *et al.*, 2005: 364)

Generally, increased segregation is most likely to occur when parents from a particular social class or race make *group-specific* choices (Bagley, 1996; Ball *et al.*, 1996; Goldhaber, 2000; Lubienski, 2005), but the jury is still out on how much of this is cause and how much is effect. Gorard *et al.* (2002) and others have found that increased school choice does *not* result in more disadvantaged students attending poorly performing schools, but more importantly, that increased marketisation cannot be shown to be the cause of increased segregation (Gorard *et al.*, 2003). Supporters of school-choice programmes go further and say that choice actually *decreases* segregation by encouraging people to choose schools other than on the basis of race or residency, and some research supports this and suggests that students from inner-city ethnic minorities do better through voucher schemes and the like than their peers elsewhere (Kozol, 1991; Howell *et al.*, 2002). They also suggest that choice programmes can *moderate* the effects of segregation where it does exist (Gorard *et al.*, 2002) and that the rise in the use of schools far from the homes of users has been of greatest benefit to children living in poor neighbourhoods (Parsons *et al.*, 2000).

However, other research points to the contrary. Gillborn (1997), Tomlinson (1997), Goldhaber and Eide (2002) and Stambach and Becker (2006) suggest that markets and competition do in some circumstances increase social and racial segregation to the detriment of disadvantaged minorities, especially those in inner-city communities. In Detroit, Michigan, for example, there is evidence that the school-choice market operates in such a way as to exclude economically deprived African-American students from the more popular schools, and that despite having significant financial incentives to recruit such students, popular schools are found to ignore them in favour of targeting students who add status. Similarly, in Spain, research on school choice and social exclusion has found that under market conditions, the middle and upper classes tend to congregate in popular (mostly private) schools, while economically disadvantaged groups and ethnic minorities tend to get trapped in the declining public sector (Bernal, 2005).

So the evidence from research is confusing, and it may be that methodology and scale are factors. Bagley (1996) and Gorard *et al.* (2003) have noted that small-scale research more frequently reports segregation effects, and that such research may be biased by changes in society rather than changes in school admissions. Additionally, segregation effects can differ even within a single educational system, such as the Dutch system, because of factors like regional religious affiliations (Gorard *et al.*, 2003),[29] or it may simply be that more complex qualitative measures are needed to get accurate information about segregation as it relates to school choice.

Generally, under conditions of competition, it is assumed that unpopular schools become 'recruiting' schools and popular schools become 'selecting' schools, because popular schools can only grow so much until they become over-subscribed. However, unpopular schools

> will only see a fall 'in the size of their intakes as long as there are places available in other schools. If schools [*sic*] closures, rising birth rates or other factors combine to keep school rolls high then, by definition, spirals of decline in terms of simple numbers cannot take place.
>
> (Gorard *et al.*, 2002: 371)

Gorard *et al.* (2002) found little evidence to support the view – as reported later by Parsons and Welsh (2006), for example – that in a school-choice market, unpopular schools lose numbers and simultaneously increase their proportion of socially disadvantaged students. They analysed data from all English secondary schools from 1989 to 1999, and found that whether falling rolls, closing schools or special measures were used as gauges, there was only one school that had both falling rolls and increased social disadvantage.

> Whatever potential arguments there are against the notion of allowing families to state their preferences for schools, the evidence . . . suggests that an increased danger of sending schools into spirals of decline is not one of them.
>
> (Ibid.: 367)

This is ironic, as Gorard *et al.* (2002) point out, since one of the few things both advocates and opponents of greater choice in schooling were agreed upon was that poorly performing schools would enter a 'spiral of decline' as a result of choice. As schools become more socially disadvantaged, the theory went, their league table position would decline, so more good pupils would go elsewhere.[30] And since league table position is related to local reputation, budget and socio-economic catchment (Thrupp, 1998), poorly performing schools would lose both quality and quantity because socially advantaged families in the catchment area would use 'their powers of exit' (Hirschman, 1970; Gorard *et al.*, 2002). Advocates of choice saw this as a mechanism for closing bad schools (Friedman & Friedman, 1980), even if that might not always happen (Pearce & Gordon, 2005); opponents saw it as penalising those who could not make informed choices (Gorard *et al.*, 2002).

In the United States, the effect of Charter Schools and voucher programmes on integration and segregation is similarly complicated and unclear. For one thing, Charter Schools have slightly lower academic attainment than public schools because of the type of pupils enrolling, and voucher programmes permit minority pupils to attend private and religious schools that also include middle-class white pupils, so it is likely that these choice programmes serve to increase the integration of autonomous schools without impacting negatively on public schools (Geske, 2003).

Critics of school-choice programmes in the United States suggest that public schools contribute to the common good by promoting the important values and attitudes necessary for a democratic society, and by implication, suggest that 'civic socialisation' is less effective in a system with choice. They further suggest that advocates and administrators of Charter Schools and parents act together to create a school system that reinforces existing social hierarchies and the interests of white, middle-class families (Stambach & Becker, 2006). Unsurprisingly, research in this area is limited, but it can be said that in private Catholic schools at least, the evidence suggests that this is not the case: there is *greater* promotion of community service and civic/political knowledge than in conventional public schools. Opponents go on to argue that any possible benefit of choice to individuals is outweighed by negative effects such as lower social integration, but supporters of choice point out that the only substantiated empirical finding from research in this area is that the parents of pupils in schools of choice are overwhelmingly satisfied with their performance as autonomous schools, although the research does not show overwhelming support among the public for choice schemes involving private schools paid for at their expense, even when it benefits low-income families (Geske, 2003).

2
School Choice and Transition

School admissions policies

In the United Kingdom, the 1998 School Standards and Framework Act, made law by the newly elected Labour Government, introduced a new framework of regulations for school admissions, which attempted to 'alleviate the problems created by the development of a largely unregulated (education) market' (West *et al.*, 2004: 348). An associated Code of Practice (DfEE, 1999) was introduced for September 2000 admissions – a later version came into force in February 2003 (DfES, 2003a) – which obliged schools to provide information and guidance for parents on admissions procedures (and in particular on selection criteria in the event of over-subscription) for use by local authorities, voluntary-aided (mostly church) schools and foundation (formerly called grant-maintained) schools. The 1999 Code of Practice stipulated that non-faith schools should not interview parents as part of their admission process, and that faith schools should interview only to establish an applicant's religious denomination and commitment. The revised (2003) code extended the interview ban to include children, except for boarding schools, but allowed for 'auditions' to take place as part of aptitude testing for places in Specialist Schools.

The 2003 Code of Practice gives schools considerable discretion in deciding their own over-subscription criteria, provided that they are lawful,[1] impartial, publicly known and geared towards providing all local children with a suitable education. Schools and local authorities are not allowed to apply criteria that have the effect of disadvantaging certain social groups. An adjudication process exists as part of the code to resolve disputes and there are rights of appeal to a Schools Adjudicator. Research by West and Ingram (2001) into admissions appeals in the first year of the 2001 code's operation – July 1999 to July 2000 – showed that the vast majority of disputes were in London and the southeast of England, and in local authorities with active education markets and a wide variety of school types. Most disputes related to testing and selection on the basis of ability, interviewing and whether families with links to the school received or did not receive preferential consideration.[2] Research also suggests that schools responsible for their own admissions use criteria designed to select certain pupils and exclude others (West *et al.*, 2004). By their nature, Specialist Schools are the ones most likely to select pupils on the basis of ability – in a particular subject area to start with – though there is considerable variation between local authorities in terms of the criteria they use to allocate places (White *et al.*, 2001). In January 1988, only 15 per cent of schools were in charge of their own admissions policies. This had doubled by 2003 (West & Pennell, 2003). Schools that are in charge of their own admissions *and* are oversubscribed are in a position, should they so choose, to select pupils who are 'likely to maximise (the school's) examination results', and avoid selecting pupils 'who are likely to have a negative impact' on league table position (West *et al.*, 2004: 347–8).

Table 2.1 shows the admissions criteria most frequently reported in research. A high proportion of schools give priority to siblings and to geographical location. Some significant differences are found between UK school types: more community/voluntary-controlled than voluntary-aided/foundation schools use as admissions criteria the presence of siblings, nearness to the school, various social needs and the school being the first choice of the applicant. On the other hand, more voluntary-aided/foundation schools use admissions criteria that mention feeder schools. Other criteria used to prioritise places in oversubscribed schools include: religious affiliation;[3] whether or not an applicant is the

Table 2.1 Most frequently used admissions criteria (from West *et al.*, 2004: 351)

Criteria used for admissions	Percentage of schools using this criteria
Siblings	96
Distance	86
Medical or social need	73
Catchment area/location	61
First preference	41
Pupils with special needs	39
Feeder schools	28

child of a current member of staff or has some other familial link with the school (despite the fact that the Code of Practice on school admissions states that giving priority to children with strong family connections to a school should *not* be used as a selection criterion as it may contravene the Race Relations Act (1976)); and whether or not an applicant would otherwise have a difficult journey to school (West *et al.*, 2004).

General academic ability or aptitude[4] at some specialism like music is a 'covert' criterion that provides an opportunity for certain pupils to be 'selected in' and others to be 'selected out' (ibid.: 352). The allowed specialist subjects (at the time of writing) are: physical education or sport, the performing and visual arts, modern foreign languages, design and technology, and information technology (DfES, 2003a). Partial selection, introduced in 1998, is permitted in schools that would otherwise not be selective – up to ten per cent of intake – and Specialist Schools may (and do) admit on the basis of aptitude in these subjects (West *et al.*, 2000; Gorard & Taylor, 2001; West *et al.*, 2004), though this might be as much a function of school type as Specialist status (see Table 2.2). Voluntary-aided/foundation schools are nearly 30 times more likely to select by ability than Community/Voluntary-controlled schools, and Specialist Schools are about three times more likely than non-specialist schools to be selecting (West *et al.*, 2004).

Opponents of academic selection in the United Kingdom see problems in the growth of Academy[5] and Specialist Schools. Although they are subject to government regulation in the normal fashion, being independent they are also responsible for their own admissions and are thus more likely to select pupils overtly on the basis of aptitude in specialist subjects and *additionally* to select covertly on other bases (Flatley *et al.*, 2001).

Selection criteria that use banding to obtain a pupil intake with a spread of abilities are, like special aptitude criteria, also covert. The School

Table 2.2 Percentage of secondary schools in England and Wales selecting a proportion of pupils by ability (from West *et al.*, 2004: 353)

Type of school	Percentage of schools selecting by ability
Foundation (formerly 'grant maintained') schools	11.2
Voluntary-aided schools	6.5
Community schools	0.3
Voluntary-controlled schools	0
All schools	2.5

Standards and Framework Act 1998 permits secondary schools to select pupils in such a way as to gain a balanced ability intake, as long as there is no deliberate skewing. Sometimes, local authorities control banding by ensuring that their secondary schools allocate places equally across the ability range, as measured by tests in its primary schools. According to West *et al.* (2004), where this takes place on a local authority-wide basis, it is to try to obtain a truly comprehensive intake for schools, but when schools do it themselves, they typically use banding to skew their intakes in favour of pupils with higher ability (Fitz, Gorard & Taylor, 2002):

> There are two main reasons why 'banding' systems used by LEAs [Local Education Authority] can be construed as being fairer than those used by individual schools. First, the LEA-wide system involves all pupils attending primary schools within the LEA ... whilst a school-based system involves only those primary pupils who apply directly to the secondary school in question. This is important, as there may be particular reasons why some parents may be deterred from applying to a particular school. Second, if the admission authority is the LEA the system is more likely to be clear and transparent as the LEA has no vested interest in the process.
>
> (West *et al.*, 2004: 355)

West *et al.* (2004) further suggest that while admission criteria used by the majority of schools are generally fair, a significant number of schools in charge of their own admissions use criteria consciously to exclude certain groups of pupils and against the interests of social justice (West, 2006). For example, children with special educational needs are less likely to be admitted to schools that operate their own admissions policies than to schools where the local authority is the admitting agent.

Factors which influence individual and group parental choice

Apart from geographical convenience (Hunter, 1991; Morgan *et al.*, 1993; Hughes *et al.*, 1994), a school's reputation – that is to say, the perceived degree of care for children and the perceived quality of the education provided – is critically important in school choice (Morgan *et al.*, 1993; Hughes *et al.*, 1994; Hammond & Dennison, 1995), although Hunter (1991) and Hammond and Dennison (1995) have found that discipline, good examination performance and to a lesser extent the curriculum on offer are also major factors. The 'good discipline' theme is echoed by Echols and Willms (1995) whose research suggests that having taken a child's own preferences into account, parents then frequently choose a (non-local) school primarily on that basis.

In the Netherlands, parental preference must be taken into account when establishing new schools; the most frequently mentioned reasons for school choice there are religious affiliation, ethnic composition, the quality of education provided and geographical convenience. Denessen *et al.* (2005) and others have categorised parental reasons for school choice into four general types – ideological, geographical, quality and non-educational – though it is thought that parental reasons for school choice might merely be indicators of their broader views on the type of school they would ideally choose, whether or not the schools on offer come close to meeting that ideal (Teelken, 1998). Denessen *et al.* (2005) suggest that when parents from different backgrounds choose a school for group rather than for individual reasons, segregation may result, and they suggest that the main influence on this is social class. Other research supports this view; that school choice is strongly related to social class (Bowe *et al.*, 1994; Gewirtz *et al.*, 1995).

Ball *et al.* (1996) identify three types of social class as it relates to engagement with school choice, determined more or less by the level of educational attainment of parents: 'privileged' or 'skilled at choosing'; 'semi-skilled at choosing'; and 'disconnected'. Disconnected parents are typically working class; parents skilled at choosing are typically middle-class professionals; semi-skilled choosers tend to be from a variety of backgrounds (Ball *et al.*, 1996). According to Bourdieu (1986a) and Coleman (1988), parents skilled at choosing have the social capital to operate successfully in the education market, and have the *nous* to use school information to compare schools with respect to the characteristics they consider important:

> [Parents skilled at choosing typically] prefer a school which suits the particular interests and personality of their child. Depending on their specific attitudes towards education, [they] may also select a school for its high quality of education, high standards of academic achievement or strong emphasis on social education. Semi-skilled choosers tend to select 'good' schools, with their choice based strongly on the school's reputation. Disconnected choosers typically choose a school with a close physical proximity to their home and schools which are a part of the social community.
>
> (Denessen *et al.*, 2005: 351–2)

Generally, research on choice and social class suggests that working-class parents tend to choose a school for geographical convenience whereas professional and middle-class parents tend to choose the school which best fits their children's abilities and aspirations, and they rate ideological factors higher (Echols & Willms, 1995; McArthur *et al.*, 1995). Table 2.3 shows some results from research in the Netherlands by Denessen *et al.* (2005) on parental reasons for choice of school ranked in order of importance.

Denessen *et al.* (2005) calculated the correlation between these reasons for school choice and the extent to which their importance was found to differ with respect to parental background. The findings suggest that quality of education is the single most important reason for parents choosing a school, and quality-related factors such as school ethos and the attention paid to individual children are the next-most important. The least important reason for choosing a school is the hope among parents that the school is populated by others with a similar social background.

The three most popular reasons for choosing a school – 'quality of education', 'school ethos' and the 'attention paid to each child' – were found to be positively correlated to one another and also positively correlated with 'order and discipline', 'getting ahead in society', 'having attractive buildings', 'class size' and 'reputation'. No correlations were found between 'quality of education' and 'social background of pupils',

Table 2.3 Reasons for school choice (based on Denessen *et al.*, 2005: 354)

Reason for school choice	Rank
Quality of education on offer	1
School climate or ethos	2
The school pays attention to each child	3
Order and discipline in the school	4
The school is within easy reach of home	5
Average class size in the school	6
The reputation of the school	7
Attractive school buildings	8
Pupils attending the school 'get ahead' in society	9
The religious denomination of the school	10
Social background of most of the pupils at the school	11
The school is considerate of our religion	12
Advice of friends	13
Extra-curricular activities on offer at the school	14
The other parents at the school are 'our kind of people'	15
Possibility of coming into contact with other cultures	16
(No other school was available)	(17)

'religious denomination' or 'distance between home and school', which suggests that there only exists a relationship between quality and school infrastructure. The two reasons for school choice based on characteristics of the school population – the 'social background of pupils' and 'other parents there are similar' – were also found to correlate positively with each other, as did the two reasons pertaining to religious affiliation. The absence of positive correlations between many of the reasons for school choice suggests, according to Denessen *et al.* (2005), that different and distinct *sets of reasons* motivate school choice.

The impact of parental background – religion, level of education and ethnicity – on school choice was also assessed. It was found that Muslim parents rate 'religious denomination' and the 'possibility of coming into contact with other cultures' as more important determinants of school choice than other parents, but for all religious parents, 'quality of educa-tion' remains the most important factor. Immigrant parents rate the 'pos-sibility of coming into contact with other cultures' and 'the school being considerate of religion' as more important reasons for school choice than native Dutch parents, but there is no evidence that school choice leads to group-specific selection of schools by those from higher social classes, and this is consistent with results from other research (for example, that by Gorard *et al.* 2003). Nor, surprisingly, is there any evidence that social class or level of parental education affects the way parents *order their rea-sons* for choosing a particular school, which is in contrast with results from research by, for example, Ball *et al.* (1995, 1996).

Advocates of school choice emphasise its beneficial effect on school improvement, even to the extent of proposing the creation of private alternatives. Enhancing parental involvement, customer satisfaction and a greater sense of community are all perceived to be part of the same mis-sion to provide choice in schooling (Chubb & Moe, 1990; Driscoll & Kerchner, 1999; Smrekar & Goldring, 1999). Market theory suggests that choice creates competition and makes for a more responsive and better service (Levin, 2002). Supporters of school choice argue that in a liberal democracy parents have the right to raise their children in a manner consistent with their beliefs, and that education is a natural extension of those preferences (Levin, 2000; Bosetti, 2004). Opponents counter that school choice results in the creation of markets to cater specifically for the needs, values and interests of advantaged groups like the middle classes who have the economic, social and cultural capital to benefit from it (Ball, 2003a), and that this in turn contributes to social fragmentation (Gewirtz *et al.*, 1995; Fuller *et al.*, 1996; Bosetti, 2004). When parents face important educational decisions, they rely on personal values and social and professional networks to collect information (Coleman, 1988). Therefore, parents without this kind of access – typically those outside the educated professional classes – are disadvantaged by greater choice in education, as indeed they are in many aspects of life.

Rational choice theory suggests that parents maximise utility when they make schooling decisions, and the most successful parents are the ones that are most proactive in getting teachers to act in the best interests of their particular children (Fuller *et al.*, 1996; Goldthorpe, 1996; Bosetti, 1998; Hatcher, 1998). However, Bosetti (2004), in research based on a survey of 1,500 parents in Alberta, Canada, suggests an alternative theory: parents invest a mixture of rationalities when choosing schools, a supposition that has been supported by other research (Bauch & Goldring, 1995; Reay & Ball, 1998; Bosetti, 2000, 2001; Reay & Lucey, 2000):

> [The] context of parental decision-making is far more complex than the result of individual rational calculations of the economic return of their investment in particular education options. Parental choice is part of a social process influenced by salient properties of social class and networks of social relationships.
>
> (Bosetti, 2004: 288)

Simple economic theory assumes that parents act rationally in school-choice matters in full knowledge of the needs of their children, and that they have clear choosing criteria and are aware of all the options available. In return for choice, parents assume responsibility for the advocacy of their children's needs and accept that they must re-engage with the market should their school of choice come up short in any way. The *quid pro quo* for having school choice is a competitive market, in which parents act selfishly in the best interest of their own children, thereby putting pressure on all schools to be more responsive. However, research has found a significant difference in what private school and public-school parents do when acting in their children's best interest (Bosetti, 2004): public-school parents typically send their children to designated schools without first seeking information; private-school parents typically seek information first. The main sources of information include talking to friends and other parents, talking to teachers and headteachers, and visiting schools (ibid.). What distinguishes middle-class parents from others is the range of information sources available and used, and the degree to which their search is deliberate and rational. Public school parents rely heavily on friends and other parents, and are less likely than private-school parents to consult published school performance league tables and the like. Private school parents are also more likely to consult with their children and teachers, but less likely to take into consideration the experience of *other* children.

Social networks play a critical role in informing parental decision-making and of course, the social networks of better-educated, middle-class parents are by definition more likely to include knowledgeable professionals. For less affluent parents, quality of information and access to it is critical:

> The challenge for administrators of programmes of choice appears to be how to infiltrate social networks to provide useful and accurate information to help parents make appropriate decisions regarding their child's education, and to increase their awareness of choice options available. However, adequate sources of information may not be sufficient to encourage families of lower socio-economic status to participate in programmes or schools of choice. These parents do not appear to have the disposition or motivation to deviate from enrolling their children in their designated neighbourhood school.
>
> (Bosetti, 2004: 395–6)

Of course, it is in the nature of markets that most customers get what they want most of the time; otherwise, another market just springs up that meets the need. So it is no surprise that research by Bosetti (2004) and others shows that the vast majority of private-school pupils receive their first choice school. However, this proportion is lower for pupils attending public schools, where among other things the need for (and lack of) suitable school transport is more of an issue. In every free market, over-subscription is the bedrock of competition, but there is actually very little competition among private schools: they simply expand or contract their provision to meet rising or falling demand. In the public sector, a smaller proportion (still a majority) of pupils get their school of first choice, though because relatively few parents actively choose schools, and those that do are largely middle class, market pressures to stimulate large-scale improvement tend not to build up.

Bosetti's (2004) Canadian research echoes that of Denessen *et al.* (2005) in the Netherlands, finding that parents choose schools for many different reasons. Non-religious private-school parents value smaller class sizes, shared values and beliefs, and academic reputation as their most important school-selection criteria. Religious private-school parents, on the other hand, mostly value shared beliefs, including the study of religion in the curriculum, and academic reputation. Both religious and non-religious private-school parents generally look for a school that addresses the individual needs of their children, whereas public-school parents value proximity to home and the fact that their children attend a school in the community with their friends as the most important factors in choosing, even before academic reputation.

Other research (Wells, 2000) suggests that families generally choose schools to associate with like-minded others, particularly in ways in which they describe their educational goals. The real difference between private (choice) schools and public (non-choice) schools seems to be that in the latter, parents are less likely to share similar values and beliefs with other parents. Bosetti (2004) suggests that this is due to the fact that although there is general agreement that the aims of education are primarily academic excellence and the development of life skills, such as confidence and self-discipline, choice parents prioritise these aims similarly whereas non-choice parents vary in their ranking.

Research shows that high parental satisfaction with school positively affects children's outcomes (Harding, 2006) and that satisfaction is highest among parents who actively choose schools for their children and among private school parents (Bosetti, 1998, 2004; Goldhaber, 1999). As an example, Table 2.4 summarises the situation in Alberta, Canada (Bosetti, 2004). Interestingly, as Bosetti (2004) points out, while parents in public schools indicate that they would still send their children to the same school if given a choice, their satisfaction levels are relatively low. It may be that they do not perceive there to be other viable schools from

Table 2.4 Parental satisfaction with schools in Alberta, Canada (from Bosetti, 2004: 399)

Factors	Public (%)	Religious (%)	Private (%)
My child enjoys school	58	69	79
The school is a safe place	48	69	69
Teachers in the school really care about students and parents	43	60	76
The school provides a challenging learning environment	25	44	62
The school helps students achieve their potential	24	51	51
The teaching strategies used at the school are innovative	23	31	51
The school provides sufficient extracurricular activities	8	18	33

which to choose, or it may be that there are other impacting factors such as school location. When parents were asked whether or not they would send their children to the *same* school if every school were open to them free of charge, twice as many private-school parents as public-school parents said they would. Forty per cent of public school parents who would change school if given the chance would stay in the state sector, which suggests strong *prima facia* support for public schooling (Bosetti, 2004). Approaching the problem from another angle, Bagley, Woods and Glatter (2001) explored the reasons for parents *not* choosing particular schools. Negative reasoning plays a significant role in school choice, even if most research on choice has concentrated on positive reasoning (Adler *et al.*, 1989; Coldron & Boulton 1991; Glatter *et al.*, 1993; Gewirtz *et al.*, 1995). Negative influences include poor discipline, bad reputation (David *et al.*, 1994; David *et al.*, 1997) and the socio-racial mix at a school (Gewirtz *et al.*, 1995; Bagley, 1996; Reay & Ball, 1998; Broccolichi & Van Zanten, 2000; Parsons *et al.*, 2000). Table 2.5 shows the main reasons for rejecting schools given by the parents in the Bagley, Woods and Glatter study (2001).

The reasons for rejection vary considerably with location; most obviously, distance and ethnic composition are more of a problem in some areas than others. Otherwise, parents frequently reject schools on the basis of the profile of students already at the school, which can relate to their unacceptable appearance, manner, attire or behaviour in public; or it can relate to ethnic composition, especially in multiethnic areas (Bagley 1996). In the United States and to a lesser extent in the United Kingdom, there is a 'white flight' in education: a drift of Caucasian parents away from multiethnic schools to predominantly white ones. School rejection can also relate to the built environment of a school – namely, its structural features such as size, age and physical condition (Bagley, Woods & Glatter, 2001) – or to the profile of staff there. Parents want teachers to

Table 2.5   Reasons given by parents for rejecting schools (based on Bagley, Woods & Glatter, 2001: 313)

Reason for rejecting a school	Rank	Percentage citing that reason
Transport or distance from home	1	84
Profile of pupils at the school	2	48
The built environment	3	34
Staff at the school	4	25
The headteacher	5	25
Ethnic composition of the school	6	25
Reputation of the school	7	21
Bullying at the school	8	18

have certain characteristics, to be neat in appearance, enthusiastic and approachable, and working-class parents especially are worried that generally teachers take more of an interest in middle-class children. The headteacher's perceived attitude to staff, parents and students is also important to parents, as is the school's reputation, though that is based mainly on hearsay and is relative to that of competitor schools, and its attitude to issues like bullying (Bagley, Woods & Glatter, 2001).

According to Bagley, Woods and Glatter (2001), parents face barriers to choice, but ways are more likely to be found to overcome these where a school

> has a special attraction that suggests the benefits will be substantially greater than attending an alternative school.
>
> (Ibid.: 320)

Parents overcome these barriers by intervening to actualise their choice of school; for example, by funding, if need be, their own school transport system to schools outside the catchment area (Herbert, 2000). Bagley, Woods and Glatter (2001) also suggest that parents actualise school choice in line with the social class and ethnic mix they consider best suits their children; this behaviour is mirrored by schools deliberately targeting middle-class and academic pupils. However, it must be remembered that choice is not a one-way process. The primary intention of school-choice programmes might be to provide greater market freedom for parents, but it also provides a parallel freedom for schools to choose pupils, within certain obvious geographical, legal and ethical constraints of course (Bagley, Woods & Glatter, 2001). Nor is choice a simple construct, as is sometimes assumed in market models. Parents do not make choices in isolation from their children's wishes, and in fact research shows that in the majority of cases, children's own choices are a major influence (Smedley, 1995).

The nature of the quasi-market in education varies from place to place, across local 'competitive arenas' (Woods, 1996), and a school's relationship with other schools in a locality effectively determines the choices that can be exercised by parents (Simkins, 1997). At worst, schools can collude to deprive parents of real choice by restricting curriculum provision, by passively accepting local hierarchies of performance to avoid competition and so on:

> Any local environment is a 'value-laden place' where both schools and residential areas inherit reputations and embedded images that affect choices, assessments and decisions.
>
> (Herbert, 2000: 79)

According to Stambach (2001), parents who involve themselves in founding Charter schools in the United States run the risk of being perceived as stepping outside their roles as carers when they are called upon both to produce and consume new educational programmes. Whereas parents have *particular* expectations of their children, teachers have *general* expectations of their pupils, which can result in a natural antagonism between the two stakeholder groups (Lightfoot, 1977). Charter school parent-founders have to produce what they themselves also want to consume. They have had to think both like public servants working in the interest of the common good and like entrepreneurs looking to sell a better product that others will want to buy.

Choice and the psychodynamic of moving from primary to secondary school

Research suggests that when pupils perceive that they have overcome the risks and dangers associated with transition to secondary school, their self-confidence grows and so does their ability to cope successfully with future transitions (Taylor & Woollard, 2003). This is especially true when the school of choice is difficult to get into. Pupils rely on established social ties to ease their transition from primary to secondary school – and indeed between schools generally – and middle-class families especially use this as an opportunity to gain advantage and bond with other families that share their values (Giddens, 1991). Education is 'anxiety-ridden' according to Shaw (1995), and nowhere is that more apparent than in the transition to secondary school (Measor & Woods, 1984; Cotterell, 1986; Youngman, 1986). It derives from the capacity of individual children to 'anticipate their futures' (Giddens, 1991) and it is an important driver in how pupils respond to change (Barbelet, 1998; Lucey & Reay, 2000) and choice, and how they deal with the preconceptions they have of secondary school, which are mostly communicated to them by stories from other children (Measor & Woods, 1984; Delamont, 1991):

> [For primary school] pupils who [are] in the process of selecting a school, the very idea of secondary school (opens) up a space in their imaginations that [is] not entirely filled by what others [have] told them. This space [provides] highly fertile ground in which half-formed, ambiguous and contradictory fears, fantasies and hopes of their own [can] be planted; a contradictory space constructed in the present around an unknown but inevitable future.
>
> (Lucey & Reay, 2000: 192)

Generally, the 'turbulence of transition' (Ruddock, Chaplain & Wallace, 1996) demands what Lucey and Reay (2000: 192) call 'emotional reorganisation', and anxiety is a central emotion in that reorganisation and to the future 'development of effective coping strategies'. Factors such as ethnicity, culture, gender and social class are also brought to bear:

> [Which] secondary school you attend is still considered a vital statistic in some corners of 'cool', 'classless' Britain (Goddard, 1998; Anthony, 1998). The significance of the transfer is not lost on working class and middle class, black and white [pupils], all of whom [regard] the imminent move [as relating] directly to [their] identity.
>
> (Ibid.: 192)

Research from the United States suggests that ethnicity (in part at least) affects parental (particularly maternal) attitudes to (and expectations of) transition to senior school – middle-class Euro-Americans value most getting along with peers, African-Americans value most academic preparation and Latino-Americans value most learning to respect authority (Harding, 2006) – but whatever their ethnicity, transfer from primary to secondary school can cause children's future academic and social 'trajectories' to diverge in line with social background (Noyes, 2006). Poor transition is linked to low social class (Nisbet & Entwhistle, 1969): the better off economically, socially and culturally effect the smoothest transition.

Knowing that a poor transition to secondary school can mean 'unfavourable outcomes on an emotional and educational level', schools can and should work to lessen the anxieties of inbound pupils (Rudduck, Galton & Gray, 1998), though 'simple policy measures' (Noyes, 2006: 57) are unlikely dramatically to improve matters (Noyes, 2004). Children sense that it is a right of passage, but it is one whose risks may be assuaged by, for example, advance visits and practice lessons:

> [Going] to 'big school' presents children with a dilemma central to the experience of growing up; that in order to gain freedom and autonomy from adult regulation one must be willing to relinquish some measure of the protection which that regulation affords.
>
> (Lucey & Reay, 2000: 202)

This is not to imply that transition must always be problematic. It can be a time for optimism too (Measor & Woods, 1984) and a time, as Rudduck (1996) says, to recognise an increasing maturity. For many children, transition represents the opportunity for greater independence (albeit with greater risk), but sometimes feelings of loss for primary school friends and former teachers can occur (Measor & Woods, 1984) to the extent that pupils are occasionally unable to imagine anything positive or exciting about the move to secondary school. In most research, pupils are found to express anxiety about the daunting unfamiliarity of what they perceive will be their new school environment (Galton & Willcock, 1983; Davies, 1986). They fear the bigger school with its strange 'informal spaces' (Measor & Woods, 1984) populated by bigger pupils, and they become 'sensitive to their own vulnerabilities' (Lucey & Reay, 2002: 258).

Lucey and Reay (2000) suggest that at the beginning of the process of transition to secondary school, parents' anxieties dominate the choice agenda as they try to actualise their schooling preferences in a highly competitive market (Gewirtz *et al.*, 1995; Noden *et al.*, 1998). At this stage too, children's knowledge is incomplete, gained mostly from friends and relatives, and horror stories and myths abound, particularly about bullying (Galton & Willcock, 1983; Measor & Woods, 1984; Davies, 1986). On the positive side, Lucey and Reay (2000: 198) point out that most horror stories are told about schools *other than the one chosen*, which suggests that pupils distance their fears as a psychological defence mechanism, and of course there are also positive and supportive stories told by friends and relatives. In particular, a consensus grows

> amongst [groups] and the emergence of a group identity around school destination ... speaks to and is an attempt to resolve the need for some sense of coherence and continuity in a time of change. It also reassures [pupils] that they have not only chosen well but that they have been chosen by the best school.
>
> (Ibid.: 199)

While schools other than the one chosen are 'demonised' by children not going there, others are idealised or 'valorised', as Lucey and Reay (2000, 2002) term it, as the pressure to get a place at a good school intensifies with marketisation (Gewirtz *et al.*, 1995).[6] For example, schools that are strict about bullying are praised at transition time by pupils who worry about bullying. As children struggle to articulate their fears, they reassure each other as a group of friends transferring together to the same secondary school (Reay & Ball, 1997; Lucey & Reay, 2000), and this positive support is bolstered by other children not concerned about bullying (to use that example) so much as concerned for getting a fresh start there and perhaps escaping bullying at primary school (Rudduck, 1996).

Crocker *et al.* (1998) suggest that demonised schools are ones whose students are perceived as deviant, violent and stupid, whose teachers are perceived to be ineffective and unprofessional and which are usually attended by a large number of ethnic minority students (Back *et al.*, 1999). These prejudices are the result both of real experience and public gossip (Segal, 1985). Children making the transition from primary to secondary school are 'acutely aware of a hierarchy of selection' and usually have 'an accurate idea of where they are positioned' in relation to it (Lucey & Reay, 2002: 256). Mostly, they fear being labelled as stupid, particularly working-class pupils who generally and historically can expect less favourable treatment in schools (Willis, 1977; Ball, 1981; Lee, 1987). It is easier for students to secure a good reputation at a new school when their social skills are those also valued by their teachers, and such pupils tend to make early and rapid progress. Working-class pupils, on the other hand, develop 'strategies for resistance' (Noyes, 2006) as a result of perceiving a dissonance between own attitudes and those espoused by the school, and because the need to work during the school year to contribute to family income depresses attainment (Gouvias & Vitsilakis-Soroniatis, 2005: 445).

Good teachers and good classroom discipline are most important to pupils concerned about school choice and transition. Prospective pupils look to teachers to provide levels of safety and order that create an environment free from violence and the threat of violence (Ganaway, 1976; Woods, 1990). However, children understand that good and bad coexist ambivalently in most schools, and fearful children hang on to the hope that the horror stories might not be true. All positive feelings are not destroyed in schools demonised by pupils who do not want to be there. In their poignant account, Lucey and Reay (2002: 260) suggest that this is more than mere 'wish fulfilment'; more than a 'desperate attempt at the kind of magical thinking that (makes) everything all right'. Reality for children faced with the prospect of going to a school not of their choosing – a demonised school – is as 'messy' as it is for most children in most other aspects of their young lives. They are driven emotionally to repair the image of the school and themselves in relation to it. In some situations, they learn to

transform a shameful reality into something good by a clever reworking of what Goffman calls 'identity information' (Goffman, 1963). But realities are constantly at play with fictions in the constitution of identity.

(Ibid.: 260)

Of course, the demonisation of some schools depends on the idealisation of others. For pupils living in the catchment areas of popular schools and who have secured offers there, the idealisation is straightforward. For those who live in the catchment areas of undesirable, demonised schools, the perfect school is always (literally) far away. The notion of an ideal school far away from a local demonised school is reinforced among friendship groups of children destined to attend the latter and by social class, academic prowess, gender and race (Allat, 1993; Gewirtz *et al.*, 1994; Ball *et al.*, 1996; Reay & Ball, 1997, 1998; West, Pennell *et al.*, 1998; Reay & Lucey, 2000, 2003). Parents in lower socio-economic group- ings traditionally place a higher value on local schools because they are uncomfortable about their children travelling long distances (Worpole, 1999), and family ties in working-class areas traditionally tend to be stronger (Savage *et al.*, 1992; Reay & Ball, 1997). It has been suggested that this is changing (Lucey & Reay, 2002: 262) and that working-class children are now willing to travel further to school, but this fact alone – as will be discussed in the second part of this book – does not mean that working-class children are doing better in school as a result of the free market (Noden *et al.*, 1998). Children, whether working class or not, seem to be innately aware of the unfairness of such a school system, but according to Lucey and Reay (2002) they are seduced by the hope that the meritocracy of having the best schools choose the best children (and of good pupils getting what they deserve) will result in them being chosen.

Gender and the transition to secondary school

Transition to secondary school is especially significant for working-class girls, according to research from Ireland (O'Brien, 2003).[7] Having secured a place, girls in particular face a 'complex web of emotional, social and academic transitions that shape and are shaped by' their social class (ibid.: 249). Research from South Africa (Walker, 2006) and the United Kingdom (Jackson & Warin, 2000)[8] supports this view and suggests that girls have greater concerns than boys about harassment and that they are less confident about transfer to mixed-sex schools, so they tend to come together for emotional support away from their male peers (Hargreaves *et al.*, 1996; Jackson & Warin, 2000; O'Brien, 2003). However, negotiat- ing choice is only part of the transition process. Pupils transferring to secondary school are also going into a more hierarchical system where working-class pupils generally do less well. According to O'Brien (2003), working-class girls regard the price to be paid for academic success – loneliness, unsociability and stress – as too great and involving a loss of solidarity with the peer group to which they feel loyalty. Secondary schools are dominated by middle-class norms (of academic success, among other things) and accentuate differences in social 'dress and style', which creates resistance among working-class girls in particular and an alienation from the ethos of success that labels working-class mores inferior (Skeggs, 1997; Plummer, 2000).

For middle-class parents choosing independent schools, the gender mix of the school is important (Jackson & Bisset, 2005), though less of a factor than the school's reputation for academic success, especially for parents who choose single-sex schools (Robinson & Smithers, 1999). Publicity surrounding the under-performance of boys in public examinations may have increased the attraction of private education for sons of middle-class families (Walford, 1986; Robinson & Smithers, 1999: 197), but the general perception prevails that single-sex schools – which in the United Kingdom continue to decline in number but are still particularly popular with girls (Jackson & Bisset, 2005: 196) – have *academic* advantages for *girls* whereas co-educational schools have *social* advantages for *boys* (ibid.).

The time immediately prior to choosing a secondary school is an emotional time for children and their families (Naughton, 1998; O'Brien, 2001). The prospect of leaving behind the familiar, of making new friends and establishing oneself with new teachers is daunting for most pupils. O'Brien's (2003) research suggests that these anxieties are particularly acute for working-class girls, as they tend to be more attached than middle-class children to their schools and local communities and the emotional comfort contained therein. Working-class girls are also found to be more concerned with issues of personal safety and bullying than other children or boys (Connolly & Neill, 2001, Reay & Lucey, 2003). Middle-class girls, on the other hand, are more likely to receive guidance (and pressure) from their parents in choosing a 'suitable' school and by and large, middle-class girls acquiesce in this 'shaping' (Allat, 1993; Reay, 1998; Walkerdine *et al.*, 2002). Working-class girls tend to 'choose' their local schools and to do the choosing themselves (Standing, 1997; Connolly & Neill, 2001) using knowledge 'gained through their social networks':

> This local experience [is] highly relevant [for working-class] students. So from [their] perspective ... the 'best' school [tends] to be the school that [is] closest and where friends are going. Parents trust the choices of their daughters because they feel they themselves lack particular knowledge about the schools.
>
> (O'Brien, 2003: 255)

Working-class children and their parents, more so than their middle-class counterparts, also tend to make school choices based on concerns about discipline and respectability (Skeggs, 1996). They want or perceive they need tough discipline and tight control over things like uniform and demeanour. However, there are financial implications for any proactive strategies that might actualise these demands, like the cost of sending children to out-of-community schools, and these costs are more likely to be prohibitive for working-class families than professional-class families (Plummer, 2000; Walkerdine *et al.*, 2002). There are emotional costs too: friendships are more difficult outside the home community and it is more difficult to join in after-school activities. Generally, being schooled outside one's community encourages feelings of difference and un-belonging, which seems to be more acutely felt by working-class children:

> Despite the apparent advantage associated with attending a well-regarded school with a good record of academic achievement, girls from outside the locality experience emotional challenges and practical difficulties that [make] belonging to that school a more complex action than might have been anticipated.
>
> (O'Brien, 2003: 256)

Girls transferring to secondary school notice more than boys the difference in discipline between primary and secondary schools (O'Brien, 2003). Discipline in primary schools is perceived by girls as 'simpler and more relaxed', though of course pupils choosing schools are aware that they are moving from being the most senior pupils in one school to being the most junior students in another, and consequently they expect a loss of freedom (Measor & Woods, 1984; Lynch, 1989; Hannan *et al.*, 1996; Lynch & Lodge, 1999, 2002). Newly transferred girls are found to notice, perhaps for the first time, that social class and academic distinction are linked: less academic girls see academic girls as different socially and so do not become involved with them in 'pro-school' activities.

Choosing a school and the transition to it also prompts concerns among pupils about the expected rise in homework and required study, particularly among working-class pupils and girls, who see it as an erosion of their leisure-time. Of course, a child's ability to study at home and to feel enthusiastic about it is significantly influenced by the material resources available there, so those living in poorer housing conditions know they will have greater difficulty. In addition, working-class parents are disadvantaged when it comes to assisting and monitoring their children's homework because of their own lack of schooling (O'Brien, 2003: 263), and they have greater difficulty controlling or restricting 'distractions' from school work because working-class children tend to have informal less-structured social activities.

3
School Choice and Globalisation

Global trade agreements and their effect on education

One of the defining characteristics of globalisation is the demand it creates for a system of global free trade and *laissez-faire* economics. Marginson (1999) argues that under it nation states are now merely junior partners for large multinational companies, and that this particular politico-economic agenda is advanced through pro-capitalist 'manoeuvres' like the introduction of the euro. The development of global markets is not a natural occurrence, but the deliberate result of specific national and transnational forces (Bottery, 2001), which have had the effect of introducing to education a new business lexicon and a new ethic. At its most basic, globalisation affects the 'financial probity of nation states and their ability to maintain adequate provision of services' (ibid.: 204) like public schooling. Critics hold that globalisation constrains what a state can do in its own interest, and although national governments still have a large degree of freedom in relation to domestic economic policy, that discretion is lessening all the time (Held, 1999). In the interim, multinational companies are creating international networks of coordinated production that pay little or no heed to national borders (Reid, 2002) and the fear of wealth fleeing from one inhospitable country to another more sympathetic one limits the de facto autonomy of national governments to act. Decisions are now increasingly made by international bodies such as the United Nations, the World Bank, the International Monetary Fund, the European Union, the North American Free Trade Association, the Organisation for Economic Cooperation and Development (OECD) and so on, in a constrained form of democracy where decisions are no longer made by elected representatives.

The relationship between globalisation – most tamely defined as the process by which countries and their citizens are increasingly drawn together (Porter, 1999; Parekh, 2003) – and education is clear, though opinion varies as to whether or not it is a good thing and how best to engage with it (Soudien, 2005). Opponents regard globalisation as the cause of public sector downsizing and creeping privatisation, and as something that adversely affects public school provision and social well-being. According to Kuehn (2001a) and others, three features characterise it: the destructive effects of global competition and rampant, unfettered capitalism; the emergence of constrained democracy resulting from the fact that governments are limited in how they can act in the interests of their own citizenries; and the prostitution of schooling whereby its *raison d'etre* is reduced merely to the human-capital approach of serving the economic good (Dreze & Sen, 1995) through a school curriculum driven chiefly by commercial considerations. Supporters, on the other hand, suggest that there are long-term gains to be had from all this and from greater competition, although critics counter by describing the reality of competition as a 'race to the bottom', where 'wages, working conditions and social programs are all caught in a downward spiral' (Kuehn, 2001a: 1).

Kuehn's (2001a) point about the downward spiral is that highly skilled jobs – not just menial, low-skilled work in textile manufacture – are chased by globalisation into low-wage regions and workers from developed countries find themselves increasingly employed without security in temporary jobs with poor prospects. Simultaneously, social benefits for the disadvantaged are being eroded while greater choice in areas like public schooling appears increasingly to benefit only the already advantaged. It seems to critics of globalisation then that the purpose – or at least the outcome – of international trade agreements is to stop governments from being able to listen to citizens and intervene in (supporters of globalisation and competition would say 'interfere with') the market on their behalf. Global business has usurped the ability and obligation of democratic government to act in the interests of its people.

As a result of globalisation, the service sector has grown enormously in developed countries. Services, rather than production, now represent approximately 70 per cent of the economy of the world's richest countries, and therefore from necessity there are now international agreements on trade in services (General Agreement on Trade in Services – GATS) similar to earlier ones on product trade (General Agreement on Trade and Tariffs – GATT). As a consequence, trade in services like public education requires a monetary value to be put on it and this is a new departure philosophically for the professionals involved in its delivery. Education has always been considered in terms of its intellectual, social and cultural benefits – in addition to its training component as a preparation for employment – rather than its unit cost to individuals. The values inherent in consumerism as an ideology are therefore in conflict with those on which public education was founded and has operated, so advocates of globalisation want and need to find new ways to commodify it; to turn the purpose of schooling to economic well-being and to turn schools themselves into commodities to be bought and sold. Molnar (2006) and others suggest that doing this will necessarily remove control of schools from the communities they serve. It is in the nature of globalisation that it should be so, but opponents like Kuehn (2001b) raise a trio of objections: that global agreements on trade in services treat education as a tradable commodity and fail to recognise that education is in essence a social capability rooted in particular 'cultural realities' and supplying the individual with other capabilities and freedoms; global agreements on trade in services are anti-democratic in that international tribunals can overturn decisions made democratically at national level; and that global agreements on trade in services are designed to stop countries changing policy or adapting policy to suit local need:

> The nature of these [international] agreements [on trade in services] leads not only toward economic integration, but toward assimilation into a conception of culture that sees it primarily as a product for sale and for export. ... Each ... has added more limits to a conception of education as primarily a social and cultural factor. Each trade deal has been part of changing the conception of education toward it being a tradable commodity.
>
> (Kuehn, 2001b: 1)

Trade in education comes in a variety of forms: privatising public sector schools and school systems; generating income from overseas students travelling abroad for education; privatising the delivery within schools and school systems of ancillary services like school administration, buildings maintenance and curriculum servicing; and vending and advertising. In schools, commercial advertising has historically taken the form of sponsorship of prizes and scholarships. It was a way for corporations to sell their products and services, and promote their points of view, sometimes on politically sensitive matters. However, there is now growing concern that such commercial activities can interfere with the academic integrity of the school, which often does not have the resources to evaluate the impartiality of sponsored materials and programmes (Kohn, 1997; Boyles, 1998). To some, it constitutes a 'pervasive informal curriculum' that 'undermines the formal curriculum' (Molnar, 2006: 630), and there is rising opposition to it. Generally, profits generated by such involvement, by definition, flow away from the communities in which they are generated to corporate headquarters and shareholders. Advocates of marketisation and greater consumerism in education, like the World Bank, support the idea of commercial sector involvement as a way forward, especially for poorer countries, suggesting (and in some cases, demanding) that schooling be demand-led rather than supply-led; that schooling be based not on policies that reflect what is appropriate for a particular society, but rather determined by consumer choice. Government still pays for it, courtesy of the taxpayer, but government no longer controls it through public provision, and a competitive market is thus created.

The changing agency of the state in education

Bonal (2003), Safstrom (2005) and others suggest that as a result of globalisation there has been a significant shift in the traditional role of the state in education (McGinn, 1997; Held *et al.*, 1999). Falk (1999) describes the new scenario as a political contest between economic market-driven *globalisation from above* and *globalisation from below*, where grass-roots movements push an alternative global civic agenda (Reid, 2002). Three categories of globalisation theorists can be identified from the literature: hyper-globalists, who hold that the nation state is effectively disappearing because global economic networks have overcome it in terms of power and influence (Ohmae, 1995); globalisation sceptics, who do not see globalisation as anything different from internationalisation and therefore that the role of the nation state at its core is unchanged (Hirst & Thompson, 1996); and transformationalists, who see the nation state as having been modified, but not destroyed, by globalisation, particularly in relation to public services like education. Others suggest that the wealthier nation states in particular are not losing control of education so much as *adapting* their education systems and discourses to service their economic and social purposes (Green, 1997; Marginson, 1997, 2002). In Sweden, for example, which has seen an explosion in private education since the introduction of a voucher scheme, the knowledge society is changing the relationship between the state and education. In fact, a new type of state is being born that Safstrom (2005) has called an 'agentic' state, which subordinates the will of the individual to its will and regards people merely as economic entities. In such a climate, educational discourse is by definition limited since philosophies that encourage individuals to seek a good life are of secondary importance to the view that education is primarily an economic imperative. Developing nations, on the other hand, are making *structural* adjustments (Carnoy, 1995; Tikly, 1999) that entail rolling back the public education provision (Matthewsa & Sidhub, 2005). Such restructuring of state intervention can take different forms, but institutional factors play a crucial role in its impact on individual schools. Dale (1989) suggests that the role of the state is to support and legitimise capitalism while simultaneously advancing social cohesion, but the identification of problems does not *ipso facto* identify the means by which they can be resolved. What is expected of the modern state is contradictory: it must levy taxes on income and employ them for the social good, but at the same time it must not endanger that which generated the wealth in the first place (Habermas, 1984; Offe, 1984):

> Within the education policy field, [this is] illustrated by the traditional tension between selective and open-access policies. Policies that would strengthen the selective character of the education system would have the predictable effect of creating resistance and contestation from those excluded by the system.
>
> (Bonal, 2003: 161)

According to Weiler (1989, 1990), states develop 'compensatory legitimation' because of the failure of educational reforms as a result of the tensions noted above. States assume responsibility for making their education systems efficient by embracing the relationship between education, economic prosperity and meritocracy (Bonal, 2003). They accept the burden of neutralising the effects on educational attainment of social class, gender and ethnicity because it is 'the only way to justify a fair but unequal social structure' (ibid.: 162). In the 1970s, as evidenced in the United Kingdom by controversies such as that of the William Tyndale school,[1] education was perceived as being in some way responsible for society's industrial and political malaise, though ironically, the then financial crisis on the one hand and the increasing demand for more and better schooling on the other made it nigh on impossible for governments to respond adequately anyway. Offe (1985) theorises about a shift in political rationality from 'conjunctural policies', which seek to maximise the adequacy of policy responses to problems such as those of the 1970s, as and when they appear, to 'structural policies', which seek to maintain a level of output while controlling demand in a way that is affordable even when resources are limited (Dale, 1989).[2]

Today, the neo-liberal economic consensus dictates that the state should be competitive abroad and facilitate a favourable pro-choice regulatory framework at home. It should create conditions for facilitating innovation and investment, keep salaries and taxes as low as possible and develop competitive modes of governance. Under these rubrics, public administration is guided by market mechanisms within the state, which must as a consequence partially withdraw from some of its traditional activities like public schooling. Quasi-market forms of provision, the drive for greater accountability and decentralisation are new forms of public sector management that are changing the nature of the capitalist state (Bonal, 2003). Within education, this process manifests itself as a policymaking strategy emphasising entrepreneurialism:

> One of the major impulses of the competition state is to minimise public expenditure ... [by] ... removing the state from all but a necessary minimum activity. ... [This] reduces, or even removes, the chronic legitimation deficit it suffers under welfare state regimes, reduces public expender and increases the scope of profit making activities. The legitimation problem becomes converted into one of efficient delivery of public services to individual citizens.
>
> (Dale, 1998: 102)

However, areas like education cannot easily be depoliticised by marketisation, especially since 'state intervention in education has been historically and politically grounded in the chronic failure of markets' (Bonal, 2003: 166). So although neo-liberalism insists on a reduced role for the state in intervening in social and economic life (Robertson & Dale, 2002), education has largely remained regulated by public bodies that have developed mechanisms through which they can reduce the state's involvement – and therefore its legitimation burden – while at the same time using new modes of intervention to force certain desired behaviour in individuals. The state is thus able to respond to a range of educational problems – school drop-out rates, teacher shortages, socio-educational problems in deprived areas and so on – by using 'local states of emergency' (ibid.); power strategies by which the state secures social control:

> If possible, the state tries to 'pass the ball' to the school and to the community in order to solve the problem, normally by using contractual

strategies that position schools and communities as responsible for school performance. Sometimes, the state cannot escape from assuming a direct role in conflict resolution, as in the case of teachers' shortages. However, this role is always presented as an emergency role. That is, once the problem is solved, the state may disappear because markets and their trickle-down effect will allocate and distribute much better than any bureaucratic body.

(Bonal, 2003: 167–8)

Bonal (2003) points to the paradox of a 'structural' mode of state intervention trying to channel demand towards the achievement of an affordable output, when accompanied by a 'conjunctural' response to dealing with risk and market failure. The paradox comes from the contradiction inherent in neo-liberalism: that the neo-liberal state must occasionally deal with its own failure and be thus forced into intervention in contradiction of its basic tenet (of non-intervention). In theory, the tensions within neo-liberalism – and the differences between it and social liberalism – should have become apparent for education in the United Kingdom with the shift in 1997 from Conservative to New Labour government. However, in practice, New Labour's policies have mainly been a continuation of Conservative ones (Power & Whitty, 1999), though Paterson (2003) suggests (perhaps optimistically) that this is an oversimplification and that there are actually three strands to New Labour's approach: a new social liberalism which has themes within it that come from the New Right of the 1980s as well as older themes from a reinterpretation of nineteenth-century liberalism; a weak developmentalism designed to promote competitiveness; and a new social democracy (Gamble & Wright, 1999) that stresses the inadequacies of unregulated capitalism and the importance of distributing power and opportunity. The New Labour aspiration to create a meritocratic system[3] is what makes its education policies more than a mere replica of Conservative ideas, according to supporters:

[New Labour] opposition to structural reform [stems] from a belief that Liberalism offers a more authentic antecedent for [its] ideology than mainstream 20th Century social democracy. It does not in fact eschew public action, partly because it does use public authority to support people who are socially excluded, and partly because that Liberal tradition would define public to include the voluntary, non-state sector. [New Labour's] Liberal instincts incline [it] to competitive individualism, real partnership between public and private, and using the state only where necessary but – unlike the New Right – certainly where necessary.

(Paterson, 2003: 173)

There are those who disagree, holding that despite protestations to the contrary, New Labour's education policy is fundamentally Conservative, and others have suggested that New Labour policy has at a minimum become a 'means for the state to reduce its obligations' (Hutton, 1999: 102). Still more argue that the morphing of Labour into New Labour can best be understood as a shift from British socialism to European social democracy, in which the free market is seen as the only efficient way of organising production and the state as the only fair way of mitigating the social consequences of such a market (Smith, 1994; Fielding, 1997).

The Conservative governments of the 1980s were the first to take educational initiatives such as cutting expenditure on universities,[4] allowing parents greater choice in schooling and introducing the Assisted Places Scheme which provided state subsidies for poor children to attend fee-paying schools. Later, the 1988 Education Act created local management of schools and a quasi-market in education. It allowed schools to switch to direct funding from central government, rather than remain funded by the local authority – in other words, to become 'grant-maintained' – and for the first time gave parents freedom to select their schools and schools the freedom to select their pupils, which some (but not most) did partly on the basis of ability. To encourage competition and accountability and to aid parents in choosing schools, league tables of examination results were published (Paterson, 2003). In addition, a new national curriculum was introduced that standardised what was taught and tested in schools, and an emphasis on basic skills and vocational training was introduced to appeal to employers. However, these school-based reforms were centralising and discouraging of local initiative and diversity. They encouraged a one-size-fits-all view of school management, which was essentially a bureaucratic, chief executive model.

New Labour thinking on education differs little from that of its predecessor, though the newly elected (1997) Labour government immediately phased out the Assisted Places Scheme and brought grant-maintained schools back under local authority control. It retained the Conservative governments' emphasis on accountability, standards and centralisation, and introduced more primary school testing and greater intrusion into teaching methods. For example, there were set-aside hours in primary schools for literacy and numeracy, schools were encouraged to organise classes according to the measured ability of students (on the assumption that mixed-ability teaching undermined standards) and teachers were discouraged from working with sub-groups or individuals. Secondary-school curriculum reforms split A-levels in a failed attempt to broaden a notoriously narrow, post-compulsory curriculum and encourage vocational and basic skills acquisition. After-school homework clubs were encouraged and a General Teaching Council established to oversee new mandatory qualifications for heads and teachers. For failing schools, the New Labour government imposed new management over the heads of the local authority, and failing authorities were required to hand over their schools to private-sector contractors.

The reliance of New Labour on a plethora of technical initiatives is, according to Paterson (2003: 170) and McElwee (2005: 20), revealed most clearly in its post-compulsory and secondary school reforms, but according to critics, they have failed to improve the structure of the education system as a whole. There is little evidence, for example, that basic skills are now any better developed or that vocational qualifications are any more favourably perceived than previously (Hodgson & Spours, 1999). New Labour policy is pragmatic rather than structural. It is an ideology-free approach that has led to private finance involvement in the building of new public schools, proposals (in the White Paper of October 2005) to privatise existing ones, support for Education Action Zones[5] funded by public-private partnerships to encourage innovation in areas of social deprivation, and the expansion of the specialist sector. Approximately 20 per cent of English secondary schools were Specialist Schools under the Conservative government that introduced them and this has risen steadily under New Labour. At the start of the 2006–7 academic year, there were 2602 Specialist Schools in England and Wales, making up 82 per cent of the maintained secondary sector (Heath, 2006). Specialist Schools rely less than Academy Schools on private finance, but they must get sponsorship of £50,000 from the private sector and in return, they get an additional capital grant of £100,000 and an additional £129 *per capita* funding for four years from the government, which for an average-sized school means an extra £600,000 in government funding.[6] Specialist Schools are also alone among public schools in England in being allowed to select pupils – up to ten per cent – according to their aptitude for the specialism in question. New Labour's support for them and for choice in schooling generally as a tenet of faith has brought it close to the Conservative policy of support for fee-paying private education.

Generally, support for private-sector involvement in schooling in the United Kingdom under both Conservative and New Labour administrations has seen a 're-agenting' (Hatcher, 2006) of the state's role in education.

Old change agents have been replaced by new change agents, like commercial companies, to drive government reform. Hatcher (2006) conceptualises this re-agenting as coming in two distinct forms: *sponsorship*, in which companies – sometimes commercial and sometimes not-for-profit charitable trusts – act philanthropically to make a financial contribution to a school and help it create a business-friendly entrepreneurial curriculum; and simple *commercial management*, in which commercial companies (like Nord Anglia and Capita in the United Kingdom and Edison in the United States[7]) take over the running of schools or local authorities for financial gain or to promote a certain 'world view' (like Global Education Management Systems, for example, which runs an international network of 65 schools – 14 in the UK – consciously to encourage a global perspective among its students). Commercial management is done exclusively and intentionally for profit through public-private partnerships. Sponsorship comes from the involvement of organisations who get nothing tangible financially out of their involvement,[8] so essentially it is 'non-profit privatisation' (ibid.) similar in nature to the traditional system of English fee-paying schools so beloved of Conservative governments.

Spending on education under New Labour is broadly similar to that under the Conservatives, although in the first term of the New Labour government, public funding of education rose less than it did under the Conservatives in the period 1991–5 (Paterson, 2003). Adjusted for inflation, the growth in spending under New Labour is only slightly higher than the average growth in spending over the years (1979–97) of Conservative government.[9]

In the face of all this sameness, Reid (2002: 571) argues for the need to 're-theorise the democratic purposes' of public schooling, which has traditionally been the primary means of ensuring that everyone receives an education that allows them to be active as citizens of a democratic society (Molnar, 2006). In many countries, neo-liberal education policies are redefining the relationship between public and private education, as governments establish a quasi-market to increase consumer choice and competition (Foskett, 1998). The very purpose of public education in the twenty-first century and its connection with democracy is being reconstructed in the midst of pragmatic upheaval. Current neo-liberal policy is based on a 'realist' conception of democracy (Reid, 2002), which assumes that democracy flourishes best in a competitive market economy with minimal state intervention (Carr & Hartnett, 1996). This view of democracy emphasises individual freedom at the expense of collective social aims. From a social democratic, anti-neoliberal perspective, democracy flourishes best in a society that is informed and active (Reid, 2002), where education is regarded as being for the common good and where the state has a large role in its provision (Carr & Hartnett, 1996; Reid, 2002). It holds that education policies that foster competition and stratification do so at the expense of developing social capital, and that schools which are free from each other and from local control must as a consequence serve the needs of exclusive subgroups based on social class and ethnicity.

Reid (2002) and others suggest that the social democratic advocacy of public education is based on an outmoded view of democracy that is no longer relevant in a globalised society. The circumstances and the contexts in which nation states operate have changed so much that it is no longer enough for supporters of public education to argue in favour of a Keynesian welfare state. Assuming support for the democratic role of public education from a past age only serves to reaffirm the opposing neo-liberal philosophy. However, the social democratic agenda is not a uniform single approach. It can be either *cosmopolitan-globalist* or *liberal-communitarian* (Reid, 2002: 580). The former is committed to a universal moral outlook based on respect for humans rights (Turner, 2002) and holds that although nation states continue to be important, the challenge in an integrated world is to create institutions at the global level that are consistent with this moral framework (Nussbaum, 1996; Held, 1999; Venn, 2002). The liberal-communitarian view, on the other hand, starts from the premise that human interests are best defined in a local context and holds that nation states must extend their democracies internally while joining with other states to address global issues (Kymlicka, 1998; Sheil, 2001). The two perspectives are not necessarily opposing, of course, and indeed there are still more alternatives (Safstrom, 2005):

> [Public] schools represent the spaces in our society where young people from a wide range of cultures, experiences and backgrounds can learn with and from one another on a systematic basis, developing the understanding, respect and tolerance that is the lifeblood of a pluralist democracy.
>
> (Reid, 2002: 581)

As a general principle, choice encourages differentiation, which is usually organised around wealth, social status and ethnicity (ibid.), and there is some evidence to suggest that the social and material effects of choice in education may damage public education for the least well-off (Whitty *et al.*, 1998; Thomson, 2001). In the United Kingdom, differentiation has meant that public schools have become less than comprehensive in their intake because the brightest and most socially adept pupils are siphoned off into private education. In practice, public schools have become second-class hierarchical institutions as they fight the top private schools in academic performance league tables and in the eyes of the public, which can be evidenced, for example, by the much lower percentage of pupils entitled to free school meals in the top 200 comprehensives (Sutton Trust, 2006: 4). They have also become more 'demutualised' as they lose their altruistic identity (Connors, 2000), and public schooling as a system has become less efficient as it loses its economy of scale. By default, in the scenario that is playing out, the dominant ethos necessarily becomes one of self-interest.

Held (1999), Kerr (2001) and others argue that the foundations of the new international political order are increasingly limited in the way it can deal with the problems created by globalisation and public sector demutualisation. Others like Dahl (1999) maintain that despite the need for politics to go global, citizen involvement is not practical at an international level (Parekh, 2003), so the challenge is to democratise nation states internally while making them work together externally to address wider issues (Reid, 2002). The free-market neo-liberal response to globalisation is based on a reduction in the protections offered to people against the whims of the market, and is done on the moral basis of welfare state inefficiency (Marginson, 1999). By presenting the welfare state as inefficient, a threat to individual liberty and an impediment to entrepreneurship, governments have been able to 'transfer public agencies to the private sector':

> [Private] activities have been legitimated above those conducted in the public sphere. Community-based activities ... and public sector programmes and institutions are constructed as less worthy, not least because they do not generate financial profits. More than this, our civil society has become saturated with commercialism: it is difficult to escape the ubiquitous presence of corporate sponsorship in many areas of community activity.
>
> (Ibid.: 578)

Those who advocate a pluralist, social democratic response to globalisation advocate greater citizen involvement in decision making, the establishment of structures that advance democracy at global level as well as at national level, 'privilege' notions of community above those of individual self-interest (Henry *et al.*, 1999; Reid, 2002), and the use of processes for negotiating diversity within a commitment to cohesion in society. The imposition of education policy by diktat from experts is not compatible with those aims or with what democracy needs to be today, and given the context of globalisation, the argument for an old-fashioned public education system is not as easily sustainable as it once was.

The rise of 'performativity' in the United Kingdom

In the United Kingdom, New Labour's emphasis on interventionist supply-side economics, criticised by opponents on the Left as paying inadequate attention to structural reform and criticised by right-wing opponents for not concentrating enough on supply, belongs more in the developmentalist than in the *laissez-faire* tradition (Paterson, 2003). By way of excuse, New Labour has come to regard interventionist supply-side economics not only as a means of creating employment, but as a means of regenerating communities and as a response to the pressures of globalisation. The belief is that demand in education can be stimulated through supply-side investment and that the United Kingdom can be made more competitive by synergising vocational education and employment policy. As Power and Whitty (1999) suggest, whereas neo-liberals attribute to the involvement of the state the failure of education to deliver economic prosperity, New Labour attribute it to the failure of the state to get involved soon enough. This aspect of New Labour's education policy differs from that of previous Conservative administrations in that it contains a strong element of moral exhortation (Paterson, 2003), resembling that underpinning 'welfare-to-work' schemes in the United States (Oppenheim, 2001). New Labour regards education as a means of building social capital by creating (and where necessary, enforcing) shared values and promoting more widespread recognition of the duties of citizenship. It is an ideological position described succinctly by Paterson as a 'renewal of social democracy' (2003: 176).

Phillips and Harper-Jones (2003) suggest that few British governments have placed greater priority on education than New Labour, at least in their first administration (1997–2001), although optimistic anticipation turned fairly quickly to despair as the role of the private sector and selection on the basis of ability were increasingly promoted (Hustler *et al.*, 2000; Fielding, 2001; Phillips & Harper-Jones, 2003). Docking (2000), Fielding (2001) and others have analysed New Labour's education policy around what they see as its dominant themes (Phillips & Harper-Jones, 2003): raising standards; modernising structures and practices; promoting choice; and most importantly as a characteristic, measuring performance.

Although modernising structures and practices in education is part of the government's wider effort to modernise the welfare state and encourage a collective responsibility for performance through more effective leadership in schools and an overhaul of teachers' pay and conditions – though more training and better headteachers do not of themselves make for better education (West, 2001) and may even stifle creativity (Gunter, 2001) – the dominant theme underpinning New Labour's education policy is not leadership but 'performativity'; the positivist assumption that it is possible and always desirable to measure performance (Broadfoot, 2001). Performativity is characterised by centralised decision-making in relation to teaching and assessment, the belief that it is necessary to assess the quality of schooling using external indicators, and that the punitive use of a 'naming-and-shaming' approach drives up standards (Phillips & Harper-Jones, 2003). Fielding (2001) and Woods *et al.* (2001) accuse the New Labour government of being obsessed with performativity to the detriment of teaching and learning. They claim it decontextualises effectiveness and makes assumptions about success and the standardisation of testing that are simply not justified. Fielding (2001) goes further in making the distinction between person-centred schools desired by the community and effective schools desired by the government, which are more concerned with results than children; more concerned with outcomes than process.

The New Labour government has also been closely associated with reform of 14–19 education. Though public primary schooling finishes at age 11 and private prep schooling finishes two years later, Pring (2005b) and others have pointed out that 14 has become the 'natural' time for rethinking curriculum provision issues. It is a time when subject choices are made and vocational options are introduced; and a time when students diversify from the national curriculum on the basis of ability demonstrated in the first two years of secondary school. The mere fact of labelling a phase '14–19' suggests that the government is seeking to inculcate a continuity beyond the statutory school-leaving age of 16. The policy aims to increase the participation and retention of young people across the social spectrum, and develop a more skilled workforce through a transformed education system in which there is parity of esteem for vocational courses and a framework by which Britain can prosper economically (Pring, 2005b). Participation and retention in the United Kingdom compares unfavourably with that elsewhere and remains below average for OECD countries.[10] Retention rates in vocational courses are now lower than in the mid-1980s and mid-1990s, though it is difficult to know how much of this 'failure' is due to the success of students leaving school for gainful employment. What can be said is that there has been an increase in the proportion of young people gaining lower-level vocational qualifications (Pring, 2005b: 77). In Britain, there is still a significant minority of young people – possibly as much as seven per cent of all 16 and 17 year olds – not in education, not in training and not employed, but there is little evidence that this problem of 'engagement' is any different in other countries with similarly large urban areas. The New Labour government believes that work-based learning is a means of overcoming this engagement barrier and is the most effective mode of learning for disaffected youth, yet 'there has been a reduction of about 12 per cent in its uptake' (ibid.: 78). The fact that the take-up of apprenticeship courses has failed to reach the government's ambitious targets may be due to the growing doubts about the quality of the learning provided by its private learning providers.[11]

The overly-complex framework for many government reforms also works against them. Different sorts of schools specialise in particular kinds of course. Sixth Form Colleges, many of which are former grammar schools, cream the best 16 year olds as they move to A-level study, and Further Education colleges pick up the residue. Unpopular 'residual schools' (Youdell, 2004: 410) thus become the repositories for pupils that over-subscribed schools choose not to admit (Marginson, 1997). To sum up:

> The [New Labour] government brought together a moral drive for greater social inclusion and an economic drive for greater prosperity. ... And yet, in all the ... practical measures put in place, there is no clear statement of educational aim or purpose, hardly any reference ... to the kinds of qualities and values which make young people into better human beings, no vision of the kind of society which a more skilled workforce should serve, no idea of the kind of learning which one should expect of an educated person in the present economic, social and environmental context. ... Certainly, young people need to learn those skills and attitudes which will enable them to ... contribute to the economic well-being of themselves and of the wider society. But not all learning is judged to be worthwhile in such a limited sense of utility. We have inherited a world of ideas through which we have come to understand the physical and social and moral worlds in a particular way. It is an inheritance, and it is the job of education to enable the next generation to gain access to that inheritance, to grasp and understand those ideas and to gain a deeper understanding of the world in which they live. The pity is that we

have been here before and yet, having no educational memory, the Labour government seems unable to learn from the past.

(Pring, 2005b: 82–3)

Between regulation and the free market: demarchical control

Globalisation can have both positive and negative effects on nation states, though perhaps it is more accurate to say that different forms of globalisation can have different effects: some forcing greater interconnectedness between nations; others forcing greater economic neo-liberalism. Olssen (2004) argues in favour of an interconnected cosmopolitan democracy – a 'thin communitarianism' – based on Foucault, wherein strategies that preserve the openness of power structures are followed (Szerszynski & Urry, 2002), and against a neo-liberalism that reduces social regulation and abolishes protection for small-scale producers of basic goods and the jobs and wages of the lowest paid. Research by MacEwan (1999), Castells (1996), Esping-Andersen (1993) and others supports the criticism that neo-liberalism undermines the stability of communities and education programmes that require a significant role for the public sector – the developed world has seen increased inequality in the distribution of wealth as a result of decreased state control – but neo-liberals offer the pragmatic retort that the 'logic of globalisation dictates a greater role for markets uninterrupted by government regulatory controls' (Olssen, 2004: 232). Government intervention, the argument goes, frightens wealthy investors who, as a consequence, take capital and savings out of that country and impoverish it. Although neo-liberals hold as a fundamental tenet that economic growth is fastest when the movement of goods, services and capital is unimpeded by government regulation (Olssen, 2004), not everyone agrees. Some commentators maintain that growth without regulation is a myth, as is the expectation that markets, which everyone accepts must be controlled in *some* way, can regulate themselves. For example, although neo-liberalism defends and promotes the free movement of goods, services and capital, there has not been an equal respect for the free movement of labour. Additionally, there is evidence that growth in the richest nations is not the result of free trade, but of regulation. Rich countries selectively protect industries when it suits them (Armstrong *et al.*, 1984; Castells, 1996) so that markets are not in fact integrated, as neo-liberals claim: capital flow is restricted by banking regulations, the mobility of labour is restrained by immigration controls and multinationals still base their operations in a 'home' country (Cohen, 1990; Olssen, 2004). From this, Olssen (2004) argues that because education and skills are crucial to the global economy, educational development must be supported from the public purse, even if many of the presumed connections between schooling and economic well-being are fairly nebulous (Wolf, 2002). Even with the shift from a Fordist production economy to a new information and service-based economy, individual nation states must resist the pressures of international neo-capitalism, and education and skills development is pivotal in this respect. This is not to argue that the nation state has a right to inefficiency and unproductiveness, nor is it to advocate that the state should be merely a 're-distributive agency' (Olssen, 2004: 234). The 'non- bureaucratic welfare state' should be decentralised and committed to increasing participation 'from student and citizen involvement in schools and public services, to consumer representatives on the boards of large business enterprises' (ibid.: 235), and it should not abandon the notion of the common good in favour of individual self-reliance and whole-scale marketisation.

There is nothing inherently wrong with arguments in favour of the devolution of authority to schools if that devolution is genuinely democratic. Olssen (2004) argues that it might even strengthen democracy as it involves an empowered, community-based welfare *society*, rather than a welfare *state* (Davey & Dwyer, 1984), but insists that such a move cannot be promoted as a 'third way' concept because it does not hold that the market is a superior mechanism for allocating resources. Despite globalisation, the state still has a role to play in education, though there are now many other agencies operating through 'demarchical' control;[12] that is to say, control by independent organisations, rather than by individuals or the state:

> [The state] is still the superior agency, hierarchically relating to all other constituents in a definite territory with clear boundaries. While it is effected [*sic*] to a greater extent in the twenty-first century by international pressures and greater interdependence, this is not a qualitatively new form of development.
>
> (Olssen, 2004: 240)

Commentators like Olssen (2004) therefore see education as the 'third estate' between the free market and the 'autocratic hand of regulation'. Its role is crucial to democracy, as schools mediate between the family and institutions of the state and its economy. Although most schools are public institutions, they are semi-autonomous; not in the neo-liberal sense where management is devolved to local schools, but in the sense that schools represent local community groups. Schools are democratic organisations, connected to local communities and empowering of families and minorities. It is where democracy, self-government, civic duty and good citizenship based on tolerance are learnt.

Between regulation and the free market: mobility and the leisure curriculum

Most globalisation theories focus on political and economic issues, at the expense of the social and cultural, but what little work there is on the latter rarely considers the implications for children (Ailwood, 2000). In this respect, Bauman (1998) raises some interesting issues of time, space and (physical and virtual) mobility. In both developmental psychology and sociology, conceptions of time and space are integral to teachers' ways of thinking about childhood and children, as is the issue of mobility and the relationship between the market and children as consumers (Ennew, 1996; Luke, 1999; Walkerdine, 1999). Walkerdine (1999) and Luke (1999) both point to ways in which new Information Technologies bring with them different conceptions of space. With greater access to Information Technology, it is not just children's physical mobility that comes into question, but also their mobility within new forms of space like cyberspace (Ailwood, 2000). The knowledge and understanding required to move effectively through cyberspace extend beyond that normally expected of young children in developmental terms. Therefore, many children who, say, have home access to the Internet arrive in primary school classrooms with a host of skills unaccounted for by traditional measures of literacy (Luke, 1999).

Walkerdine (1999) refers to the regulation of middle-class children's time and mobility through extra-curricular activities organised by adults as 'the full-diary syndrome', and Ennew (1996) discusses the control adults have over children's time – their 'leisure curriculum' – and how it is organised around adult needs and used as a means of developing cultural capital for middle-class children. The central issue implicit in these discussions is the control of physical mobility, since children obviously need transport to participate:

> [Parents] who have the means are increasingly under pressure to fill young children's time beyond ... school with private lessons of some description. The multiple layers of perpetual motion in the life of a ...

child is the fertile soil that grows effective consumers. It could be argued that the carefully targeted advertising and images in children's media ... [showing] the ultimate in children's culture is beamed via television across many a household, and via the internet ... The consumption of computers, music lessons, sports and other activities costs money, as does the transportation of children between activities. For many young children and their parents, even being a member of the local sports team is a struggle, and thoughts of computers with games and internet access are but a pipe dream.

(Ailwood, 2000: 109)

Questions must therefore be asked regarding the links between globalisation and education policy with respect to children's mobility. Globalisation maps onto local practice in unpredictable ways, so the development of education policy is tied to the process of translating and transforming global trends to a local context (Lingard, 2000). In both the United Kingdom and Australia (Queensland), for example, the pro-globalisation political environment has enabled policymakers to prescribe a curriculum, even for children as young as pre-school, which 'pushes the processes of surveillance and testing downward' (Ailwood, 2000: 110) and forces teachers and children to engage with schooling outcomes – in the case of pre-school children, readiness for primary school in terms of literacy and numeracy skills – rather than with learning processes.

Globalisation and school improvement

Mortimore (2001) suggests that globalisation undermines traditional educational objectives: the passing on of knowledge accumulated over generations; the development of skills from basic literacy and numeracy to advanced intellectual analysis; and the appreciation of culture. He suggests that school-effectiveness research has failed to establish better the relationship between schooling and culture, and that Porter's (1999) simple definition of globalisation (referred to previously), which conjures up a 'vision of a peaceful coming together and renouncing of individual interests' masks a 'mad scramble for domination by the powerful' over the rest (Mortimore, 2001: 230). Globalisation, to those who share this critical view, is but another form of colonisation, and not an entirely new phenomenon at that (Kelly, 2001, 2004). As Robertson (1992) points out, globalisation has been evolving since the fifteenth century, taking off between 1870 and 1925 (Ailwood, 2000); the current phase is merely one of 'uncertainty', which term seems especially appropriate given the decline of the traditional nation state and the emergence of post-national politics (Appadurai, 1996; Ailwood, 2000).

Fundamentally, globalisation has come about through the search for more profitable markets, while technological advances have simultaneously made knowledge less precious and more freely available in real time (Kelly, 2001). This has both promoted and enabled an 'escape' from national regulation, which according to Mortimore (2001) is characterised by four relatively new phenomena: international capital can move freely around the world in pursuit of profit; more countries are forced by free-trade to compete on the basis of price, which in turn diminishes the protection national governments can offer native industry; commercial companies can employ from a world-wide pool; and production and service can move to low-wage and 'friendlier' tax environments without any adverse effect on output quality. As a consequence of these phenomena, the economic power and freedom to act of nation states has been reduced, perhaps even to the extent where democracy is under threat (J.Beck, 1999), while multinational corporations have become more powerful. This has implications for education, which has traditionally been the remit of individual states. According to Porter (1999), western democracies have retreated from their traditional political commitment to education in favour of a 'drive' for basic skills based on the imperative of economic prosperity.

Against this backdrop of encroaching globalisation, Mortimore (2001) traces the development of school-effectiveness research from that by Coleman *et al.* (1966) and Jencks *et al.* (1972), which famously concluded that if all American high schools were equally effective, differences in attainment would be reduced by less than one per cent (Ouston *et al.*, 1979). Following this, in the United Kingdom, Rutter *et al.* (1979) embarked on what Mortimore (2001: 236) regards as the 'first phase of school effectiveness research', finding (like Edmonds, also in 1979) that the influence of schooling on students' life-chances, while small, was significant even when account was taken of the differences in the students themselves. The 'second phase of school effectiveness research' in the 1980s focused on replicating earlier research with students in a variety of settings and found that different schools had different degrees of effectiveness, but that those serving disadvantaged students could, despite their constituencies, still be effective (Mortimore *et al.*, 1988; Sammons *et al.*, 1995). The research emphasis then shifted away from school effects to action on school improvement, until we arrive today at what constitutes a fourth phase of school effectiveness research, focusing on the global comparison of schools in different cultural settings (Mortimore *et al.*, 2000).

'Fourth Phase' studies have found that though different schools in different countries use similar strategies, 'the different contexts in which they operate' – including cultural attitudes to education and intelligence, and the motivating effect of better career prospects in some places – 'mean that similar actions do not always produce similar results' (Mortimore, 2001: 239). Therefore, despite the pressures of globalisation and the pressure on emerging nations particularly to adopt a universally approved approach, school improvement techniques must, according to Mortimore, 'fit with the grain of society'. There is no one size to fit all contexts. Additionally, research suggests that change should be initiated and implemented by schools themselves and not by diktat from the centre, though of course schools cannot lift society up by its own bootstraps. Schools alone cannot overcome the link between social deprivation and low educational attainment. In all cultures, it is likely that those from disadvantaged backgrounds will generally perform less well in competitive examinations than their more advantaged peers.

Mortimore (2001) lists the challenges for schooling in a globalised future: whether or not schools should continue to be part of a national network run by government, at what cost and under what sort of regulation; how best to plan the building of new schools, and the design and implementation of new systems of curriculum and assessment; and how best to group learners.[13] The trend over the last 25 years has been for governments to set schools free from government control. The argument in favour of schools being independent is straightforward: that neither national nor regional government knows best what is good for schools and local communities, who should properly feel a sense of ownership of schools if society is to be genuinely democratic. The argument in favour of *national* government control is that it ameliorates the adverse effects of uneven local spending; the argument in favour of *regional* government control is that it ties schools to communities, insofar as that is ever possible, and stops schools from selecting pupils on an 'easy-to-teach' basis to the disadvantage of society generally.

Globalisation, managing change and teacher professionalism

The congruence of various national educational initiatives and the effects of global neo-liberal governance by powerful political and financial organisations has established a managerialist agenda characterised by a desire for accountability, entrepreneurialism and effectiveness measurement (Angus, 2004). Bottery (2001) and others have examined transformational leadership in this context, where success by headteachers is defined mainly in terms of their achievement of government-imposed targets, and suggests that the situation is exacerbated by a professional culture of compliance. In the United Kingdom and elsewhere, the government's preferred model for school leadership is a transformational one, and Bass (1985) and others consider this a necessary ingredient, along with scientific managerialism (Day *et al.*, 2000), of effectiveness. Whereas transactional leadership relies on the exchange of favours, transformational leadership relies on the ability to inspire:

> The argument for transformational leadership seems at least in part to be that individuals generally dislike change and will resist it until they can see good reason to be committed to it. However, in an age of continual change, it is now an essential function of leadership to generate this commitment by providing a vision of the change mission, and the means of achieving it.
>
> (Bottery, 2001: 200)

Transformational leadership creates – critics might say 'imposes' – a vision and with it the confidence and trust of followers. In many ways, it is a micro-response to macro globalisation pressures and in schools it is underpinned by the belief that leadership should involve the widest participation of stakeholders (Leithwood *et al.*, 1999; Day *et al.*, 2000). It lends itself, as Bottery (2001: 201) says, to 'rich conceptions of the pedagogical relationship between teacher and student', which make it superior to commercial and market-based models of headship. Transformational leadership is sensitive (and specific) to political and economic contexts (Shah, 2006), so its parameters can be defined by the forces of globalisation (Bottery, 2001) even when there is disagreement as to the exact effect of such forces. Green (1999) and Marginson (1999), for example, argue that although globalisation predicts the destruction of the nation state and the demise of public systems, nation states still retain considerable control of taxation, policing, health care provision and education, and globalisation forces are generally mediated by governments and cultures. This is not to deny the existence of global influences and pressures: there is certainly a drive today towards a polity beyond that of the nation state, which relocates areas of traditional responsibility into larger transnational bodies; and there is an accelerating trend towards a global capitalism and free-trade that pressurises citizens to identify with localities rather than with nations (Naisbett & Aburdene, 1988; Parsons, 1995). Yet there are discernable opposing forces, working against the trend towards globalised uniformity, which advocate and have the effect of increasing cultural diversity within nation states. While these trends all have their effects, pro-globalisation economic trends have the most immediate and greatest impact on services like education, so that governments are forced primarily to devise coping strategies to deal with the huge financial clout of a growing number of large multinational corporations and in particular their ability to switch production at the drop of a hat to more favourable (i.e. cheaper) location (Brown & Lauder, 1997):

> [There is] a 'global auction' [in which] corporate investors play off nation states one against another in the game of driving down wages and taxes in exchange for investment in local jobs. This can lead, particularly in the developing world, to what Brecher (1993) has called a 'the race to the bottom'.
>
> (Bottery, 2001: 204)

An alternative strategy to auctioning cheap labour is for states to move to the hi-tech end of the market, like Singapore (Ashton & Sung, 1997), but this requires a huge investment in expensive education programmes to provide a flexible and highly skilled workforce. Domestic markets alone do not provide employers with sufficient incentives to invest in skills enhancement for employees, so governments must intervene in education and training. The belief that the purpose of education is to act as a driver for economic well-being has implications for school leadership: concerns for social cohesion assume a secondary importance; education becomes increasingly centralised; the distinction between public and private sectors becomes blurred; and headteachers become merely 'implementers of governmental policy' (Bottery, 2001: 206) or apparatchiks. Educational change is mediated by culture and structure in the same way as global change is mediated by individual nation states (ibid.), so there are limits to the kinds of leadership possible. At a school or college level, permissible leadership styles are bounded by, among other things, organisational maturity and the extent to which participants are willing (or able) to create a culture of shared values. The nature and acceptance of followers is important as well, increasingly so as change becomes more complex. Bottery (2001) argues that in the United Kingdom over the last two decades, headteachers have had to cope with many and various changes: the introduction of the National Curriculum; the creation of an internal market in which student numbers have a direct bearing on school income; examination league tables; assessment at various Key Stages; Office for Standards in Education

(OFSTED) inspection; a plethora of literacy, numeracy and skills initiatives; and the introduction of performance-related pay for teachers. So naturally the nature of school headship has changed too, from patristic (authoritarian) leadership in the transmission of moral and cultural values, via social democratic (collegial) and entrepreneurial chief executive (collaborative) leadership, to today's outcomes-focused transformational leadership (Grace, 1995). New Labour government policy views the quality of senior leadership in schools as crucial to the success of their policy reforms. It sees headship as a solitary activity, so it has moved to a system of qualification, rather than experience, for headteachers. This ties school inspection to notions of effectiveness, which in turn are linked to measures of economic prosperity in a competitive global environment and which constrains headteachers' ability to 'adopt a truly transformational role' (Bottery, 2001: 211). The consequent increase in administration and bureaucratic tasking does not of and in itself prevent the emergence of transformational leaders on an individual basis, but it has had an adverse effect systemically:

> There will always be remarkable individuals who fight against systemic constraints, and who do remarkable things for and with their organizations ... Yet a reliance on this kind of individual is inadequate, simply because it is not enough to expect these exceptional individuals (or their schools) to counter the effects of a system-wide emphasis on and reduction to technical efficiency, market responsiveness, and outcomes fixation. ... So whilst circumstances do not need to be perfect for the exercise of transformational leadership, the political and cultural context does need to be supportive if widespread development is to be possible.
>
> (Ibid.: 212)

The influence of professional culture in constraining transformational leadership is linked to followership. Transformational leadership in schools requires a supportive followership, despite the fact that teachers are restricted in their view of professionalism in that they see their role as being primarily to impart knowledge to students and this prevents them from taking a wider view of their own leadership potential. This view is not confined to public-sector teachers of course. Earlier research by Bottery (1998) suggests that as teachers in public schools come face to face with the kind of competitive pressures faced by private-sector teachers, their values change and they begin to see expertise in terms of competitive advantage.

Bottery and Wright (2000) suggest that schools do little to help teachers develop a wider understanding of the pressures (like those of globalisation) on education. Schools tend to concentrate only on enabling teachers to do a better job in the classroom, ignoring the bigger picture. This is not solely the result of legislation: there appears to be an inherited professional culture that leads teachers to 'collude in their de-professionalisation' (Bottery, 2001: 214). There is clearly a need to recognise the importance of a 'culturally and politically contextualised' approach to leadership and it must be recognised that while local education leaders have their agenda imposed by central government, so do national governments have their agenda imposed by new globalising super-national organisations. Just as policymakers attempt to mediate globalisation effects, so educators attempt to mediate government legislation (ibid.). For transformational leadership to be realised in schools then, teachers and school managers must develop greater political appreciation, which historically their professional culture does not encourage.

The deterministic notion that globalisation is homogeneous in its effects around the world implies acceptance of a structure that imposes its irresistible will on people and circumstances without any possibility of local moderation (Angus, 2004; Edwards *et al.*, 1999). This is not a credible theorisation, though there is widespread acceptance of it with the growing dominance of international over national politics. In schools, globalisation is conceptualised as an external phenomenon that results in competition (Gewirtz & Ball, 2000) and the replication of policies on accountability, inspection and effectiveness around the developed and developing world (Dale, 1999). And conversely, in the United Kingdom at least, local government is conceptualised benignly as aligned with old-fashioned welfarism. Unsurprisingly, some see this as an over-simplification. Angus (2004: 25) and others (Dale, 1999, 2000) suggest that the sense of professional partnership that existed in pre-Thatcher Britain was not simply a 'gift of government', but the result of 'contested educational politics'. Nor is it clear that the new super-technocrats in transnational organisations like the OECD and the European Union are initiating change according to their own agenda rather than simply responding to changing circumstances beyond their making (Bacchi, 2000). Angus (2004) suggests that commentators make educational change seem the result of 'mysterious networks' rather than the 'hard graft of power and politics in which we are all implicated', and that these descriptions of educational change rely essentially on unfounded generalisations about globalisation. Educational change is concerned with the negotiation and contestation of educational meaning and politics, and although contemporary conceptualisations of globalisation have been widely 'asserted as regimes of truth', meaningful educational change is achieved in the real world by 'complex human agents'.

Many of the pressures that have reshaped conceptions of teacher professionalism have resulted in the disempowerment of teachers and a shift in the relative status of professional values. Despite this, many teachers retain their enthusiasm and acquiesce in the new managerialism only to maintain an influence in what they care passionately about. Part of being a member of a profession is being able to define that profession in terms of its cultural and symbolic capital (Angus, 2004). Therefore, although professional norms may be contested from within, the profession's legitimacy rests largely on a sense of its own distinctiveness. The importance of competition and performance is a pragmatic imperative, threatening the autonomy of teaching's cultural capital, but the blame for re-culturing schools and education cannot be entirely laid at the door of globalisation:

> [The] everyday ... politics in ... schools ... are connected to, but not determined by, the macro-politics of globalization, the weakening of the nation-state, ... the reduction of education to a site of economic planning, the control of schools and teachers by neoliberal governments, and the like. The reconstruction of education as a social institution fits neatly into the neo-liberal cultural agenda, but we are all complicit in such reconstruction in particular sites.
>
> (Ibid.: 39)

The narrow notion of 'agency' – the ability and willingness of teachers to *resist* unfavourable agendas – used to argue in favour of globalisation as the cause of managerialism in education is overly simplistic. Teacher agency is also the exercise of engagement in ways that occasionally *support* external agendas: 'we exercise agency when we comply just as much as when we resist' (ibid.: 40). The challenge is to identify how and why teachers and heads resist the globalisation agenda, the circumstances and ways in which they sometimes comply and the effects of both on school performance.

4
School Choice and Marketisation

The General Agreement on Trade in Services

The increasing number and influence of global trade agreements is evidence that education has not been commodified in one fell swoop, but progressively over many years. Nevertheless, it is possible to identify several significant milestones on the road to commodification. In 1944, finance ministers met in Bretton Woods, USA, for the United Nations Financial and Economic Conference. Within two years, the International Bank for Reconstruction and Development (the 'World Bank') and the International Monetary Fund (IMF) had been established. Today, the latter operates through 'Structural Adjustment Programmes' – economic advice packages put together by IMF advisors – which typically impose public sector cost-cutting measures on governments through the privatisation of expensive public services and which critics suggest causes problems because it creates systems copied from outside in countries facing financial difficulty without proper acknowledgement of local traditions.

The original aim of the Financial and Economic Conference was to establish three organisations, but attempts to found an International Trade Organisation were rejected by the United States Congress. Instead, a General Agreement on Trade and Tariffs (GATT) was instituted to decrease tariffs on the import and export of industrial goods and to achieve a liberal world market based on free trade. Today, GATTs are typically negotiated in 'rounds of talks' and ratified later by member countries. A World Trade Organisation (WTO) was eventually established at the start of 1995 to improve trade and investment conditions, stabilise trade relations and achieve progressive liberalisation (Bienefeld, 2001). Situated in Geneva and currently with 149 members, the WTO oversees two main treaties in addition to the GATT: the Trade Related Intellectual Property Rights (TRIPS) and the General Agreement on Trade in Services (GATS), which is of particular interest to those involved in education and choice in schooling.

The GATS covers service areas from telecommunications and finance to education, and came into force at the same time as the organisation itself was established. It is based on the 1948 GATT and the (never-ratified) Multilateral Agreement on Investment (MAI). It facilitates an international trade in services more or less free from restrictions on suppliers and applies to all services – including public services, which are defined as services not provided on a commercial basis or in competition with other suppliers – except services supplied 'in the exercise of government authority' (Article I, Section 3b) (World Trade Organisation, 1994). Education, however, is not so identified. It is seen as a knowledge *industry* rather than a social service (Consumers International, 2001).

The GATS recognises four categories of trade, in education as in everything else: cross-border supply, like delivering distance learning programmes using the Internet; consumption abroad, like student-exchange programmes; commercial presence, like opening branch campuses or partnerships abroad; and the presence of persons, like overseas recruitment of lecturers and researchers. Each service sector can be either 'generally' or 'specifically' committed to GATS. *General Commitment* essentially confers a 'most favoured nation' status and service providers from such countries are treated equally with national providers (Article II). *Specific Commitment* means that the sector is fully signed-up to GATS and is expected to maintain the highest degree of liberalisation and market access, which in essence means that suppliers from all other WTO member states have unfettered access (National Union of Students in Europe, 2001). The key requirement for Specific Commitment is to agree to abstain from measures that modify the conditions of competition, in law or in fact, in favour of a member's own domestic service industry, and critics like Wainwright (2003: 178) warn:

> The long-term consequences of GATS are drastic. If it is allowed to go through, it will open up all public services worldwide to private corporate investment. Most human activities will become, in the fullness of time, profit oriented commodities.

Education is one of the least 'committed' service sectors, but the European Union, on behalf of most of its member states, has earmarked education as a Specific Commitment even though education legislation in the European Union falls under the jurisdiction of national governments.[1] There are 30 commitments on primary education, 35 on secondary education, 32 on higher education, 32 on adult education and 20 on other education services. There are more limitations placed on primary and secondary education than on higher and adult education. But there is mounting pressure from the United States, Australia, Japan and New Zealand, which until very recently followed a very aggressive policy in favour of a free market in schooling, for the European Union to make more liberalising commitments on market access to all levels of education, including primary and secondary. Large English-speaking countries like the United States and the United Kingdom raise substantial revenues from exporting education. They sell education services abroad, especially to China and other Asian countries with big market potential. For example, Nottingham University has branded extensions in China and Malaysia, as does Shrewsbury (private) School in Thailand. The commodification of education in a liberalised market regime suits 'producer' nations very well.

Critics suggest that the increased pressure to privatise education poses a threat to academic freedom and internal democratic subsidies, which Article XV of GATS states are 'trade-distorting' and should be declared illegal. Critics argue that globalisation and privatisation transforms education from a public good to a private privilege (Molnar, 2006) and there is also a suspicion that licensing schools abroad, of the type done by Shrewsbury School in Thailand, is harmful to poorer countries because it inhibits the growth of indigenous, culturally-contextualised native schools of a similar quality.

Some governments have decided that deregulation is the most politically painless way to ease the burden on the treasury of increased participation, especially in higher education, and GATS goes a long way towards establishing a framework for transnational education, where suppliers offer education in countries other than their own. The movement of education suppliers, students, lecturers and researchers are all covered by the agreement, which has provision for setting up an international regulatory body for licensing and assuring quality, though Article VI 4(b) stipulates that regulation should be kept to a minimum. However, as the National Union of Students in Europe (2001) points out, there are no provisions for the mobility of welfare and student support: GATS concentrates on 'developing trade and not on developing excellence'.

The emergence of state-market partnerships

There are those that suggest that 'new market-states' (Bobbitt, 2002) are replacing nation states across the globe and that this can be seen most notably in the governance of education, where a new devolution of provision to non-governmental agencies is replacing local government delivery by welfare states. The belief that society has entered a new post-capitalist phase is widely held (Clarke *et al.*, 1994), providing a foundation, in the United Kingdom at least, for the post-modernist belief that 'reconciling the state and the free market transcends capitalism and socialism' (Ainley, 2004: 497). Bobbitt (2002) proposes an elaborate typology of state formations, from the Princely State and the Kingly State, through the Territorial State and the Nation State, to the Market State, whose emergence (and the start of globalisation) can be traced to the end of European communism in the late 1980s (Ainley, 2004: 499). Nation states exist in order to benefit the people they govern: the 'flow of legitimacy' is from the governed to the state (Bobbitt, 2002). Whereas a nation state, with its system of welfare and free public education, guarantees the well-being of the nation, a market state promises instead to maximise individual opportunity and to make 'representative government less influential and more responsive to the market' (ibid.: 211). A legalist orientation is being replaced by a marketist orientation. The market state offers no welfare entitlement for its citizenry; rather it depends on international capital and capitalists, and perceives its role as a 'minimal provider' (Ainley, 2004: 500) of opportunity (rather than wealth) in a classless society. Supporters claim that market states are empowering and reward the most dynamic of their people so as to allow them the opportunity to generate wealth for everyone, but classless societies have not materialised with their emergence. Rather, a new under-class to replace the old manual working class has emerged, which is:

> increasingly segregated from the rest of society not only by its growing poverty ... but by the lack of any worthwhile academic qualifications. Education and training has, thus, played a large part in contributing to and now sustaining this new social situation. The new market-state, therefore, becomes also the workfare state and the penal state for those from whom the guarantee of social insurance against unemployment has been removed.
>
> (Ibid.: 501)

Critics further suggest that the market state represents a new social contract between the state and its citizens, and that the old division between the public state and private enterprise has been blurred by the fact that some 'critical infrastructures' like education are now 'in the hands of the private sector' (Bobbitt, 2002). Supporters of the welfare state oppose this privatisation of education because it removes the cultural aims of schooling from the nation state, but Bobbit (ibid.: 242) suggests that the days of mass public education are numbered and that American-style voucher systems, wherein the state gives greatest support to the most popular schools, are likely to become the norm both inside and outside the United States.

In the United Kingdom, the change from nation state to market state, established by successive Conservative governments in the 1980s and 1990s, and strengthened afterwards by successive New Labour governments (Ainley & Corney, 1990), stemmed from the rapid rise in unemployment in the recession following the oil crises of the mid-1970s. Early Conservative governments introduced Youth Training Schemes and other employment initiatives managed by the Manpower Services Commission. Later, in 1986, the Department for Education and Science set up City Technology Colleges as a solution to the crisis,[2] which heralded the start of the transfer of power away from local authorities to the central state. It was a move away from a national system locally administered, and continued years later with Incorporated Polytechnics and Further Education colleges (Ainley, 2004).

State-induced enterprise is a means of privatising problems and decentralising responsibility while retaining power centrally (Wallace & Chandler, 1989). It is a means by which government can retain control of policy while distancing itself from delivery, and remain flexible enough to expand and contract its bureaucracy in response to circumstance:

> In this new 'mixed economy' of private and state capital ... indiscriminately mingled together, ... former services provided by the local or national state are taken over and sold off to private companies, [and] other public services are retained by the state as semi-independent agencies to be run at a profit. Citizens are then re-defined as consumers with individual rights enshrined in the contractual relations of 'Charters'.
>
> (Ainley, 2004: 504–5)

The market state can reconfigure existing services like education or it can create entirely new services 'from the bottom up' to provide more comprehensive provision or to tackle problems like social exclusion (Ainley, 2004). Such a cycle of deregulation and reconfiguration is common in education and training, particularly in private- and voluntary-sector services funded (in part at least) by the state. Targets might be set centrally, but local providers have discretion to vary them in response to local needs and priorities. Different social groups can be targeted with 'flexible and discriminating' approaches (ibid.: 506), though the long-term agenda is that models of best practice and differentiated local provision are developed that can be replicated across all schools (Barnes *et al.*, 1998):

> The new arrangements ... extend across the whole new or post-welfare state to dynamize and differentiate the 'one size fits all' national entitlement provision of the old welfare nation-state. As seen, a feature of the new social polity is that it indiscriminately mixes together private and public provision, offering state-subsidies to the private and voluntary sectors at the same time as semi-privatizing the state sector.
>
> (Ainley, 2004: 506)

Education policy in the United Kingdom seeks to encourage competition between schools through a variety of initiatives. From the 1980s, a 'locally managed zonal system of allocation' (Adnett & Davies, 2003: 398) was replaced by a system in which parents could express a preference for certain schools. In addition, league tables were introduced to provide parents with objective information regarding individual school performance, though of course the measures of effectiveness used were crude. Although the data used to compile league tables is still not completely understood (West & Pennell, 2000), they are still widely used by parents to guide them in school-choice decisions (Woods *et al.*, 1998).

The underpinning belief that competition raises standards does not always result in consistent policies, nor is it the case that competition was always top of the government's list of priorities. Earlier reforms at the beginning of New Labour's reign promoted cooperation instead. The first New Labour white paper on education in July 1997, *Excellence in Schools*, hinted at a shift away from the Conservative government's competition agenda. Education Action Zones, typically involving two or three secondary schools and their feeder primary schools, and the

Excellence in Cities scheme launched in 1999, both promoted innovation and cooperation rather than competition in areas of high deprivation. Similarly, Beacon Schools introduced in 1998 and Specialist Schools (introduced in 1994 by a Conservative government but subsequently greatly extended by New Labour) received additional government funding to spread best practice and were encouraged to use their expertise as a resource for local communities rather than as a means of gaining competitive advantage (Adnett & Davies, 2003).

Whatever the rhetoric and notwithstanding the contradictions, British governments of every hue are increasingly committed to the principle of choice between private and public provision, and to the view that the role of the 'partnership state' is to guarantee (by regulation and supervision) access to basic public goods and services, but not necessarily to provide them. It admits the need for the state to provide welfare, but to do so by a mixture of private, public and voluntary contracts (Whitfield, 2001). Specifically, in relation to education, Ainley (2004) and others highlight a notion developed by Hatcher and Hirtt (1999) of a business agenda for schools and a schools agenda for business. In the United Kingdom, schools are encouraged to act like businesses under the Education Act of 2002, whereby their governing bodies may constitute themselves as private companies to sell services and deal with the private sector; and businesses are encouraged to develop an education agenda by taking over failing schools and local authorities. However, Ainley (2004: 511) points to an inherent contradiction in all this; between on the one hand commodifying qualifications, and on the other, the inability of those same (mostly irrelevant) qualifications 'to guarantee secure employment'.

The calculus of choice and risk

The fact that pupils and parents can choose schools 'has implications for their self-identity' and lifestyle (Giddens, 1991). However, there are associated individualised risks, which Gewirtz *et al.* (1995) and Taylor and Woollard (2003) suggest may encourage the commodification of social relations:

> [The] dominant tendency is for choosers to attempt to colonize the future by drawing on their social and cultural capital. If more equitable choice processes and outcomes are desired therefore, attempts must be made to collectivize risk.
>
> (Ibid.: 617)

Studies from New Zealand support these concerns (Waslander & Thrupp, 1995; Pearce & Gordon, 2005). An education market works as a class reproduction strategy for the middle classes (Ball, 2003a), which in part at least explains why school choice has gained such popular acceptance there (Kenway & Bullen, 2001). Its effects are difficult to measure and different social groups are likely to take up different positions (Dehli, 1996), but school choice seems particularly important to parents who demonstrate greater awareness in a risk society. According to Giddens (1998), a risk society is one living on a technological knife-edge that no one completely understands and which generates a myriad of possible futures. Beliefs are challenged and rendered less certain by scientific advances, which in turn creates greater risk that must somehow be minimised (Beck, 2000):

> To live in [a modern society] is to live in an environment of chance and risk, the inevitable concomitants of a system geared to the domination of nature and the reflexive making of history.
>
> (Giddens, 1991: 109)

There is a general feeling in today's risk society that career paths no longer follow a 'natural' progression and that tradition no longer provides a safeguard against chaotic influences. The individual becomes the 'basic unit of social reproduction' (Beck & Beck-Gernsheim, 2002) and traditional social class inequalities lose some of their significance (Scott, 2000; Taylor & Woollard, 2003). Taylor and Woollard's (2003) research suggests that students no longer consider traditional career paths in their constructions of identity through choice. They tend, unlike their parents, to dissociate their schooling and their careers, and they do not see either schooling or career as part of greater family betterment. The contrary view is that while risk and attempts to control it are pervasive, risk awareness is related to social position and varies across gender, age, ethnicity and nationality (Douglas, 1992; Elliott, 2002; Lupton & Tulloch, 2002; Ball, 2003a). Crooks (1999), for example, suggests that neo-liberalism, which emphasises individual freedom and individual responsibility, is particularly appealing to policymakers because the role of the state is then only to provide 'accountability information' to encourage individual self-reliance. Yet the idea that the risk involved in school choice is purely individualistic must surely be an over simplification (Elliott, 2002; Lupton & Tulloch, 2002) since at a minimum, individuals consult family and friends when taking what they perceive to be risky decisions (Douglas, 1992).

Today, society presents individuals with a range of choices and they are increasingly held responsible for their own self-actualisation, even if not everyone has equal access to equally profitable routes (Giddens, 1991). Those from poorer socio-economic backgrounds tend to make passive choices from necessity; better-off families actively engage with choice and cultivate risk as part of who they are (Kenway & Bullen, 2001). Nevertheless, middle-class parents still remain ambivalent and find stressful the burden of school choice and associated information gathering (Crooks, 1999; Ball, 2003a):

> [Failing] to be the ideal rational consumer leaves [parents] with a sense of not being good parents. But despite the impossibility of knowing whether one has ever made the 'right' choice, the market assumes that responsible parents will invest a great deal of time and energy in trying.
>
> (Taylor & Woollard, 2003: 623)

Attitude to school choice may be related to lack of knowledge among parents about the magnitude of the risks involved (Taylor & Woollard, 2003). The extent to which parents construct school choice as momentous – that is to say, critical to their children's future prosperity (Giddens, 1991) – varies from family to family, but the ability of some parents to intervene in support of their children in the transition to secondary school is significant (Ball, 2003a, 2003b). It is a 're-appropriation of knowledge and control' (Taylor & Woollard, 2003: 624). The middle classes typically want more than the merely adequate (Ball, 2003a) and wherever there is competitive selection for school places, there is a middle-class need for 'committed, opportunistic action' in the struggle to 'colonise the future' (Giddens, 1991). Middle-class pupils are also more aware of themselves as consumers and regard the process of choosing a school as empowering. They believe that it is they who construct a school's environment, though they are aware that not everyone enjoys the same choices or benefits (Taylor & Woollard, 2003).

Of course, middle-class parents and pupils do not constitute a single homogeneous group, though Ball (2003a) suggests that the individualism of the school consumer is mediated through a collective memory and expectation that is sensitive to the habitus of individuals (Bourdieu & Wacquant, 1992). The middle classes are largely dependent on education to acquire and maintain their position (Power, 2001), so according to Ehrenreich (1989), they tend to be more apprehensive both as a group and as individuals. Families from lower socio-economic groupings tend to be more fatalistic and unlike middle-class parents, do not spend time using their social capital to manage risk on behalf of their children (Ball & Vincent, 2001; Ball, 2003a). Research by Taylor and Woollard (2003) suggests that middle-class parents in particular rely more on the 'hot' knowledge derived from social networks of shared values to provide reassurance about risk, than on the 'cold' formal information provided by and about schools (Ball, 2003a), which is the staple diet of working-class families.

In Canada, school choice is also a key theme in educational reform (Robertson, 1998; Levin, 2001). In Alberta, for example, it centres on open enrolment, local management of schools and the introduction of Charter Schools (Taylor, 2001b). Taylor and Woollard (2003) describe Edmonton, a city in Alberta of nearly one million inhabitants, as a leader in the movement for marketisation and greater school choice. The city sees choice as the foundation of its approach to school improvement, beginning with open catchment areas to allow parents and pupils to select the learning environment of their choice. However, Taylor and Woollard (2003) suggest that improvement in school performance in Edmonton may in fact be due to legislative changes at provincial (rather than at city) level (Alberta, 1988), which include new allowances for home schooling and private schools, and rights for parents to enrol in any school willing to accommodate their particular linguistic, cultural, religious or curriculum needs. These legislative changes, it is suggested, work because they introduce competition to the public-school sector, and between public and private sectors. According to Taylor and Woollard (2003: 620):

> [Public schools] have actively forestalled the establishment of charter schools and outflow of students to private schools by responding to requests for alternatives from parents and interested individuals. For example, Christian programmes were introduced in 1996 and three formerly private Christian schools became part of the (public school system) in 1999. Alternative programmes currently address religion, culture and language groupings, special interests (fine arts, sports, military, technology), modes of delivery (home schooling, virtual schooling), gender (all girls), and exceptionality (students with disabilities, gifted). Some programmes are offered in almost every high school in the district ... while others are dispersed across the city.

Catholic schools in Edmonton have acted in a similar pre-emptive way, so competition across the publicly funded school system has increased, as has the movement of pupils between public schools.[3] The idea of reinventing schools or schools reinventing themselves in advance of imposed restructuring – similar to schools in the United Kingdom getting a fresh-start as Specialist Schools – is used in Edmonton as a way of revitalising the system and moving away from old-fashioned 'blue-collar' programmes to modern specialisms, though Ball (2003a) and others suggest that this is pandering to the professional middle classes and adapting public schooling to meet the perceived needs of that minority.

Features of the student population such as ethnicity, which potentially can increase segregation, are important factors in differentiating between schools. Thrupp (1999) has suggested, in another context, that given the comprehensive nature of most high schools, choice can be as much about *who else* chooses the school as anything else, and Taylor and Woollard (2003) confirm this. Parents have been found to be concerned with the notion of school community, but typically they also want control over the social and ethnic mix that their children experience in school and they tend to relate school quality to pupil intake (Ball, 2003a). Neither increased competition between schools nor the promotion of self-interest is likely to foster the kind of school community valued by parents, so there is an obvious tension between what parents want for their children and what they say they value. Research also suggests that irrespective of ethnicity, pupil identities are constructed through school choice, insofar as cultivating risk through actively choosing (rather than passively accepting) a school provides a feeling of control. The reputation of a school is also important in the choice process and parents generally respond to stress by selecting a traditional one (Kenway & Bullen, 2001) even when they do not always encourage traditional educational and societal mores in their children (Taylor & Woollard, 2003).

Markets individualise risk though they may also strengthen social inequality (Douglas, 1992) as the more privileged move out of poor neighbourhood schools to better ones further away, which in turn leads to further decline in the neighbourhood. Individual attempts to find personal solutions to minimise the risk of choice by drawing on resources not available to everyone may result in increased disadvantage for already vulnerable groups (Douglas 1992) and reinforced social divisions (Ball, 2003a). It opens up what Ulrich Beck (1999) calls a 'threatening sphere of possibilities' and can fuel the anxieties that some families feel about the future. The middle classes, whose enthusiasm for advancement is an important driver in the school-choice movement, do not generally question the fundamental principles of choice and risk, even when they result in what are perceived to be unfavourable outcomes, like community breakdown and increased segregation. Rather, they utilise their personal resources to safeguard the future for their offspring, because choice favours the more privileged and the more academic (Taylor, 2003). In that sense, the middle classes are locked into participation, or as Taylor and Woollard (2003: 632) put it, they find themselves 'caught within the discourse'.

As a counter-measure to redress these inherent inequalities, Thrupp (1999) suggests offering higher pay to teachers working in schools serving disadvantaged areas to encourage teacher mobility, but this kind of intervention is despised by free marketeers and may even be contrary to GATS and EU free-trade legislation. Increased segregation remains a significant moral stumbling block for the pro-choice lobby, but the middle classes do not have it all their own way. Ball (2003a, 2003b) points out that additional risks arise for families by the very act of engagement with school choice and this is especially true for middle-class families. They face the haunting prospect of 'generational decline' (Parkin, 1979; Ball, 2003a) in a society that is increasingly preoccupied with futures. Greater school choice has the effect that the middle classes must work harder to maintain their advantage going forward (Halsey, 1995), though of course and by definition, they have more advantages to start with. School choice and neo-liberalism in social policy opens risk to everyone. The middle classes can do no more than use their capital advantages as strategically as possible and 'predispose' their children to reproduce their success (Ehrenreich, 1989) – 'the domestic transmission of cultural capital', as Bourdieu (1986b: 244) put it – and sometimes this includes opting out of public welfare provision (Giddens, 1998). So while marketisation confers advantage on middle-class families, the uncertainty experienced by them in relation to social reproduction is greater:

> The market has a degree of openness and unplannedness which constantly threatens to overwhelm the orderliness and planning, the futurity, which denotes many middle-class households.
>
> (Ball, 2003b: 165)

Not all commentators agree. Some like Gleeson and Keep (2004) suggest that the very idea that education reproduces social class is spurious because it implies that education 'operates in a subservient relationship to the economy'. In fact, wider cultural, global and familial factors are equally, if not more, important:

> Far from being subservient, education has the capacity to mediate contradictory tensions between the economy and society, and to challenge or promote new ideas which serve the interests of both or either.
>
> (Ibid.: 39)

Choice can be a matter of 'uneasy compromise', wherein the citizen-consumer is knitted into various allegiances while appearing merely to be making choices (Rose, 1996). They are 'drawn into the ontology of the market' (Ball, 2003b: 165). For middle-class families, too much choice carries the increased 'possibility of unsuccessful choice-making' (ibid.: 166), the objective for middle-class families being to minimise the risk of poor social reproduction and maximise control of the future. So there is a tension between, on the one hand, the dynamic choice of the market where responsibility and resourcefulness are celebrated in the midst of uncertainty, and the 'one-size-fits-all solution of neighbourhood comprehensive schools':

> which [are generally] perceived by ... middle-class parents, as engendering the risks of levelling ... in relation to their projects of social reproduction and differentiation.
>
> (Ibid.: 166)

Media condemnation and political criticism of public schooling systems provokes anxiety and insecurity, especially among those in the middle classes who have the resources to exercise choice and who typically expend great (and sometimes unnecessary) amounts of time and effort in gathering and discussing data:

> Distrust, self-interest and the over-supply of information within market societies are a heady and unstable combination. This may be a paradox of reflexive modernisation, on the one hand the idea that information is related to control, and, on the other, the idea that all information is potentially unreliable ... Market systems produce (information) which is not to be trusted – tradition is displaced by new ... forms of 'knowledge' – promotion, advertising and aggressive accounting, for example.
>
> (Ibid.: 167)

The upshot for middle-class parents is an education market wherein the exercise of choice is known to be imperfect and risky in terms of what middle-class parents want by way of social reproduction. Less and less is there a logic to 'doing the right thing', as the state shifts from being in a welfarist sense the provider, to being in a neo-liberal sense both the regulator and the source of comparative data. The fact that this comparative data is acknowledged to be incomplete and unreliable imposes a sceptical imperative on the middle classes to check it ... endlessly and without conclusion. Ball (2003b: 168) captures this Catch-22 dilemma very nicely: all information is considered but none is trusted. Information gathering to supplement government information is itself supplemented by visiting schools and socialising within middle-class networks to exchange information and acknowledge each other's self-reliance, but information may not be enough. For parents racked with doubt, mistakes can be 'low probability' but 'high consequence'.

Perception of the risk inherent in school choice varies with type of person and geographical location, which of course is why some families relocate to areas with good schools. Other families stay where they are but use their resources to pay for extra tuition; for example, in the run-up to public examinations or for private interview preparation in advance of university selection procedures. It is as true in the United States as it is in the United Kingdom, both having seen a similar growth in such services since marketisation. It is part of what Elliott (2002) calls the commodification and privatisation of risk. One person's risk is another's commercial opportunity (Ball, 2003b: 169).

In terms of risk, school markets are of course different in different localities. Local catchment areas differ by social class, level of integration and political leanings, and therefore how education is delivered and with what emphasis. These constitute what Ball (2003b: 169) calls 'spaces of subjectivity' and what Butler and Robson (2003: 25) call 'narratives of the areas'. In some catchments, there is a critical mass of collective desire for the same thing; other catchments have more socially disparate groupings. And within reason, schools just reflect their own socio-geographic locations.

For parents who regard public sector schooling as a risk too far, private schools provide the answer. In that respect, private schools are 'enclaves' of social class, social reproduction and culture (Teese, 2000; Sedden, 2001). However, they are more than that; they are enclaves also of aspiration and protection from uncertainty:

> [They] work to export risk of failure to state schools. They protect and reproduce classed 'communities of destiny'. In effect choosing the private sector, as a response to the risks of the state sector, can be seen as a different, older, form of risk management.
>
> (Ball, 2003b: 170)

Private schools provide boundaries that prevent the kind of mixing that dilutes middle-class aspiration and work ethic. They are places where 'neo-liberal policies do not operate', though of course they come at a financial cost to those who choose them (Crook, 1999; Ball, 2003b).

The riskier society is perceived to have become, the more those who can afford it turn to tradition. Ball (2003b) points to an 'enterprise of education within the family' as a particularly middle-class response to the risks associated with school choice, but such an enterprise carries with it at least two opposing senses of social guilt: for choosing private schooling which not everyone can afford; or for not choosing private schooling and thereby failing to provide for one's children to the best of one's ability. This caricature of guilt-ridden, middle-class habitus is one of hard work, prudence, ambition and reproducing in children the values and aspirations of their class. The middle classes look to the future on their children's behalf and while the commodification and marketisation of education through greater school choice, both private and pubic, may have increased exponentially the permutations, it has also increased for middle-class families the risks and consequences of being wrong.

Hierarchies and local markets in schooling

Competition between schools is related not only to relative performance but to social class. Working-class parents are fearful to engage in what is a middle-class discourse, so critics of school choice allege that it exacerbates existing differentials in power and information (Reay & Ball, 1997). However, there are other important factors at work according to research by Taylor (2001), which include the geographical, spatial nature of competition and the movement of pupils between schools.[4]

Local education markets in the United Kingdom are hierarchical in that competition between schools is related to examination performance and the physical whereabouts of other schools in the 'competition space' (Marsden *et al.*, 1998). Considering geographical locations and breaking them into smaller competition spaces allows the specific characteristics of local markets to be taken into account (Taylor, 2001). A competition space or 'local competitive arena' (Glatter & Woods, 1994) is an 'area of interaction between schools in the marketplace' (Taylor, 2001: 199). It is more than a catchment area, and some competition spaces, like those of religious schools, are not based simply on schools being adjacent to one other. Nor is it the case that schools always pursue the greatest number of pupils in its 'arena'. In the case of choice programmes in the United States, for example, schools have been found to respond as much to local as to national incentives, sometimes to the detriment of socially disadvantaged and ethnic communities. In Detroit, Michigan, for example, schools and districts open and close their boundaries to non-residents depending on their proximity to poorer communities and on their relative status within the local market hierarchy (Lubienski, 2005). Generally, in an intense local arena, schools target high-status students.

According to Taylor (2001), calculating the number of pupils who do *not* attend their nearest school gives an indication of the degree to which parents within a local authority are responding to marketisation. The research suggests that parents are more likely to reject their nearest schools in urban authorities, that the majority of schools have competition spaces of between four and nine other schools and that the size of competition spaces also depends on the extent of parental activity in the marketplace. Taylor (2001) proposes three possible bases for competition between schools. Firstly, it may be based on rejecting the nearest school in favour of the next nearest school. Research shows that nearly a quarter of all 'gains' take place between schools and their nearest competitors, which is significant since most schools compete with between five and nine others, and the local authorities with the highest proportion of 'proximity gains' are rural ones. Secondly, the extent of competition between schools may be determined by their relative position in local examination league tables. Schools mostly gain pupils from others below them in the league table, which creates a hierarchy within the local market. Research shows that slightly more than half of all gains are made by pupils in order to move up the league table, which means conversely that a very significant amount of competition – just less than half – is non-hierarchical (probably because there is only a finite supply of places in 'better' schools to cater for the greater demand). Thirdly, diversity of school types within the marketplace – how like or unlike independent private schools they are – may also be a factor in competition between schools. Schools can have varying levels of access – religious, academic and gender based – which create markets operating in parallel with each other: faith with same faith; boys only with boys only; and grammar schools with grammar schools. In Taylor's (2001) research, more than two-fifths of gains were to self-governing schools, but the significance of this varies with the number of such schools in the area.

Different schools have different 'levels of engagement' in the education marketplace. Well-performing faith and selective schools have very little competition from other schools that rely on local intake (Ball *et al.*, 1995; Gorard, 1996; Taylor, 2001) and competition between dissimilar-type schools is often not as significant as it is between similar schools:

> Clearly, attempts to diversify schooling in the UK have only created a new tier of competition. This may be blurring the boundary

between LEA- and self-governing schools that existed before the (1988 Education Reform Act), but it continues to sustain the parallel nature of competition, which in turn could ensure LEA-maintained schools will never be as popular as the more 'exclusive' state schools.

(Taylor, 2001: 211)

Voter support for marketisation and competition in education

In May 2001, Nord Anglia, a commercial company, took over the management of a state school in England. Since then, it is increasingly accepted that public services can better be delivered by a mixture of public and private means (Brighouse, 2003). It is claimed that public schools run by commercial companies on a for-profit basis will improve by importing the culture of the marketplace, and that market discipline will reduce inefficiency, encourage innovation and increase attainment. Public opinion for and against such marketisation largely reflects the 'anticipated personal cost and benefit': parents across the social spectrum are generally in favour; teachers are generally against (Belfield, 2003: 155). However, it is not correct to assume that marketisation is always the result of government policy and that public opinion is incapable of driving its own course. In Ireland, for example, despite the government's reluctance to adopt the competition agenda enthusiastically, middle-class parents are found increasingly to be using their economic capital to *create* a private sector to 'secure the class futures of their children' (Lynch & Moran, 2006: 221). Schools collude in this by encouraging (or discouraging) certain kinds of entrants in order to gain competitive advantage, but the rationale for it – for greater choice in schooling – did not come as in other countries from government-driven neo-liberal ideology, but from domestic constitutional pressures (ibid.: 232) and a booming economy. In Ireland, perhaps uniquely, secondary education is undergoing marketisation from forces *outside* the state system and *without* the government's encouragement or support.

Situations like that in Ireland is one where public preference is reflecting perceived utility and an economic model for understanding this is described comprehensively by Belfield (2003). Utility is a function of education, and individual families seek to optimise it even when constrained by financial considerations:

Education may be thought of as a proxy good, reflecting all the beneficial attributes for the household that are associated with greater levels of education (e.g. earnings capacity, job prospects, social skills); social human capital is also valued by the household on the assumption there are positive externalities from others' education.

(Ibid.: 156)

Since education must be paid for by families, indirectly in taxes or directly in school fees and out of the same budget as general goods, any increase in the price of general goods reduces both the amount available for education and a family's willingness to spend or support public spending on it. Small families in particular reap fewer benefits from tax-funded welfare programmes like public education, and so perceive themselves as subsidising larger 'under-paying' and 'over-consuming' families. Belfield (2003: 157) suggests therefore that improving public education is equivalent to 'lowering its price', and goes on to outline a number of possible policies for reforming the school system:

- The first is to increase the proportion of government spending on education, although the effectiveness of this approach has been questioned by others (Hanushek, 1998). Families that under-pay for education – larger families, typically – will favour this policy, as will teacher-families on the assumption that it will raise their incomes. Families that under-consume public education – those without or with few children and those on high rates of tax – will oppose it. It is possible to increase spending on education either by reducing spending on other public services and keeping taxes the same, or by increasing taxes and maintaining other services at current levels. Those who under-consume public education are likely to prefer the former.

- Another possibility is to improve the efficiency and effectiveness of the current system by increasing competition (West *et al.*, 1998) and giving greater freedom of choice to parents. Families that under-consume public education will be in favour of it; those who under-pay will be against it, 'unless they expect it to increase the quality of provision' (Belfield, 2003: 158).

- A third possibility is to encourage selection on the basis of ability. Such a policy is likely to raise 'productivity', but there are adverse side effects on social capital and freedom of choice for those 'less able'. The most likely opponents of selection on the basis of ability are those who obtain social benefits; the most likely to support it are those with high incomes or those with academic children.

- A fourth option is to eliminate private schooling altogether, which would mean raising taxes and hence the price of education, but it would raise the quality of public education since the more academically able would then *per force* enrol in a truly comprehensive public school system.

> Private schooling may be thought of simply as a higher quality version of public schooling, but it may also be thought of as a different good.
>
> (Ibid.: 158)

For each of these possibilities, both advocates and opponents may choose to disguise their true interests:

> either with reason or with appeals to fairness; households may only report socially desirable responses to such proposed reforms.
>
> (Ibid.: 158)

Belfield's (2003) research, using a sampling frame based on postcodes to examine respondents' views on possible policies for education reform, suggests that nearly three-quarters of parents think that the government should spend more money on education, and more than half think that they should raise income tax in order to do it. Only one-quarter think it a good idea for schools to be made to compete against each other for pupils and only one-fifth think that the government should abolish private education, but nearly half (particularly those with 'identifiable religious belief') are in favour of selection on the basis of ability.[5] Female voters and parents tend to favour greater investment in education, and single and elderly people tend to oppose it, with income having only a weak effect. Generally, homeowners are against increasing taxation to pay for greater investment in education, while younger individuals and those with little education are in favour of extra spending, but like homeowners are against raising it from higher taxation. In fact, only two-thirds of all those who favour greater government expenditure on education are in favour of raising income tax to do it.[6] Belfield (2003) suggests that strongest support for competition and selection of pupils by ability comes from families with children, from families whose children have been or are in private education and among older respondents. Opposition comes largely from teachers and others who work in education, but again, income has little effect.[7]

Like the general public, academics are divided on issues relating to privatisation in education. Brighouse (1998, 2003), for example, argues convincingly against both contracting out the management of schools to private companies and voucher schemes,[8] claiming that the former cannot yield greater efficiency because the contracting process is insufficiently competitive, and the latter cannot work because the private sector in the United Kingdom is unwilling to participate fully in a sector with such high 'social justice' and democratic accountability expectations, though at least with voucher schemes, according to Brighouse, parents rather than governments make the choices and private schools are thereby drawn into the 'public mission' (Brighouse, 2003: 42). Others argue in favour of commercial companies being given a fair chance at delivery or more extremely, the complete privatisation of education (Tooley, 2000) on the basis that competition generates innovation and improves productivity. Pollock *et al.* (2002) argue against this: that profits made by companies from public-private partnerships 'represent a net loss to the service' (Brighouse, 2003: 37) and that profits must by definition come from employees working harder without getting higher pay. Other critics claim that without some form of government involvement in delivery of education, it is difficult to assure quality:

> Markets in schooling are troubling for two reasons. First of all, efficiency is only desirable within the constraints described by justice: it may be inefficient, for example, to educate children with disabilities. ... The second problem ... is that educational markets are by their natures highly imperfect.
>
> (Brighouse, 2003: 37)

It is difficult to gauge the success of private sector involvement in public schooling in the United Kingdom because the government provides substantial subsidies in the case of each privatised (previously failed) school. At any rate, long-term government underwriting is not sustainable for purely fiscal reasons (Brighouse, 2003: 37) and because the contracts awarded to private companies involved in running failed public schools are necessarily short-term in case the initiative fails and to ensure competition in the re-tendering process. The companies involved also face a regulatory regime in perpetual flux so they 'lack incentives for long-term planning and investment, since they have no guarantee of reaping the benefits' (ibid.: 39); and teachers employed by such companies are no longer motivated by the traditional public service ethic to work for less in exchange for job security:

> Unless contracts are terminated, or not renewed, reasonably often, contractors have good reason to rest on their laurels. The relative paucity of competitors for contracts will not help.
>
> (Ibid.: 40)

In the United States, the involvement of commercial companies in the management of public and public Charter Schools is no more promising. When Edison Schools Inc., the largest such commercial company, was launched in 1991, the plan was to open 200 privately operated schools within five years, but it was later reorganised as a firm simply to manage public and public Charter Schools (Molnar, 1996). The fundamental premise of the business was that it could save money through economies of scale and greater efficiency, and raise achievement while spending less per pupil than ordinary public schools (Symonds, 2000; Levin, 2001; O'Reilly, 2002). The Edison strategy was therefore to gain a large number of schools and to standardise their operation so that they could significantly lower *per capita* administrative costs. However, by March 2002, Edison hinted that this economic model was 'not viable' (Molnar, 2006: 627) and there is a lingering suspicion that similar difficulties beset other firms (like 'Knowledge Universe' and 'K12 Inc'.) operating in the sector.[9]

Generally, it is difficult to see how commercial companies undertaking the management of public schools can make profits large enough to balance the significant risk involved. How this will affect government programmes to privatise public schools is anyone's guess. If commercial companies will not get involved, it may be that governments must offer more and bigger subsidies; or it may be that the schemes will be shelved for lack of public acceptance of such subsidies.

5
School Choice, Competition and Performance

Quasi-markets in education: competition and cooperation

The market in education is a quasi-market because the government, not the consumer, makes market decisions in the belief that both competition and cooperation promote higher levels of academic attainment, although the introduction of greater school choice may increase differentials between schools in that respect. 'Coopetition', defined by Adnett and Davies (2003: 393) as competing in some markets and cooperating in others, is the dominant strategy in the business sector, but until recently policymakers in education have been slow to recognise the need to promote it in schools. Policy in relation to school choice in England now promotes both competition and cooperation: some policies, such as open enrolment and league tables, aim to stimulate competition; other policies, like Beacon Schools aim to share best practice, Excellence in Cities schemes and Education Action Zones to encourage partnerships, and Specialist Schools to stimulate community-wide initiatives (Bagley, 2006), aim to encourage cooperation. The three-year (1993–6) Parental and School Choice Interaction (PASCI) Study in the United Kingdom showed education markets to be complex and localised, wherein managers adopt a variety of coping strategies. A follow-up study ten years later by Bagley (2006), one of the original researchers, measured the effect on the market of later government drives towards mixing competition and cooperation (Adnett & Davies, 2003; Bell & West, 2003). It found that, despite the 'discursive shift in political rhetoric', there was little evidence on the ground of greater inter-school cooperation (Bagley, 2006: 357). In addition, in the time between the two studies, parental consumerism, school responsiveness and rivalry were all found to have intensified.

The interaction between competition-inducing policies and cooperation-inducing ones generates 'complex responses in local schooling markets' (ibid.). Historically, in the United Kingdom, self-reported competition between secondary schools increases (Foskett, 1998) as cooperation decreases (Power *et al.*, 1997), and headteachers still tend to see the two as mutually exclusive conditions (Ribchester & Edwards, 1998). Supporters of competition assume that stakeholders act in their own self-interest and therefore that competitive markets create 'incentives that align self-interest with general welfare'. Supporters of cooperation, on the other hand, suggest that competition increases inequality and therefore believe that both individual and public interest is best 'aligned by strengthening teachers' professionalism' (Adnett & Davies, 2003: 394). It is likely that both competition and cooperation have desirable and undesirable properties (Finkelstein & Grubb, 2000), so some have argued for schools to identify appropriate and different 'foci' for each:

> Competition is more likely to promote short-run efficiency and co-operation is more likely to promote long-run dissemination. Whether competition or co-operation is more likely to promote effective innovation depends on the strength of market hierarchies, first-mover advantages, and the resources required for successful innovation.
>
> (Adnett & Davies, 2003: 394)

League tables are important to competition and in that sense they have three important characteristics: they give different weightings to different outcomes of schooling; they attach different weightings to different intake characteristics and peer effects; and the success of (and reward for) a school in a local market depends on its *relative* performance. Critics suggest that the overall effect of league tables has been to narrow the focus onto school targets, to restrict cooperation between schools and to encourage duplication of effort. To counter this, a number of policies have been introduced instead, which provide financial inducements for cooperation, but generally these have been uncoordinated and inconsistent at school level (Adnett & Davies, 2003).

Advocates of marketisation in education say that state restriction of school choice allows some schools to maintain a captive market in their catchment areas, and that consequently schools have no need to innovate or act responsively to consumer demands (Shleifer, 1998). They hold that open enrolment – in other words, the effective abolition of catchments – allows parents and pupils to choose the type of school best suited to their 'abilities and aspirations, and the needs of the economy'. Competition thus raises pupil attainment, increases efficiency and reduces principal-agent friction because teachers are incentivised to act in the interest of their school and its managers, and not in their own interest.

In competition, there are always advantages to acting first (Kelly, 2003). The innovator can prevent other schools from acquiring the necessary expertise or resources to overcome the bureaucratic inertia that accompanies second-comers. Secondly, the innovator school is more likely to secure a reputation and capture a market, especially if there are insufficient numbers seeking a particular type of education to justify the government subsidising provision in more than one place (Adnett & Davies, 2003: 395). And thirdly, innovators can simply sell their innovation to others or at the very least, make money from its dissemination. Counteracting these innovator advantages, Adnett and Davies (2003) identify five characteristics of education markets that 'create problems for the implementation of market-based reforms':

- Most of the goals of public education are either unknowable or not easily measured, making it difficult to gauge the extent to which a school is adding value.
- Schooling markets involve multiple stakeholders with diverse preferences regarding the relative importance of different educational outcomes, so increasing the influence of one faction in the marketplace reduces that of others. This in turn leads to changes in educational outputs even when the government thinks it has retained control over what it deems educationally desirable and what it requires schools to achieve.
- Teachers and headteachers are not motivated solely by self-interest. They are to a greater or lesser extent motivated by professionalism and altruistic considerations. Market-based incentives, which are premised on selfishness, may therefore produce dysfunctional effects within the collegia that operate in schools.
- Education markets are by and large local, at least in the public sector. Parents and children do not travel very large distances to access schooling, unlike in the private (usually boarding school) sector. Therefore, in a public sector market, a small fixed number of schools compete for a fixed number of pupils. They acquiesce in that arrangement and the behaviour of one school has a huge influence on the behaviour of others in the locality (Davies *et al.* 2002). In addition, each school has total market power over those families who cannot afford to vote with their feet.

- Equating 'popular' with 'successful' is problematic for schools (Vandenberghe, 1999; Walford, 2001; Adnett & Davies, 2003). Those that are highly successful in social or academic terms – that is to say, are successful in being well-liked or perform relatively well – attract more parents and pupils who value those aspects of schooling. So these schools become ever more popular without necessarily adding ever greater value. They succeed in creaming the best of the cohort and taking credit for the subsequent success of students without having done anything other than maintain the illusion of effectiveness. In competition, nothing succeeds like success.
- Competition in education 'assumes that under-performing schools face credible threats to their viability, not least through expansion by rivals'. In practice, as the New Zealand experience shows (Pearce & Gordon, 2005), this is not so because the expansion of good and popular schools is not unlimited: there are financial and physical constraints on their expansion, just as there are political constraints on the government's ability to close unpopular ones.

In the commercial sector, cooperation and competition are perceived to be at opposite ends of the operational spectrum, with the added complication, as Adnett and Davies (2003: 397) point out, that in business, cooperation is essentially 'collusion aimed at subverting consumer welfare'. Occasionally, in the private school system in the United Kingdom, 'cooperation' is similarly engaged. In 2006, 50 of the leading English private schools, all registered charities, were fined a total of £3.5 million by the Office of Fair Trading (OFT) for fee-fixing. The OFT ruled that the schools had for a number of years been in breach of chapter 1 of the Competition Act (1998) by exchanging detailed information about fee structure and being in concert to restrict and distort competition (*The Guardian*, 15 September 2003; *The Times*, 9 November 2005; *The Daily Telegraph*, 25 February 2006).[1] This is all in stark contrast to the public school system where cooperation between teachers and between schools is regarded as a good thing, reducing costs by sharing specialist resources and avoiding duplication of provision while providing a wider range of subjects. It also encourages the dissemination of good practice, though research indicates that this is not happening on a large scale because very good schools have no incentive to risk innovation, and poor schools do not have the resources (Adnett & Davies, 2000). Ironically, while competition between secondary schools has reduced cooperation, it has resulted in an increase in cooperation between secondary schools and their feeder primary schools (Levacic, 1995).

For example, it is now common for specialist secondary schools to provide science and language tuition in their feeder primaries.

Brandenburger and Nalebuff (1997) originally used the term 'coopetition' to describe the mix of competition and cooperation that sometimes makes for optimal strategies in business. Cooperation is not always the enemy of competitive success, but sometimes market forces – or in the case of schools, government regulation – can militate against it. Since school league tables, for example, benchmark a school's success against the average performance of other schools in the same area with similar intake characteristics or contexts, it is relative and not absolute performance that determines success in the marketplace. Naturally, such a scheme forces schools to adopt a zero-sum attitude against cooperation: there is little incentive for a school to help another or to share good practice if doing so only serves to drag the better school back towards the average and thereby make it less successful relative to the benchmark (Kelly, 2001). Against such a backdrop, cooperation only makes sense when all cooperating schools benefit equally and they all benefit relative to non-cooperating schools, and even then not every school that might benefit from cooperation will engage in the cooperative.

According to British government metrics, schools are improving and more children are achieving more (Bradley & Taylor, 2000). However, this success, insofar as the measures are valid at all, may not be the result of increased competition, as is sometimes claimed. It may be that the measuring instruments are not accurate enough or are inappropriate; it may be that expectations have dropped; it may be that students are achieving more but only in the measurable outcomes like examination success and not in other equally desirable areas, like cultural awareness say; or it may be that schools are 'teaching to the test' more and ignoring the wider aims of education. Also, what parents and teachers understand by competition varies with the extent of the competition. Efficiency gains and the perception of competitiveness are higher where there are more schools competing in the local market (Foskett, 1998). Research by Bradley *et al.* (2000) suggests that examination performance across a group of local schools has an influence on the performance of any single school, especially in urban areas. They also found that a (large) improvement in examination performance leads to a (small) increase in enrolment, and within reason, schools increasing in popularity as a result of examination success do manage to increase capacity to cope with the increased demand (Bradley & Taylor, 2000), so that there is some substance to the claim that government competition policies in education are working. In addition, Gorard and Fitz (2000a, 2000b) suggest that at national, regional and local level in the United Kingdom the impact of open enrolment and competition is to reduce (rather than increase) segregation and stratification of students by social class, although of course not everyone agrees (Gewirtz *et al.*, 1995; Bradley & Taylor, 2000; Gibson & Asthana, 2000). There is growing acceptance, though there is no conclusive proof yet that there is an increasing gap between the performance of students in the highest and lowest ranking schools (OFSTED, 1999; West & Pennell, 2000; Davies *et al.*, 2002) and that the reduced role of local authorities has isolated schools from each other and has reduced cooperation and access to external expertise:

> [Co-operation] is more likely when a public service ethos dominates the local schooling market. In this case, heads and their governing bodies welcome co-operation and the perceived needs of all the children in the local community drive school behaviour. Alternatively, where schools are part of a wider network sharing a common ethos and mission, for instance catholic schools (Grace, 2002), voluntary co-operation may extend even outside of the local market.
>
> (Adnett & Davies, 2003: 401–2)

The impact of marketisation on student attainment

Across the developed world, there has been widespread experimentation (Adnett & Davies, 2000) with policies aimed at marketising the allocation of resources to schools (Whitty *et al.*, 1998), which reflects concern over:

> the comparative performance of national state schooling systems together with a recognition of the increased importance of educational achievement in determining national economic competitiveness. Reforms have also been fostered by: public-choice critiques of state education (Chubb & Moe, 1988); the weakness of the relationship between government expenditure on schools and levels of educational attainment; ... and empirical evidence of the consumer welfare gains from deregulation and privatization in other industries.
>
> (Adnett & Davies, 2000: 158)

School choice advocacy is then usually based on one of three arguments: the neo-liberal idea that choice in education is a good thing *per se*, as it is for other commodities and services, which (it is argued) explains why choice programmes are popular (Willms, 1996); the egalitarian notion that school choice programmes promote social mobility and extend to the many what would otherwise only be available to the few (namely, the ability to pay or the convenience of living in the right catchment area); and the notion that extending parental choice in secondary schooling drives up standards because poor schools become unpopular and close (Gorard & Taylor, 2002). However, convincing though some or all of these arguments may be, as Gorard and Taylor (ibid.) point out it is difficult to prove causality between school choice and higher student attainment because of the difficulty in defining and measuring standards of attainment. In the compulsory phase, popularity cannot be the gauge at all and even in the post-compulsory phase, there are many and various complex socio-economic determinants at work (Rees *et al.*, 2000; Gorard & Taylor, 2002). The obvious measure of effectiveness is examination performance, but it is not easy to compare qualifications over time (Gorard, 2000): course content changes, as do assessment procedures and grading structures. In the United Kingdom, it is even difficult to know whether the same qualification is equivalent across the different examination boards in any given year (Gorard & Taylor, 2002), and sometimes standards rise simply because marking is more lenient.

Then there is the issue of deciding which background contextual factors to take into account when making comparisons (Willms, 1992). There are clear differences in attainment between social groups, yet many of the identifiable factors are merely proxies for each other and for various antecedent variables:

> For example, ... there are clear differences in attainment by ethnic group, but once other background factors, such as class, are accounted for then ethnicity has little direct effect. Similarly with pupil mobility (turnover within years between schools). Standards in some of [the] poorest regions appear to be affected by high pupil turnover (Dobson & Henthorne, 1999) ... but ... once other indicators of disadvantage and pupil prior attainment are used, then the direct effect of mobility disappears. Once prior attainment is accounted for at student and institution level, there is no difference between the effectiveness of different school types such as grammar and comprehensive.
>
> (Gorard & Taylor, 2002: 8)

With this in mind, Gorard and Taylor (2002) discuss the theory of selecting appropriate control groups and factoring socio-economic background into the equation when assessing the impact of school choice on attainment.

The simplest way of expressing improvement over time is to consider the prevalence of particular qualifications over successive age cohorts.

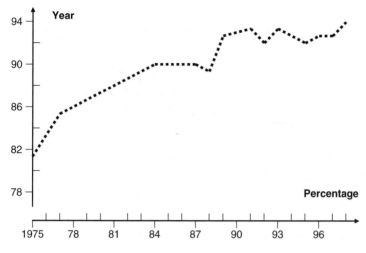

Figure 5.1 Low levels of attainment: the percentage attaining one or more GCSE grade G or better (from Gorard & Taylor, 2002: 9)

Figure 5.1 shows the proportion of the age cohort in the United Kingdom obtaining one or more GCSE[2] (grade G or better) for each year between 1975 and 1998. The rise in 1989 is unlikely to be attributable to the impact of the Education Reform Act of the previous year because it would not have come into effect in time (the first cohort recruited in the school choice era following the 1988 Act took their GCSEs in 1993). The attainment figure for 1992–7 is lower than that for 1991 and the improvement rate before 1988, represented by the gradient of the curve, is greater than that after 1988, so the introduction of market choice with the 1988 Education Reform Act appears to have had little, if any, beneficial impact on school standards at low levels of attainment.

The trend for higher levels of attainment – five or more GCSEs at grade C or better – on Figure 5.2 is different from that on Figure 5.1 for low levels of attainment. Before 1988, there is only very small (if any) annual growth; after 1988 there are significant year-on-year increases, but the growth appears too early (i.e. before 1993) to be the result of the 1988 Act.[3]

> Since 1988, there is clear evidence of change over time. Not only is the entry cohort for examinations increasing as a proportion of the age cohort, the grades awarded to them are improving year on year. Nevertheless, because of concurrent changes, we are unable to attribute these improvements to market forces.

> (Gorard & Taylor, 2002: 11)

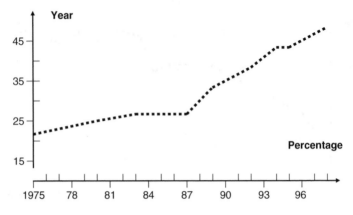

Figure 5.2 High levels of attainment: the percentage attaining five or more GCSE grade C or better (from Gorard & Taylor, 2002: 10)

Gorard and Taylor (2002) suggest that what is needed is a more sophisticated experimental control group; perhaps using the fee-paying, private school sector, where the Education Reform Act of 1988 has had no direct effect.[4] Generally, the examination results of students in private schools are better than those in public schools (see Table 5.1 for the six years from 1992 to 1997), but public schools have been marginally catching up. According to Howson (2000), the trend continued after 1997, though this may in part be a consequence of regression towards the mean, because private school results are already near maximum and public school results are starting from a much lower base. Nevertheless, Table 5.1 suggests that reforms within the public sector since 1988 have led to some improvement relative to the private sector, as well as across the board.

A third way of assessing change over time is to see whether or not children from poor families are now more likely, than in the past, to 'obtain their fair share of the qualification spoils'. Data derived from a series of regression analyses and from other research both in the United Kingdom (Hackett, 2000; Atkinson & Gregg, 2004) and abroad (Duru-Bellat & Kieffer, 2000) suggest:

> If anything, the link between the explanatory variables such as poverty and outcomes scores such as GCSE results is growing slightly stronger.
>
> (Gorard & Taylor, 2002: 13)

Table 5.1 Comparison of results by sector (from Gorard & Taylor, 2002: 12)

Year	% ≥ 1 GCSE A*–G		% ≥ 5 GCSE A*–C		Average A-level points per candidaterte	
	State schools	Private schools	State schools	Private schools	State schools	Private schools
1992	76	86	34	70	13.4	17.3
1993	77	86	36	73	13.6	17.7
1994	80	87	39	75	14.5	20.0
1995	80	90	40	80	14.9	19.2
1996	80	91	41	79	15.5	19.3
1997	81	89	43	83	16.0	19.9

Approximately 90 per cent of the variation in student achievement can be explained by background characteristics and characteristics of the school such as its gender mix, the percentage of pupils eligible for free school meals (i.e. whose parents receive some form of Income Support), the existence of a sixth form, the proportion of students with English as a second language, and so on, and this figure is relatively constant over time:

> [There] is little variance ... left to attribute to a school, or even a school system, effect. The possibility of discovering an improvement in this relatively small school effect over time would seem difficult enough. To partition out any of this improvement that is a direct result of market forces would appear nearly impossible. In this, we agree with the conclusion of Plewis (1999) that the most effective way to tackle inequality in education is by addressing poverty.
>
> (Ibid.: 14)

So strategies for system-wide improvement, like marketisation, are 'likely to fail'. Socio-economic, rather than educational, factors can and will explain nearly all the variance in student performance (Thrupp, 1998; Goldhaber *et al.*, 1999). If there has been any system-wide improvement in the United Kingdom since the 1988 Education Reform Act, this is most likely due to changes in the nature of assessment and 'changing patterns of socio-economic segregation between schools' (Gorard & Taylor, 2002: 14) rather than to the act itself or to the impact of market forces resulting from the act (Gorard & Fitz, 2000b).

This research by Gorard and Taylor (2002), which suggests that marketisation has had a nil effect, represents a new finding because in earlier research, Gorard and Fitz (1998a, 1998b) had found, to their surprise, that secondary schools had become *less* segregated since marketisation under the 1988 Act.[5] The Gorard and Fitz research used eligibility for free school meals as the indicator of poverty. They examined the spread of students eligible for free school meals across secondary schools and found that disadvantaged families had been 'liberated from the iron cage of selection by mortgage' (Noden, 2000: 372). In Noden's view, their findings presented a major challenge to the view of the time that marketisation offered

> further advantages to already advantaged families and that, consequently, such market reforms [led] to increased social segregation in schools.
>
> (Ibid.: 371–2)

Noden (2000), by way of response to Gorard and Fitz (1998a, 1998b), but ahead of Gorard and Taylor (2002), and using a new 'decomposed isolation index' but still using eligibility for free school meals as the main indicator of social disadvantage, suggests that there was in fact an increase in segregation in the United Kingdom during the period following the marketisation act of 1988.[6] The supply-side reforms of the 1988 act introduced incentives for schools to attract high-attaining pupils (Gewirtz *et al.*, 1995) and 'the devolution of control over school admissions increased the power of schools' to achieve this (Noden, 2000), thereby increasing segregation and concentrating disadvantage. In the era of marketisation, parents typically select schools with high educational standards and avoid those with disadvantaged intakes (David *et al.*, 1994; David *et al.*, 1997; West, Noden *et al.*, 1998), but without having the information to take into account the prior attainment of school intakes. Thus it is difficult for parents to differentiate between schools with high-ability students and poor teaching, and those with low-ability students and good teaching.

The Gorard and Fitz–Noden measurement debate, so succinctly elucidated in Noden's (2000) paper, proves only that segregation and marketisation are complex notions, not universally defined or easily measured, but best understood at local rather than national level:

> Even though this paper has reported a rise in social segregation in schools ... the [rise] ... may be relatively trivial. ... It may be that the detrimental effects of bureaucratic control over admission numbers have been underestimated and that, therefore, despite the rise in segregation, ... a larger number of disadvantaged families have now

been freed from the 'iron cage'. The introduction of open enrolment may have had a substantial and beneficial effect on the opportunities available for disadvantaged families.

(Ibid.: 383)

The dynamics of local competition

In localised markets with only a few providers, increased competition generates a variety of different behaviours and an assessment of something like the intensity of competition depends on the particular indicators chosen (Davies *et al.*, 2002). Promoting consumerism in education is 'intended to generate greater inter-school competition' (ibid.: 91), but a small localised market such as exists in schooling (Waslander & Thrupp, 1995; Gibson & Asthana, 1999), where local schools compete for market share, does not make for a uniform response. Certainly it may result in a kind of constructive competition, but it may also result in a suspicious cooperation.[7]

Davies *et al.* (2002) provide a theoretical framework for understanding that it is largely the structure and conduct of local conditions that determines the extent of competition in a marketplace. Of the different types of competitive behaviour possible in education – and not every type of competition is possible when the market in non-commercial[8] – schools can try to reduce costs (Levacic, 1998), be more aggressive in promoting themselves (Maguire *et al.*, 1999), change the quality and nature of what they provide like becoming a Specialist School say (Fitz *et al.*, 1997), or get in and out of different markets as it suits them (Barrow, 1998; Lauder *et al.*, 1999). In any case, economic theory suggests that schools will behave in such a way as to

> reflect the nature of the market in which they operate. In markets with restricted exit and entry, competitive behaviour is predicted to be stronger if the total size of the market is low relative to the producers' capacity, [but] evidence for this is [contradictory].
>
> (Davies *et al.*, 2002: 93)

Theory also suggests that the more providers there are in a marketplace, the greater is the competition (Foskett, 1998; Bradley *et al.*, 2000), but there are dangers:

> More generally, in oligopolistic schooling markets, providers have a greater ability to subvert market forces ... through reducing the

number of rivals in the market (by forcing them out of business, take-over or by creating a niche market) or by co-operation or collusion with rivals.

(Davies *et al.*, 2002: 94)

Schools can reduce competition by differentiating themselves from rivals, by responding to consumer preference or by creating niche markets (Hesketh & Knight, 1998; Davies *et al.*, 2002). Glatter *et al.* (1997) note that competitive pressures are least in markets with a small number of widely dispersed schools. They suggest that competition, which in theory depends on the number of providers in a marketplace, effectively no longer exists when the number of providers is very small, as is the case in education, and others have gone so far as to suggest that this may work against the interests of parents and pupils by incentivising collusion (Davies *et al.*, 2002: 94). Though Foskett (1998) and others (Grace, 1995; Raab *et al.*, 1997) have found that the most intense competition exists where there is a dearth of collegiality amongst head-teachers, advantage accrues (as it usually does in such situations) to those who make a pre-emptive move in abandoning agreement (Kelly, 2003). For one thing, first-strikers can stake out their territory of expertise or specialism, rather like university academics do, though in blazing a trail they make it easier and cheaper for others to follow and compete in a then established market.

Competitive behaviour varies with the nature and history of local markets, and different types of competitive behaviour have different effects on educational outcomes. Market forces 'do not always encourage a congruence of interest between schools and pupils' (Davies *et al.*, 2002: 104) and rivalry between providers does not always act on their behalf. Markets sometimes create incentives for providers to adopt policies that reduce competition and produce an 'interdependence of producer behaviour'. Therefore, the overall effect of market forces on attainment is dependent on the process of local competition, which may or may not be influenced by government policies and which in any case encourages both cooperation and competition.

Headteachers' perceptions of competition and student attainment

Those who suggest that there is a causal link between a quasi-market structure in education and student attainment assume that heads and teachers are motivated by self-interest and not by vocational selflessness. It is possible that a greater professional ethic prevails in the public sector than advocates of competition like to admit, such that schools can perform in the interests of parents and students as things stand without the necessity of introducing a market. Opponents further suggest that greater competition between schools stratified by ability and social class results in lower average attainment *across the whole system* (Feinstein & Symons, 1999).

Belfield and Levin (2001), in a review of research, mostly from the United States, on the impact of competition on student attainment, and research in the United Kingdom by Bradley *et al.* (2001), both conclude that competition and school efficiency are positively correlated and perhaps increasingly so, but that effects are small-scale. Much depends on how competition and markets are defined. Belfield and Levin (2001) measure competition using the Herfindahl Index, which Levacic (2004: 189) describes as 'the sum of the squares of per school enrolments over total enrolment in the local market'. Other simpler measures of competition include the relative enrolment of public and private schools in the local market, the number of schools per thousand students (say), and the number of schools within a given political or geographical area. In a study of headteachers, Levacic (2004: 179) measures competition based on participants' *perceptions* of it, on the basis that the link between market structure and competitive behaviour cannot be assumed to exist in schools, even though public choice theory 'attributes equally self-interested motives to managers of public service organisations, such as schools, as to those in the private sector'. Levacic found that the number of competitors in a local schooling market is positively and significantly related to school performance in terms of the percentage of students obtaining five or more higher grades (A*–C) at GCSE, but not in terms of the percentage obtaining five or more lower grades (A*–G). She also found that the structural features of a market do not determine competition behaviour. It is the values and norms of headteachers and managers that determine it.[9]

The *types* of school in an area and their spare capacity is a good predictor – a negative predictor in the case of spare capacity – of how headteachers perceive competition. The actual *number* of schools is not significant. Being a single-sex or a faith school has a positive and significant impact on student attainment (GCSE), but having a sixth form or having a relatively large number of students entitled to free school meals has a negative impact. Overall, Levacic (2004: 186) concludes that there is

clear evidence that competition does have a positive impact on GCSE performance. This is consistent with the findings of Bradley et al. (2001). It is unlikely that the causality is in the reverse direction, although the possibility that headteachers in more effective schools are more aware of competitor schools is a possibility that cannot be ruled out.

Competition and curriculum diversity

There is no known relationship between the extent of competition in schooling markets and the degree of curriculum diversity and innovation. Competitive markets do not necessarily encourage greater curriculum diversity – indeed, as seems to have happened in the United Kingdom, it may (initially at least) encourage greater conformity – nor does greater diversity in governance of itself make for a wider curriculum. Adnett and Davies (2000) suggest that marketisation can initially increase curriculum conformity in local markets, especially when it coincides with the introduction of a compulsory nation-wide curriculum, but in theory and over time marketisation offers greater incentives to innovate and diversify. Nevertheless, while the pressures to diversify are most keenly felt in schools that cannot afford it, and while the rise in curriculum conformity is slowing down, the trend in the United Kingdom is not consistent with the predictions of marketisation advocates (ibid.: 158). Tooley (1996) suggests that this is because full marketisation has not yet been achieved – there is only limited choice in schooling and the national curriculum restricts what they can offer – though Burtless (1993) and others argue that education markets should perform well even when they are incomplete. Additionally, schooling markets are dominated by a hierarchy of successful schools delivering a traditional academic curriculum, and encouraged to do so by the existence of government league tables. Increased competition may create incentives to diversify and innovate in curriculum areas where consumer demand has been neglected, but evidence suggests that a stable, league-table hierarchy is the enemy of innovation.

Supporters of school choice suggest that it encourages parents and students to take responsibility for their own decisions and encourages schools to 'differentiate their offerings to appeal to particular clienteles' (Levin, 1991: 148). Thus it is hoped that marketisation can satisfy wide-ranging demands, and encourage diversity and innovation while increasing efficiency (Tooley, 1993). However, curriculum diversity also depends on the size of the local market, the 'distribution of parent and pupil preferences', the cost of change and economies of scale, and incentives and regulations concerning school funding and admissions (Adnett &

Davies, 2000: 159). In any case, in the United Kingdom, it is generally agreed that diversity of provision has *not* increased with the advent of the National Curriculum and that levels of conformity may actually have increased. For real diversity, a wide range of schooling alternatives must be available to parents. Creating demand alone is not enough. Sometimes new-style institutions start out by mimicking traditional established patterns so as not to frighten away parents and pupils – as Adnett and Davies (ibid.: 161) put it, schools 'fear to challenge the dominant model' – and older style institutions can be reluctant to discard winning ways (Barrow, 1996; Fitz *et al.*, 1997; Halpin *et al.*, 1997). More particularly, any devolution of budget to schools when coupled with pressures to perform in public examinations means that resources are typically diverted away from broadening curriculum areas like social education (Adnett & Davies, 2000) towards traditional ones. Woods *et al.* (1998) and Davies and Adnett (1999) suggest that to some extent, marketisation reforms to date may have

> re-worked traditionalism, with schools becoming more willing to utilize modern ideas ... to reflect particular local market circumstances. For example, schools have begun to emphasize the technological aspects of their curriculum or links with local employers to compensate for their inability to directly compete with the academic prestige of the local market leader. Similarly, under-subscribed schools in poorer areas ... are becoming more inclined to develop a vocationally oriented curriculum.
>
> (Adnett & Davies, 2000: 161)

Parents and pupils base their market behaviour on the utility they expect to gain from their investment in schooling, so curriculum conformity most probably arises because there is conformity in parental preference. This in turn comes about, according to Bishop (1997), from the 'signaling benefits associated with a single system of curriculum-based external exit examinations':

> Such network externalities can lead to the dominance of a single national system of exams ... and by locking-in students, colleges and employers, restrict the demand for diverse and differentiated curricula.
>
> (Ibid.: 162)

It has been argued that in the United States, where parents are less certain about the abilities and ambitions of their children, there is demand for a common broad curriculum as a means of shedding risk, which produces greater curriculum conformity (F. Brown, 1992). However, as Adnett and Davies (2000) cleverly point out, this logic contains an inherent contradiction: career uncertainty reduces as students progress through school, so it follows from the argument that curricula should diversify in line with students getting older. Theory suggests that all schools should tend to offer a curriculum broad enough to attract those (usually middle-class) parents willing to think and act along careerist lines – that is to say, increased competition should encourage all schools to cater for parents whose children are career-minded – and research from England supports this, suggesting that schools increasingly target the children of active middle-class parents, and that such parents typically demand a relatively narrow academic curriculum (Gewirtz *et al.*, 1995; Whitty *et al.*, 1998; Woods *et al.*, 1998; Adnett & Davies, 1999). Additionally, Walford (1996) points out that parental pressure for more choice is not about diversity of curriculum, but about choice between schools offering the *same* curriculum, according to their league table ranking:

> It follows that the consolidation of a [league table] hierarchy of schools in a local market, all offering similar traditionalist academic curricula, [is not] a response to a general consumer demand based upon risk-shedding. Instead it may result from schools in a local market responding largely to the preferences of a minority, those middle-class parents who strongly emphasize instrumental-academic schooling outcomes (Woods et al. 1998).
>
> (Adnett & Davies, 2000: 162–3)

The extent of curriculum innovation in schools, when it does occur, depends on cost. Headteachers and local education managers must deliver the curriculum within budget, so the use of purely financial criteria in the allocation of resources increases with the devolution of financial power to schools (Tuckman, 1998). Schools are further limited in what they can do with the curriculum by the constraints on teachers' time and effort. This suggests a *gradual* adjustment by schools to competition and that minor curriculum changes are more likely than major ones, which are more likely to occur in schools facing challenging circumstances or failing. The Canadian experience supports this view (Levin & Riffel, 1997): innovation is more likely in schools losing market share, though this is rarely matched by sufficient enabling resources since funding depends on enrolment.

Schools and headteachers tend to rely on the behaviour of other schools and headteachers in the marketplace, and on informal networks, to inform their decision-making (Ball & Vincent, 1998). So smaller and less successful schools, rather than differentiating their curricula, exhibit 'strategic imitation' of larger and more prestigious market-leading schools (Adnett & Davies, 2000). Essentially, local education markets are net-worked markets, where reputation and track record are important predictors of future success (Besen & Farrell, 1994). Consequently, neither the market-leading schools nor the imitating ones have much incentive to innovate. Everyone is locked into existing patterns of organisational behaviour (Katz & Shapiro, 1994), for which government regulatory frameworks provide the rationale. Additionally, the success of competition depends on the validity of the indicators used to gauge its effect on improvement. As Adnett and Davies (2000: 164) put it:

> [Reliance] on performance indicators leads to reduced co-operation and distorts school production. In the particular case of the UK, the narrow range of indicators chosen and the failure to produce value-added measures increases the pressures towards curriculum conformity. Schools are unable to trade-off achievements against targets in pastoral or social education against those for academic attainment.

6
Actualising Choice in Schools and Communities

Assumptions about choice and school organisations

Oplatka (2004) and others have raised concerns about the core principles that underpin choice and marketisation. For example, some 'institutional elements' in schools are oversimplified as obstacles to diversity and improvement, and the market itself is assumed to be simple and neutral. Education markets consist of a supply side from schools and local authorities, and a demand side from parents and pupils. Oplatka (2004) suggests that these are characterised by some unjustified assumptions about choice, diversity of supply, competition and responsiveness:

- Choice. The core assumption is that parents select schools, within or outside their local neighbourhoods, on the basis of properly informed and appropriate criteria.
- Diversity. The assumption here is that the market differentiates schools from each other, and the ability of parents to interpret this diversity is what makes choice work.
- Competition and responsiveness. The assumption is that schools improve their own performance by striving to increase market share, and that this makes them more sensitive to market demands.

Criticism of marketisation is two-fold: from a sociological point of view, greater choice only serves to reinforce existing socio-economic advantage; from an organisational point of view, education is fundamentally different from other consumables and commodities (McMurtry, 1991; Cookson, 1994; Grace, 1994; Henig, 1994). Schools exist in weak technical, but strong institutional, environments (Meyer & Rowan, 1977) and are 'likely to conform to institutional rules' in order to 'gain legitimacy with stakeholders' (Oplatka, 2004: 146). They also tend to

- Conform to society rules in order to promote an image of success.
- Conform to institutional rules and become isomorphic (more like one another) in the belief that conformity guarantees long-term survival without necessarily increasing efficiency or performance.
- Decouple (or loosely couple) internally to provide a buffer between inefficient teaching and learning, and the school's formal structures and environment.
- Normative decision-making, which imposes social obligations and constrains choice.

The corresponding difficulties raised by these features include: concerns about whether the improvements that allegedly result from competition are fundamental or cosmetic; concerns about whether or not diversity of provision follows from marketisation; concerns about whether parents in a market make informed decisions based on complete information; and general concerns about the rationality of parents' choices and the extent to which they act in self-interest or are influenced by collective values (Oplatka, 2004).

The link between greater school choice and school improvement is at best unproven (B.Brown, 1992; Gorard, 1997; Whitty, 1997; Woods *et al.*, 1998; Plank & Sykes, 1999), due in part to parents' lack of information (Rapp, 2000). Some commentators have questioned the view that choice improves schools in any significant way, given that schools can 'adopt image-based changes which conform to institutional rules and, in turn, promote their survival and social legitimacy' (Oplatka, 2004: 148). Schools tend to adopt innovations that carry 'endorsement from legislatures or professional agencies' and such changes by their nature gain acceptance on the basis of cultural beliefs (Meyer & Rowan, 1978). Consequently, school structures and processes mirror the norms and expectations of society (Hoy & Miskel, 1996), and schools that wish to increase market share tend to adopt strategies that maximise their image as good schools in the sense that they conform to society's image of what is 'good'. This is reinforced by the government in the way schools are funded, which in turn is tied to enrolment and has led to the image and reputation of schools becoming all-important (Youdell, 2004). The upshot is that schools in competitive situations tend to implement cosmetic changes that 'mirror their environment's beliefs' rather than adopt fundamental changes that improve teaching and learning (Oplatka, 2004: 149).

The basic premise that conformity to institutional rules promotes the long-term survival of an organisation without necessarily increasing its efficiency or improving its performance (Meyer & Rowan, 1977; DiMaggio & Powell, 1991; Scott, 1995) contradicts rational models, which hold that performance is the main determinant of success (Oplatka, 2004). In order to survive, schools must strive to maintain their status as successful schools, promoting the superficial symbols of success rather than being better at teaching and learning (Meyer *et al.*, 1992; Fitz *et al.*, 1993; James & Phillips, 1995; Foskett, 1998; Levin, 2001; Oplatka, 2002; Oplatka *et al.*, 2002). Failing schools are therefore, almost by definition, those not conforming to 'socially legitimated' expectations and norms (Oplatka, 2004: 150).

Advocates of choice assume that schools in competition, left to their own devices, will become more responsive to the market (Chubb & Moe, 1990), but Oplatka (2004: 151) suggests that this responsiveness itself might be just symbolic:

> It is possible that in the early days of marketization, schools adopt image-based innovation[s] ... that are replaced over time by new organizational practices in response to new institutional rules (e.g. less image-based changes, new curriculum).

Competition is also supposed by advocates to increase diversity as schools seek niche markets, but research suggests that this has not (yet) happened (ibid.), perhaps because marketisation has not been fully implemented. In Australia, for example, moves to greater school choice have only been partial, with school catchment areas remaining the first (but not the only) criteria for admission to the majority of public schools (Youdell, 2004). Oplatka (2004) suggests that organisational isomorphism – the fact that by obeying the same rules and following the same path to success, organisations resemble one another – is a better explanation, but one ignored by choice advocates.[1] Pressures to conform come in many guises (DiMaggio & Powell, 1991; Scott, 1995): coercive pressures, which come from government regulation like inspection and prescriptive curricula; imitative pressures, which come from schools emulating responses from other schools they regard as superior in order to reduce uncertainty (Ball, 1994; Oplatka, 2004); normative pressures, coming from the fact that all teachers receive more or less the same formal training and thus bring similar norms into their profession;[2] and cultural pressures, which provide a dominant template for 'good' schools to copy (Gewirtz *et al.*, 1995; Woods *et al.*, 1998).

In terms of the tension between coercive and imitative pressures, both loosely coupled (Weick, 1976) and decoupled (but not tightly coupled) schools buffer or protect teaching and learning processes from the formal bureaucracy of schools (Meyer & Rowan, 1977), thereby resolving 'the contradiction between pressures for efficiency' and regulation:

> In order to remain apparently conforming to institutional beliefs and myths ... schools are likely to conceal their non-conformity. ... Schools, for example, may ... adopt a certain policy or educational programme as a symbol of innovative schooling ... but by doing so school headteachers may conceal the proliferation of traditional classroom practices.
>
> (Oplatka, 2004: 153)

Loose coupling means, in effect, that the structure is disconnected from activity, and activity is disconnected from effect. Loose coupling and decoupling might buffer teaching processes from bureaucracy ones, but they also make information more difficult for parents to get and more difficult for them to interpret. Parents receive 'ceremonial and symbolic' information, but not about 'what is going on within the classroom' or 'how the school is being run'. So parents choose schools:

> not because of any objective measure and information on teaching, but due to their satisfaction with teachers' replies to their questions at a marketing event.
>
> (Ibid.: 155)

A major assumption of choice advocacy is that parents are rational choosers and make informed choices about selecting schools for their children (Elmore, 1987; Chubb & Moe, 1990; Witte, 1990; Tooley, 1992; Cookson, 1994; Foskett & Hemsley-Brown, 2001). However, critics suggest that in reality parents lack sufficiently clear information (Grace, 1994; OECD, 1994; Ogawa & Dutton, 1994; Gorard, 1997; Lauder *et al.*, 1999; Rapp, 2000). Information gathered about schools by prospective parents – most frequently from visits to schools, from friends, from school brochures and from examination league tables (Gorard, 1999; Bagley, Woods & Woods, 2001; Foskett & Hemsley-Brown, 2001) – is typically limited to the emotional, intuitive, visible and image-based structures of schools, rather than about innovations at classroom level or the like (Maddaus, 1990; Gewirtz *et al.*, 1995). Most of the time, parents simply do not have the time, resources or know-how to do other than make ideological choices, strongly influenced by 'collective norms and values that impose social obligations on them', rather than on self-interest or maximising utility.

Education triage and school markets

Youdell (2004) suggests that in a market dominated by individualism, educational triage (Gillborn & Youdell, 2000: 134) – the commonsense if callous act of using scarce resources only when and where they will do the most good – becomes both acceptable and necessary. Educational triage selects pupils based on the perceived likelihood of them attaining benchmark grades and Youdell suggests that this takes place at all levels in schools: at the bureaucratic level, at the institutional level and at classroom level.[3] The practice is 'underpinned by discourses' on pupil ability and selection, pupil conduct, schooling marketisation and individualism. With the advent of marketisation, school practices generally have become more centralised despite 'policy reform being framed' by 'decentralisation and market forces' (Youdell, 2004: 409), and with greater parental choice comes a scattering of government funding to facilitate, what is hoped will be, greater diversity of provision. The new marketplace is underpinned by an individualism that locates responsibility for educational success and failure with the individual student, not the school, just as it locates individual school success and failure with the school and not with the system (Apple, 2001).

Under market pressure to perform competitively against neighbouring schools, according to Gillborn and Youdell (2000) in a chilling allusion, pupils are triaged by both system and teachers into categories: 'safe', in that they are good learners perceived by the school to be already on track to achieve good grades; 'hopeless', in that they are perceived to be neither able nor willing to learn and are predestined to get poor grades; and 'suitable for treatment', in that they are perceived to be willing or able to become good learners and are thus likely to achieve good grades if provided with proper resources and good teaching. Not surprisingly, given the various research findings referred to earlier, these triage categories tend to be characterised by social class, race and gender:

> White middle-class students and girls [are] disproportionately allocated to the safe group; working class, minority ethnic, particularly black students, and boys [are] disproportionately allocated to the category of hopeless cases; and white middle class boys [are] disproportionately allocated to the treatment group.
>
> (Youdell, 2004: 411)

The idea that individuals should take sole responsibility for their failure in school affects who is thought worthy of triage. When resources are scarce, they are directed only towards those who promise the best returns, which in turn engineers the local market. Within the classroom, individual teachers use constructs of ability and conduct to categorise pupils according to desirability; that is to say, to triage along the lines described above and to constrain the particular identities of pupils.

In a system-wide sense, say within local authorities, schools can be brought together in clusters to partner each other and to partner private sector businesses in a bid to triage improvement in a different way. In the United Kingdom, there are Education Action Zones and Excellence in Cities Action Zones, and there are similar arrangements in Australia. Both 'remove duplication, enable specialisation, and delete surplus places' (ibid.: 414) by changing the way schools go about their business and by inserting competition into the local market. Just as there are 'safe', 'hopeless' and 'suitable for treatment' *individuals*, so there are 'safe', 'hopeless' (or 'residualised') and 'suitable for treatment' *schools*. 'Safe schools' are those performing adequately with a secure client base; 'hopeless schools' are those not performing well, without a secure client base and perceived to be without the potential to improve; and 'suitable for treatment schools' are those not performing well and without a secure client base, but perceived to have the potential to improve. 'Suitable for treatment schools' are the ones encouraged by government policy to become effective competitors in the marketplace, adjusting their positions locally while being constrained by available resources and nation-wide regulatory frameworks.

School choice and school closure

According to Gorard *et al.* (2002), there were 90 school closures in England between 1995 and 1999 – about 2 per cent of the total – and 40 per cent of these faced a significant drop in size in the run-up to closure. In the United Kingdom, when it has been decided to close a school, enrolment is usually reduced incrementally year-on-year by not admitting new intakes. The fact of closure is known within the local community – the regulations oblige schools facing closure to consult and notify – so there is necessarily a simultaneous decline in confidence among parents (Gorard *et al.*, 2002).

Schools in the United Kingdom put into 'Special Measures' – that is to say, schools requiring special attention because they are failing to provide an acceptable standard of education (ibid.: 378) – are a special category as far as closure is concerned. The scheme was first introduced in the 1993 Education Act and reinforced in the School Inspections Act, 1996. Not surprisingly, schools put into special measures quickly lose their best pupils to other schools, from which not-so-capable pupils are simultaneously excluded. Research suggests that falling enrolment in such schools tends to be the greatest near inspection periods because parents use inspection information to choose schools, which suggests that

> the market, as a general phenomenon, may not itself lead to 'spirals of decline', but that the announcement of the label of 'failing' is ... likely [to be a] cause of falling numbers.
>
> (Gorard *et al.*, 2002: 378)

Schools with falling rolls tend to have unpredictable, volatile intakes. It is not the case that they simply take more and more socially disadvantaged pupils, despite the widely held belief that such schools are invariably in 'spirals of decline':

> the notion of spirals of decline resulting from increased market forces ... may be dismissed in practice. As ever, it is not the case that absence of evidence is evidence of absence, but it would be unparsimonious to continue to assume the existence of spirals of decline on this basis. Even where we focus ... on ... 'failing' schools, ... there is still little evidence that market forces are leading to a fall in roles [*sic*] and an increasingly polarized intake. To some extent, the lack of change as a result of introducing a policy of increased school choice is hardly surprising ... and others in the USA are beginning to discover

that competitive schemes such as the Cleveland Voucher Experiment and the Milwaukee Charter Scheme have produced no obvious reaction ... and little discernible change in ... publicly-funded schools. It is sometimes easy for commentators to exaggerate the significance of national policies in education.

(Ibid.: 382)

Gorard *et al.* (2002) suggest that Local Authorities in the United Kingdom directly and indirectly control student numbers in such a way as to keep most schools supplied with a reasonable number of students: they ensure that schools provide for the needs of local children and thereby encourage parents to choose a local school and reduce the movement of pupils between schools (White *et al.*, 2001); they maintain enrolment in individual schools by rearranging provision within their areas so that 'official' surpluses are low; they operate school transport schemes in such a way as to limit accessibility to schools outside the area (for example, by only providing buses to the nearest school); they manage admissions and resources by incentivising cooperation between schools, by preventing schools from exceeding stated admission ceilings, by modifying admissions criteria and by changing the feeder school network to create new channels of pupil transfer to less popular secondary schools (Gorard *et al.*, 2002). However, despite this *modus operandi*, school closures *do* result from the free movement of pupils, even when that freedom is curtailed by local authority activity. When they do occur, research shows that they impact negatively on teacher attitudes and behaviour, just as they do with employees in commercial companies (Medoff & Harless, 1996). Ultimately, school closures, no matter what the cause, lower productivity among distracted, anxiety-ridden teachers, who 'spend less time on their preparatory duties' (Rapp, 2000) and work less effectively with children as a consequence.

The practice of school headship in the education marketplace

Schools in the United Kingdom operate like small businesses, and in areas where supply (of places for pupils) exceeds demand (number of pupils), they are in competition with one another (Gewirtz & Ball, 2000). The quasi-market thus created has implications for school headship, which can be seen in its shifting discourse: Angus (1994) and others (Considine, 1988; Bottery, 1992) suggest that school administration is becoming more managerialist and technicalist, and less professional and welfarist (Clarke & Newman, 1997); Grace (1995) suggests that a 'social democratic phase of school headship' is being 'superseded by a market phase' (Gewirtz & Ball, 2000: 253–4); Yeatman (1993) suggests that the influence of humanistic intellectuals is being replaced by those of a technical intelligentsia; Storey (1992) suggests that collectivism is being replaced by individualism; and Gewirtz and Ball (2000) suggest a shift from a learner-needs perspective to an institutional-needs one.

Welfarism is characterised by bureaucratic professionalism (Newman, 1998), which couples administrative rationality and professional expertise, and protects professionalism and the neutrality of the welfare state. The welfarist headteacher is a humanist intellectual and a public servant (Yeatman, 1993), mindful of theory and committed to collegiality and the practice of delivery within the welfare system.[4] Managerialism is characterised by the efficient implementation of strategies for achieving educational aims, which are decided outside the school and not open to amendment by headteachers. The managerialist headteacher regards bureaucratic and collegial systems as 'repressive of the enterprising spirit' and a barrier to corporate and individual competitive success (Newman & Clarke, 1995):

> The new management discourse in education emphasises the instrumental purposes of schooling – raising standards and performance as measured by examination results, levels of attendance and school-leaver destinations – and is frequently articulated within a lexicon of enterprise, excellence, quality and effectiveness.
>
> (Gewirtz & Ball, 2000: 255–6)

In practice, welfarist headship aims to help students equally with their personal relationships and social development, and aims to meet the needs and abilities of all students. Managerialist headship, on the other hand, concentrates on achieving the highest academic performance. Whereas welfarist headship views education as an instrument of social transformation, managerialist headship seeks to make performance-focused schools transform individual student lives. Welfarist headteachers seek to maintain consultative and non-hierarchical modes of management; managerialist heads act in a chief executive style to tie school objectives to government-determined measures of performance.

Managerialist heads are concerned with marketing and entrepreneurship, and use the language of commerce, but this is not to imply that they have less lofty aims than welfarist headteachers. It is more a question of approach and lexicon:

> There is no doubt that benefits may arise from the task-centredness of [managerialism]. Ossified and ineffective practices ... [are] challenged and loosened up. However, ... its performance-related ... [focus suggests] ... a reorientation of the school ... away from its primary emphasis on the immediate needs of its current community to 'improvement' by intake manipulation whereby highly valued clients [are] sought out at the expense of the needy ... In this way, new managerialism functions as a 'relay' (du Gay, 1996: 66) for the implementation and dissemination of the post-welfarist project. It ... asserts management's right to 'manipulate and ability to generate and develop resources' (Legge, 1989: 40).
>
> (Gewirtz & Ball, 2000: 265–6)

In many ways, welfarist management is the basis for how managers initially behave in public-private partnerships; that is to say, in private companies working in the public sector. Woods and Woods (2005) speak of an 'adaptive public service' model of management and suggest that a basic commitment to a public service ethos is common in the early stages of commercial sector involvement, though it becomes more target-driven as time passes. They also suggest that outsourcing elements of public education generates improvement, but not enough to overcome some serious deficiencies, which finding is 'consistent with the experience of private participation in public sector education' generally (ibid.: 23). The management of private sector companies involved in public education involves 'public-orientated strategic engagement' and 'bounded loyalty'. The former uses private sector practice as a means of developing public sector values while remaining committed to public sector ideals and ethos;[5] the latter is where senior management retain a sense of vocation that transcends the interests of the organisation because of its value to society. Private sector managers working in public education aim to transform school culture so that teachers subscribe to the idea of entrepreneurship and modernisation through distributed/ transformational leadership, even if they do not always subscribe to the notion that commercial sector involvement is *per se* a good thing. That re-culturing also aims at 'nurturing' risk-taking while building self-confidence and technical competence (ibid.: 31).

However, in practice, re-culturing is not as extensive, entrepreneurial or bureaucracy-free as is sometimes portrayed or as headteachers would like it to be. Research in the United Kingdom suggests that most of the time there is little difference between schools run by local authorities and those run by public-private partnerships as regards bureaucracy and financial/hard-asset management. Neither is there compelling evidence that commercial companies (or their larger parent companies) draw on all their resources and expertise to improve the schools they run in public-private partnerships:

> The modesty of improvement in some areas and failure to improve others is consistent with experience of private participation generally ... The linking of the company's income to performance measures, and the fact that the company like any other private sector organization is dependent on meeting market criteria for its success, creates an institutional constraint.
>
> (Woods and Woods, 2005: 34–5)

School choice and the role of headteachers

In the United States, competition between public schools is not new (Witte, 1996). Minnesota launched a programme in 1985 that permitted students to spend their final two years of high school at any institution in the state, and followed it two years later by a policy enabling pupils at all age levels to attend any public school of their choice (Rapp, 2000). Of course, for the better-off, school choice has always existed because those parents could and did choose schools by moving home (Schneider *et al.*, 1997) or by going private (Rapp, 2000). In 1995, more than 11 per cent of American parents sent their children to private schools (Rapp, 2000). In a similar way, competition has always existed in the United Kingdom too. In London, for example, house prices differ hugely – by as much as one-third for primary schools and one-fifth for secondary schools (Cheshire & Sheppard, 2003) – even along the same street, because different houses belong to different school catchment areas: *on average* in the United Kingdom, living in the catchment of a good school adds £16,000 (£24,000 in London) to the value of a house (RCIS, 2006). However, the advent of free choice *in public schools* under the 1988 Education Reform Act added a new dimension, not least because headteachers were 'cast into managerial roles' (Herbert, 2000: 79) on the basis of their ability to retain and attract pupils and exercise entrepreneurship. Herbert's (2000) research suggests that where choice is exercised (in Wales at least), it is mediated by managerial attitudes in schools. Headteachers are key players in the process. They have significant levels of discretion on the admission of pupils, where local management of schools has diminished the executive power of local authorities:

> A key feature of the British system of school choice is that although parents have the right to exercise choice under open enrolment, there is no guarantee of places outside their catchment areas.
>
> (Ibid.: 82)

Admission to a school ultimately depends on the availability of places therein and the main gatekeeper is the headteacher (Fidler *et al.*, 1997). When schools are desirable because of their location and reputation, headteachers typically try to build success in public examinations; headteachers of schools with poor reputations are more 'constrained' by their situation (James & Phillips, 1997). The headteachers of secondary schools that gain from choice – those with better academic reputations – see their schools as successful because of their ethos, academic performance, discipline and co-curricular activities (Herbert, 2000). The problems facing headteachers of schools that lose out in the education marketplace tend to centre around issues like falling rolls and the need to maintain staffing levels to service the curriculum and provide adequate facilities for the dwindling student population. When such schools lose students, they lose the better ones, so that children with less choice get stranded in sink schools whose heads resent the 'inequity of a system in which the budget is pupil-oriented rather than curriculum-oriented' (ibid.: 93). Avoiding student loss is always a priority in these situations and headteachers therefore take an absorbing interest in the strategies of competitors and the allegiance and support of heads in their feeder primary schools. Research shows that headteachers who have to counter their school's negative image tend to publicise research that highlights the relevance of social background to student attainment, and typically are bitter and disillusioned by the over-zealous promotional activities of competitors.

Local education authorities and regulation

Fitz, Taylor and Gorard (2002) have found that the impact of market reforms on British schools since the 1988 Education Reform Act has actually resulted in a *decrease* in segregation[6] (Gorard & Fitz, 1998a, 1998b,

2000a, 2000b), though it remains high and there are regional and local variations.[7] Local authority admissions policies regulate this, though they have done little to

> redress the advantages [of] grant-maintained and church-affiliated schools ... nor have they broken the mould of 'selection by mortgage' where residential segregation gives rise to schools with very different socio-economic intakes.
>
> (Fitz, Taylor & Gorard, 2002: 125)

In the United Kingdom, local authorities have a historic function in the management of school admissions policies and they have a statutory duty to provide places for all children of compulsory school age, though for a long time – since 1944 in fact – parents have been able to express (but not exercise) a preference. Local authorities constitute the 'primary framework of school choice for parents' (ibid.: 126) and have the main role in interpreting and contextualising national policy, though of course parents have the right to dispense with their provision and go private or choose religious schools if they wish.

Local authorities must maintain some system of allocation of children to school places in order to fulfill their statutory obligations, though allocation procedures can vary across authorities and over time. In the quarter century between the 1944 Education Act and the introduction of comprehensive schools, the 'eleven-plus' examination taken by pupils at the end of the primary school cycle 'distributed secondary school children between schools on the basis of ability'. From 1970 (approximately) onwards, allocation has been on the basis of catchment areas or 'geographical proximity', but in their different ways, both the distribution of pupils on the basis of ability and their distribution on the basis of proximity are 'ways of balancing choice and the responsibilities of Local Education Authorities' (Fitz, Taylor & Gorard, 2002: 128).

The 1988 Education Reform Act introduced increased parental choice to education and with it, more open enrolment. Under the act, each school was obliged to admit pupils up to a certain threshold ('Standard') number, which was in effect the greatest number of pupils that the school could physically accommodate. Parents could express a preference for a particular school and could appeal against unfavourable local authority allocation decisions.[8] Under the act, schools acquired the right to opt out of local authority control and be maintained by a direct grant from central government ('Grant-maintained' now called 'Foundation' schools). Thus, local authorities with grant-maintained schools lost their power to alter the social composition within and between individual schools.

Under the financial provisions of the 1988 act, resources were linked inextricably to admissions using a funding formula that incentivised schools to select pupils on the basis of the funding captured (Fitz *et al.*, 1993). In some areas, nearly all secondary schools opted out of local control and local authorities were left merely monitoring whether or not every child had acquired a secondary school place (Fitz, Taylor & Gorard, 2002). Multiple individual school admissions policies 'diminished Local Authority capacity to match pupils to places', which task was made even more difficult by a 1989 legal judgement – the so-called Greenwich judgement – that enabled parents also to express a preference for schools *outside* their local authority area. Opt-out schools, especially ones in large cities where it did not cost as much for parents to send their children outside a catchment area, effectively acquired unbounded catchments as local authorities sought to maintain the 'geographical' scheme. In some cases, local children could not gain entry to local schools as places were going to out-of-catchment families drifting in. In London, whole cohorts drifted westward and northward as a result of being displaced by others drifting the same way.[9]

The School Standards and Framework Act (1998), introduced by the then recently elected (1997) New Labour government, sought to curtail the recruitment of pupils by grant-maintained schools. Codes of Practice on school admissions were introduced by which schools and local authorities were required to publish and consult with each other about their admissions criteria (White *et al.*, 2001), and disputes were to be resolved by ministerially appointed adjudicators. Experience since the introduction of the act has been that most appeals have concerned local children failing to be placed in local schools, and most have been resolved in favour of parents, so the School Standards and Framework Act as a piece of legislation has 'restored the capacity of Local Authorities to address the worse excesses' of the market, especially by forcing changes to the admissions policies of non-authority public schools:

> LEAs remain important arenas within which school choice operates because they define [the] kinds of choice available to parents in, and adjacent to, their administrative boundaries. ... Their policies define the diversity of secondary schools available to parents. In some LEAs academically selective schools are a central feature of provision, in others the majority of schools ... lie outside the direct control of the LEA while others have predominantly comprehensive community

schools. To some degree the particular mix has historically determined whether middle class parents stay in the state system or exit
for fee-paying selective education.

(Fitz, Taylor & Gorard, 2002: 143)

Today, local authorities/Children's Services exercise almost total control
over school admissions, provided their criteria are published and made
known to parents, and provided they are otherwise legal. However, neither the 1988 Education Reform Act nor the 1998 Schools Standards
and Framework Act have been implemented uniformly across all local
authorities. Fitz, Taylor and Gorard (2002) suggest that the acts have only
changed the basis for (and not the fact of) segregation, from geographical
allocation policies to ones favouring choice and self-governance. And
while popular non-authority public schools have used their admissions
policies to 'maintain the proportion of pupils from relatively privileged
backgrounds', there is little evidence to suggest:

> that social class patterns of choosing, reported elsewhere (Gewirtz
> *et al.*, 1995), have intensified or diminished since the introduction of
> market-driven policies.

(Fitz, Taylor & Gorard, 2002: 141)

The effect of educational markets introduced by legislation has been
'muted' by legislation. Local authority admissions policies still maintain
a pattern of segregation based on 'selection by mortgage', and although
they try to 'equalise the distribution of pupils and resources across their
schools', their very existence in parallel with opt-out public schools is
problematic (ibid.).

The self-selection of pupils between schools

Robertson and Symons (2003) suggest that when schools and children
are free to seek each other out in the marketplace – 'free-matching
equilibrium' – it leads to 'perfect' segregation on the basis of intellectual ability. They suggest that a competitive system most easily (and
usually) produces the optimal allocation of children to schools, and
assuming that children arrive at school endowed with a certain ability,
any increase produced by the school depends only on the average ability of the child's peer group.[10] This contention raises the fundamental
issue of whether it is better to mix or segregate students by ability. The
answer according to Robertson and Symons is that it depends on

whether there are increasing or decreasing returns – in terms of raising attainment – to peer groups: in diminishing returns it is suggested that children should be mixed by ability; in increasing returns they should be segregated. The scenario of diminishing returns is thought to be the one more likely to prevail today (Henderson *et al.*, 1976; Robertson & Symons, 2003) and Robertson and Symons (2003: 260) suggest that in such circumstances, the optimal solution can be achieved by competition between schools to which students pay fees or from which they 'receive inducements'.

Robertson and Symons (2003) also consider the theoretical effects of allowing pupils to bid for places and schools to bid for pupils. The pupil supplies a 'service' to the peer-group and receives in return a portion of the services supplied by others. Both of these activities are supported by a competitive system, and the price charged for the net gain – services received minus those supplied – supports the desired outcome. However, a combination of parental choice and free selection of pupils by public schools most probably leads to a 'bad' result: bad schools become populated mainly by the worst students, and very good schools become populated by very good students. In the Robertson-Symons (2003) model, a shift of children from very good schools to bad schools effects a net welfare gain because the loss of the very good cohort is more than compensated for by gains to those in the bad schools. But maximising the welfare gain by other means – like compulsorily allocating pupils to schools – would not result in Pareto improvement because there would be an incentive for the 'losing pupils' – those good pupils forced into bad schools – to leave the public system altogether. Anyway, mixing most likely produces as many losers as winners, so that it would be difficult to sustain a majority in favour of a compulsory system (ibid.).

According to Robertson and Symons, instituting greater choice and simultaneously allowing schools to charge fees leads to the optimal result – perfect mixing and an unambiguous pareto improvement – but unfortunately, in an unregulated competitive market, the least academically able pupils would end up paying the highest fees:

> In these circumstances the competitive solution would clearly need to be supplemented by a scheme to enable the poor to pay market fees. If the state were able to identify the least able and provide them with some sort of dowry, ... the welfare optimum could be achieved. In practice, means-tested vouchers may approximate.
>
> (Ibid.: 270)

Aside from macro-economic considerations, there are issues relating to individual choice, self-selection and social background; principally, who is actually making the choice. Research suggests that the involvement of children in choosing schools is more typical of working-class families (Woods, 1996). Some studies (Thomas & Dennison, 1991; Forster, 1992) find that although the majority of children claim to have made the choice of school themselves, they do not really have the final say: to a greater or lesser extent the child is part of the choosing process, but it is the parents who actually make the decision (Woods, 1992; David *et al.*, 1994; David *et al.*, 1997). Gorard (1997) proposes a three-tiered model for the involvement of children in the choice process. In the first, parents alone decide on the school; in the second, they consider and discuss alternatives using formal and informal sources of information; in the third, parents and children come to an agreed decision by considering alternatives together (Carroll & Walford, 1997). Research by Smedley (1995) on choosing schools distinguishes between 'process criteria' like human relationships within schools, and 'product criteria' like examination results. Parents tend to stress the latter and also convenience factors like location and proximity, which are particularly relevant for low-income families (Gorard, 1997); children tend to stress the former and also things like having friends at the school and the availability of sports facilities (Forster, 1992).

Schools and employers under marketisation

The commercial sector has a significant influence on government education policy in most of the developed world, particularly as it relates to vocational education and training. Gleeson and Keep (2004: 37) suggest that this constitutes a 'voice without accountability that has shifted regulation and responsibility onto the state and education, and away from the workplace'. It is part of an emerging consensus between the state and employers that has allowed the latter to increase its influence over the direction of education policy. High quality education is generally agreed to be a means of achieving economic prosperity in the face of global competition, just as in previous generations it was a means of escaping poverty for individuals. However, the relative responsibilities of schools and employers has not yet been agreed in a world where education is becoming less autonomous. In fact, Gleeson and Keep (ibid.) suggest that there are many implicit and explicit misapprehensions among policymakers about the motivation and influence of employers acting in the sphere of education, and of course there are tensions within and between different interest groups. Gleeson and Keep (2004: 39) give a telling example of such a tension. Individuals want to maximise benefit from acquiring a skill or a qualification while minimising the opportunity for others to obtain the same advantage because there is a limited supply of desirable related jobs. They also wish to minimise the cost to themselves, in terms of time and money, of acquiring such skills and qualifications. Employers have different priorities: they want (within reason) to create an over-supply of skilled workers to keep wages down, and they want the state to pay for it. They also want employees to acquire only non-generic skills – skills useful solely to their own individual enterprises – in order to minimise the risk of training them to see them leave or poached by competitors. The state, acting as the agent for society at large, has a third set of priorities, which are (probably) more long-term and (possibly) less utilitarian. So individual learners, employers and the state want different outcomes from schooling in relation to social reproduction, attitudinal and economic indoctrination, and forcing skills development into schools at public expense but without any educational benefit to the state or to students.[11] And all this, as Gleeson and Keep (2004) point out, depends on a Senge-like discipline of communication between providers and users. If employers do not communicate coherently what they require from vocational training, everyone loses.

The state (and schools and colleges) needs detailed, accurate forecasts of future-employer demand for skills, but unfortunately:

> there are good reasons for doubting whether employers can deliver what is needed. As long ago as 1989 the main national employers body – the Confederation of British Industry – argued that 'few employers are able to predict their medium term skill requirements with any confidence. The uncertainties over technology, exchange rates, and future corporate strategies are simply too great (CBI, 1989, p. 33).
>
> (Ibid.: 56)

On a more general political point, in relation to the goals of education:

> Nations that have strong traditions of social democracy and well-developed notions of citizenship, for example, the Nordic countries, are more liable to maintain wider, societal goals for education ... than nations where such strands of political thought are weakly developed and where notions of citizenship have very limited political

and cultural resonance (e.g. England). [In] countries with narrower conceptions of what education is for, the tendency will be for economic imperatives to provide the key rationale for educational activity, and this in turn will tend to legitimise the right of those who represent low trust economic interests to have a major say in what happens in the classroom.

(Ibid.: 41)

In Germany, for example, the roles of schools, trainees, the state and employers are understood and specified (Culpepper & Finegold, 1999), whereas in the United Kingdom there is vagueness and ambiguity (Gleeson & Keep, 2004).

The factors that have influenced the change in interaction between employers, schools and the state (ibid.) include increasing diversity in competition strategy and the demand for skills, the changing nature of skills themselves, the growing role of education in securing economic competitiveness and social inclusion, the decline in work-based training, the participation expansion in further and higher education, and the tension between the needs of the aspirant middle classes and the needs of industry. The growing role of education at the heart of social and economic policy, and societal values concerning the aims of education, are important in determining the influence of the 'employer voice in educational decision making' (ibid.). The nature of the relationship between employers and schools has resulted in the latter playing a subordinate role (Reeder, 1979):

Although the term partnership is often deployed, ... the norm as far as the state is concerned, has been to assume that education needs to listen to and learn from business. ... This asymmetry, overlain by recent Private Finance Initiatives (PFI), has been the source of many problems, as it undercuts any likelihood of establishing a democratic discourse or division of rights, responsibilities and roles, and often leaves education in a responsive mode.

(Gleeson & Keep, 2004: 44)

In the United Kingdom, local Learning and Skills Councils have responsibility for funding state-sponsored post-compulsory vocational education, and employers have nearly half the seats on the councils, 'making theirs the largest interest group'. Gleeson and Keep (2004) point out that demand for skill comes in the first place from the ways in which organisations seek to fulfil their primary purpose, whether it is generating a profit or delivering a service, and ultimately, developing skills is not the primary purpose of organisations outside education:

> From this fundamental misapprehension a number of academic and policy fault lines flow. One such fault line is the frequent tendency to assume that skills are extremely important to the competitive success of all employers. There is a large and growing body of evidence that, at least within the UK context, this is not universally true. Many employers are able to generate the profits they desire with a relatively lowly-skilled workforce which they treat as a more or less disposable commodity.
>
> (Ibid.: 46)

Policymakers also rely on qualifications to perform tasks for which they were not originally intended and automatically correlate qualification levels with skill levels:

> Research has indicated [that] the vast bulk of learning and skills development taking place in the workplace is informal and almost invariably uncertified. It therefore tends to remain invisible to policy makers. Second, the shift away from manufacturing towards service sector work has, as one consequence, tended to boost the importance of informal and contextually based skills which are not easily amenable to formal certification. And, third, qualifications are not a particularly good indicator of skill level or learning, despite their association with power, selection and cultural capital.
>
> (Ibid.: 46)

Government enthusiasm for more qualifications is generally not shared by employers, who place only limited emphasis on them. So by gearing vocational education and training to the achievement of more qualifications, governments have produced systems that do not fundamentally meet the needs of employers. Nor are the achievements of employers as trainers evaluated. For all the targets in vocational training, there are no targets for employer activity and even basic information is lacking (Fuller & Unwin, 2003). Employer interaction with education tends to be indirect, mediated by the state and its agencies, and 'takes the form of a deficit view' of education:

> which tends to legitimate employers' lack of responsibility by blaming most or all ills on a lack of skills among [recruits] ... [which] then

causes resentment and bad faith in the education system, which as a result acts defensively.

(Gleeson & Keep, 2004: 50)

Schools must simultaneously be sensitive to the disparate needs of students as consumers, be efficient in delivery and provide employers with what they need for the economy to prosper. As Gleeson and Keep (2004) put it, education has become 'an arm of welfare and social security', regulating access to a cheap labour market through various vocational education initiatives for students who have failed in mainstream schooling.

In many countries, but less so in the United Kingdom and the United States, the ability of employers to act unreasonably with employees is constrained by the influence of trade unions and statutory employment leglislation.[12] In the United Kingdom, working hours are long, and there is widespread dissatisfaction and anxiety about discrimination, harassment and victimisation in the workforce (R.Taylor, 2002). According to Gleeson and Keep (2004: 52), there is also evidence that 'a desire for compliant workers underlies at least some employer demands for skill'. In recent times, most skills qualifications have been achieved through the education system, rather than through employers in the workplace. There is an apparent unwillingness on the part of employers to support work-based routes to vocational qualifications (Keep & Payne, 2002; Fuller & Unwin, 2003). Essentially, the state has underwritten employer liability using Further Education colleges and private training providers. Employers have even proved reluctant to provide work experience for students, though it is clearly in their stated interest to do so (Huddleston & Unwin, 2002).[13] Essentially, schools are being asked to develop in their students skills that are 'heavily' bounded by the 'varied, non-educational organisational contexts in which they will be deployed' (Gleeson & Keep, 2004: 55), even though the classroom cannot fully mimic or anticipate the workplace in terms of the development of skills like 'working with others' and 'problem-solving' (Stasz, 1998; Guile, 2002). It is simply too 'out-of-context'.

Gleeson and Keep (2004) and others argue that many of the changes in British vocational education have been 'a form of displacement activity', and when education has responded to employer demands, the practical response has been disappointing. The expansion of the education system has partly been a substitute for action by employers, who want 'many different and conflicting things from education and from the state' (ibid.: 57). Anyway, 'employers are not the only customers of education: students and communities also have interests', which diverge from those of employers but are no less legitimate:

> [The] needs of the economy ... is not the sole function of education and ... other societal and personal agendas and goals may be important. A less narrowly utilitarian approach would help put employer demands in a wider civic perspective, rather than their being seen as the be all and end all of the educative process. This would add broader meaning to recently advocated notions of the 'knowledge economy' and 'learning society'.
>
> (Ibid.: 60)

Part II Adapting Sen's Theory of Capability to School Choice

7
Well-Being and Capability

Social choice

Research on the commodification of education and schooling,[1] some of which has been described in detail in the preceding section, has largely been concerned with the relationship between education as a commodity and pupils (or parents acting by proxy) as customers with choice. Typically, the research has investigated how (and the extent to which) pupils and parents can establish command over the commodity that is education. The judgement as to whether or not the education market is 'properly' supplied is a question particularly relevant today to the public provision of schooling, and related to fundamental concerns about commodification is the question of how student well-being can most accurately be judged and levels of personal benefit from education measured.

There are many different approaches to understanding choice and self-interest, and to judging whether or not students are doing well: the extent to which they are happy in school and with their education; the extent to which society is well served by what schools are doing; the extent to which there is enough choice in the system; the extent to which the market can get what it wants and where it wants it; and so on. How choice is understood is something that has occupied the minds of great economists over the years, none more so than Amartya Sen, Nobel laureate in 1998, who suggests that the impact of choice on poverty and quality of life goes 'to the very foundations of democracy'.

The early origins of social choice theory can be traced to work by the eighteenth-century French mathematician, the Marquis de Condorcet, but it was in the 1950s that the theory 'took its modern form' as a result of work by Arrow and others (Wallace, 2004: 4). Social choice theory provided Sen with a new basis for measuring social progress, which until then had relied on macro-measures of societal wealth such as Gross National Product (GNP) and Gross Domestic Product (GDP). Sen regarded such measures as intrinsically flawed because they did not capture how income was *distributed*; nor did they take account of the many influences on well-being that have little or nothing to do with income, such as diversity, equity, disadvantage and circumstance (Sen, 1992, 1999). Sen, by way of an alternative, developed an approach that focused on the freedom of individuals to pursue their own values and interests: his now famous 'Capability' approach (much lauded but which has its critics).[2] He also developed a measure of poverty that took relative deprivation into account, and a measure of social welfare, the Human Development Index, which went beyond GNP and GDP to take into account various 'observed features' of opportunity and well-being.

Sen suggests that certain features of democracies, like freedom of information and overt public criticism of government, are by their nature a bulwark against economic disaster because they both demand and facilitate a quick response by government to extreme events. Democracy is as much about public debate as elections, particularly if that debate involves people disadvantaged by illiteracy, poor health and lack of economic mobility and opportunity (Wallace, 2004). Of course, debate is not harmonious when the choices facing a society are controversial: when opinions differ and are strongly held, the problem is to find methods for bringing them together. Social choice theory is about linking these individual and societal choices in such a way that collective desirable outcomes can be derived from the desirable outcomes of individuals. This is crucial to developing 'meaningful measures' of well-being, 'helping public sector decision making' (ibid.: 6) and generally measuring how well a society is doing in light of the selfish interests of its disparate members. For Sen, freedom is about letting people choose what they value:

> [Development] requires the removal of major sources of unfreedom: poverty as well as tyranny, poor economic opportunities as well as systematic social deprivation, neglect of public facilities as well as intolerance or overactivity of repressive states.
>
> Sen (1999), cited in Wallace (2004): 7

Individuals in society, particularly decision-makers, are always faced with the choice of doing what is best for themselves or doing what is best for the collective, and consequently choice theory's main focus is on economic principles like that of self-interest (Buchanan & Tullock, 1962). It suggests that although self-interest can lead to benign results in the marketplace, it can also produce pathology in political decisions (Felkins, 1997) and all kinds of manoeuvring by voters to get their hands on public funds. Coalitions frequently form in order to gain advantage from the public purse or to get favourable legislation enacted, but unsurprisingly such coalitions are rarely formed by under-privileged members of society, for whom seeking advantage would only be fair remediation. Instead, they are formed by the groups most likely already to have advantage, such as large commercial companies involved in public-private initiatives to deliver services like education. These companies encourage big spending by government while at the same time calling for lower taxes and public sector restraint. This situation only adds to societal inefficiency as organisations expand pre-emptively to justify ever-larger applications for public money.

The behaviour of bureaucrats is also at the heart of choice theory. While they are supposed to work in the public interest, putting into practice the policies of government as efficiently and effectively as pos-sible, they are in reality 'self-interested utility-maximisers' (Felkins, 1997) motivated by factors like salary, power, reputation, patronage and an easy life (Niskanen, 1973). Bureaucrats in both public and private systems act, at least partly, in self-interest and some are motivated solely by it (Downs, 1967), although of course motives such as pride in per-formance, loyalty and altruism also affect behaviour (Downs, 1967; Niskanen, 1973; Sen, 1977).

In *The Wealth of Nations*, Adam Smith (1776) postulates the concept of 'an invisible hand', which leads individuals to further the common interest through the pursuit of self-interest (Felkins, 1997). The success of free (as opposed to controlled) markets in private goods is a good example of this, but the appropriateness of extending Smith's invisible hand concept to public goods is not clear-cut. The pursuit of self-interest may simultaneously promote the common interest when deal-ing with private goods and services, but it usually does the opposite when dealing with public goods and services:

> [All] too often we are less helped by the benevolent invisible hand than we are injured by the malevolent back of that hand; that is, in seeking private interests, we fail to secure greater collective interests. The nar-row rationality of self-interest that can benefit us all in market exchange can also prevent us from succeeding in collective endeavours.
> (Hardin, 1982)

Choice theory examines the options involved in solving the many social dilemmas that come from living in a society. It addresses the challenges of finding the best of the many imperfect solutions to the problem of delivering public goods and services like education when a simple free market does not work.

The meaning of utility

There is a tradition in economics of theorising with a single 'utility' measure of self-interest and achievement, and the corresponding field in education has similarly focused on summative (and perhaps crude) judgements of school-level and pupil-level attainment such as national league tables of examination performance, percentage of school-leavers progressing to university, rates of literacy and so on. There has been little interest in a 'plurality of foci' in judging student and parent self-interest.

Utilitarian economists define utility either as satisfaction/happiness (Crocker, 1992), in line with the classical view of Bentham and others (Edgeworth, Marshall, Pigou, Ramsey), or as desire-fulfilment, in line with the modern utilitarianism of Sidgwick (Hare, 1981; Sen, 1984a). They all claim empirically that these interpretations coincide with Pigou's (1920) interpretation in terms of 'desiredness':[3]

> It is fair to suppose that most commodities, especially those of wide consumption that are required ... for direct personal use, will be wanted as a means to satisfaction, and will, consequently, be desired with intensities proportional to the satisfactions they are expected to yield.
>
> (Ibid.: 24)

However, utility can also represent what a person values most or it can represent a person's well-being, however that is judged, which vagueness has frustrated attempts at analysis. As Sen puts it:

> Mathematical exactness of formulation has proceeded hand in hand with remarkable inexactness of content. The difficulty does not lie in defining 'utility' as something other than 'happiness' or 'desire-fulfilment', the traditional meanings of utility ... so long as one makes one's usage clear ... The real problem lies, partly, in trying to transfer the established concern with 'utility' in the traditional sense to a similar concern with the newly-defined 'utility'.
>
> (Sen, 1985a: 3)

A difficulty with utility as a mechanism for analysing the provision of schooling in an education market is that of giving it different meanings at the same time, and thereby making the implicit empirical assumption that these meanings are in reality coincident. For example, both students' perceptions of their own welfare and the choices they make can each be called 'utility' without any great difficulty, but if both are called 'utility' simultaneously and treated as being the same, then it is implicitly assumed that what students always choose is their own selfish welfare, which is not true. It is quite common for students to sacrifice their own study concentration to help classmates, for example.

Education policymakers and advocates of school choice generally take an economic view of schooling by regarding parents and pupils as 'rational fools', unable to differentiate properly between the choices available to them (Sen, 1973, 1977; Hirschman, 1982; Margolis, 1982; Akerlof, 1983; Basu, 1984). In contrast, Sen's work, as adapted here, follows an approach whereby motivation behind pupil choice is treated as a parametric variable that may or may not coincide with the pursuit of self-interest. The focus is not on actions or behaviour *per se*, but on judging self-interest.

Well-being and advantage

'Well-being' is a way of viewing student self-interest; 'advantage' is a way of viewing the fulfilment of those self-interests. The former is concerned with achievement; the latter with the freedoms and opportunities a student has compared with others. Opportunities are not judged solely by results, and therefore not just by the level of well-being attained. It is possible for a student to have real advantages and not to make good use of them in a selfish sense; for example, to deliberately sacrifice own well-being for altruistic reasons or out of sympathy (Sen, 1977), and not to make full use of own freedom to achieve the highest possible level of well-being (Sen, 1985a: 5). It is possible to have lots of opportunity but not to achieve.

The notion of student opportunity is intrinsically linked to choice, but the two are not synonymous. Opportunity cannot be defined simply as whether, for example, entrance to an oversubscribed sixth form college is a realisable choice for a student, but rather whether say the particular student's family can afford to support the student financially for another two years at school. There is a real opportunity cost for poor families in having children stay on at school into the post-compulsory stage, most obviously in a loss of income that may not be recouped

(Dearing, 1997; Brennan & Shah, 2003). And setting the issue of cost to one side for a moment, simply having the choice of going to a good school is not an opportunity if the student cannot benefit from the curriculum on offer there. This is a real difficulty in the United Kingdom with the proliferation of Specialist Schools. It seems at a superficial level that developing such localised expertise provides greater opportunity to students in the catchment area, but that is not necessarily the case. Many students may not have the wherewithal to engage with that expertise to their own benefit. Advantage may well be, in Sen's words, a freedom-type notion, but freedom must be even-handed for students to take advantage of it (Sen, 1985a: 5).

Measuring self-interest is crucial to measuring educational opportunity, analysing social disadvantage and instituting public policies to counteract bias. Sen suggests that in economics it is unlikely that there is one single measure of self-interest superior to all others and applicable in all contexts, and this is likely also to be true in education and for student well-being in schools. However, the purpose is not to find such a metric. It is rather to

> clarify the ... limitations of different concepts of self-interest, and to fill in what may well be important gaps in the conceptual apparatus of self-interest assessment and the judgment of advantage and well-being.
>
> (Sen, 1985a: 7)

Commodity and capability

Commodities are best seen in terms of their desirable properties and securing a quantity of a commodity gives a consumer command over its desirable properties or characteristics (Sen, 1985a). Schooling gives a student access to the commodity that proponents of choice suggest is education, which can be used to satisfy intellectual curiosity, provide social advancement and opportunities for friendship and open the door to economic prosperity. However, the mere acquisition of such a commodity (or some quantity of it) does not guarantee the acquisition of the desirable benefits associated with it, nor does the possession of the commodity reveal what the acquirer can and cannot do with it (Yaari & Bar-Hillel, 1984). A student with a learning disorder that makes formal classroom learning difficult may suffer from poor educational outcomes even though he or she may attend the same lessons as another student who benefits in all the desirable ways from the same exposure.

In judging the well-being or 'self-interest achievement' of students, their 'functionings' and not just the desirable properties or characteristics of education must be considered. The functioning of a student is what the student actually succeeds in doing with his or her schooling. Admittedly, the ownership and command of a commodity like education is personal – even if it is sometimes jointly owned by the family – so the size and extent of the desirable properties associated with it do not vary from student to student no matter how much or how little they benefit from it; in other words, the innate desirable properties of schooling and education are unaffected by whether or not particular students benefit equally from it because of learning disorders or whatever. Nevertheless, in gauging the well-being of a student, functionings and the number and extent of the characteristics at his or her command still need to be taken into account: a student with a learning disorder may not be able to do things other students can with the same access. This is one of the difficulties with Higher Education access policies in the United Kingdom.[4] It is not enough to discriminate positively in favour of students attending 'poor' secondary schools and thereby open the doors of elite universities to them. There must also be a commensurate enhancement of functionings to enable those students to derive the same level of benefit from attending elite universities as students from 'good' schools (and overcome their legitimate belief that Higher Education is not necessary to achieve the things *they* value).

A functioning is a personal achievement (Sen, 1985a: 10): what a student does with the desirable properties or characteristics of the commodity under his or her command; what the student manages to do or be. A functioning is derived from a desirable property of a commodity, but functioning and characteristic is not one and the same thing. A functioning is distinguishable from the well-being it generates. Learning is not the same as having a school to attend, and the physical act of going to school in the morning is not the same as deriving benefit from the intellectual curiosity satisfied by being there.

> A functioning is ... different both from having a commodity and its corresponding characteristics (to which it is posterior), and having utility in the form of happiness resulting from that functioning (to which it is prior).
>
> (Ibid.: 11)

A student's achieved functionings depend on his or her 'utilisation functions', which reflect particular choices of schooling that the student has the freedom actually to make. The happiness that the student then enjoys is a function of the set of achieved functionings; in other words, of whether the student is well educated, socially skilled, employable and so on. 'Well-being' is the *evaluation* of this set of achieved functionings and indicates the kind of being or existence the student is achieving. The exercise of evaluation is simply one of ranking; in other words, of attaching a scalar value to each achieved functioning to represent how relatively good it is. The happiness function can similarly be valued by attaching a scalar. It represents how happy a student is with his or her set of functionings, though it does not reveal how good that way of living is or even how good a student thinks it is.

A student's set of feasible functionings is his or her 'capability', which represents the student's command over schooling and the commodity of education; in other words, it represents the freedom the student has and the various combinations of functionings that he or she can achieve, and ultimately his or her freedom to decide what kind of life to lead (Dreze & Sen, 1995). While it is possible to characterise the values of well-being that can be achieved, students will not necessarily choose the highest value. There are other social tensions and altruisms at work:

> [The] highest value [of well-being] will not necessarily be chosen, when such a maximum exists, since maximizing one's own well-being may not be the only motive for choice. Given other possible objectives and possible 'deontological' requirements (related, say, to one's obligations to others), it is quite possible that a non-maximal may in fact be chosen [which] will introduce an additional problem in the evaluation of a person's capabilities.
>
> (Sen, 1985a: 14)

In gauging capability, which is a type of freedom, it is difficult to equate the value of a whole capability set with the value of its biggest element, even when that element can be chosen. Consider the following two scenarios. In the first, a student has a capability set within which the biggest element (representing the best available school, say) may be chosen in order to yield a certain well-being, but a smaller element is chosen for some social, familial or altruistic reason. In the second, the biggest element is actually chosen, but from a reduced set of possibilities; in other words, the student has fewer choices available than in the first scenario, but can and does choose the biggest. In either case – by not choosing the biggest element or by choosing it from a reduced set of feasible functionings – it is difficult to argue that the student's 'freedom' has been reduced in the sense that he or she is worse off. Certainly, there are fewer (what might be called) degrees of freedom in the latter case, but this is not of any great importance if the biggest element is to be chosen anyway. By analogy, in relation to school choice, having a very good school available to students who do not have the social capital or know-how to avail of it does not increase their capability. What use is the freedom to attend a good school outside the catchment area for those without the means to organise family life around travel? And equally, it is of little benefit to increase the number of schools available to students by giving parents the 'freedom' to add poor schools to their sets of feasibilities.

In preparing to make a selection from their capability sets, students (or parents on their behalf) must assess the relative value of the elements therein. Sen (1985a: 16) observes that it is possible to rank one functioning over another without being able to rank *all* available functionings, even in pairs, but such an insistence on completeness is unnecessary anyway. It makes more sense to accept the less ambitious partial orderings than to insist on arbitrary completeness, and both well-being and advantage fit the partial ordering format more naturally than they do the more exacting requirements of complete ordering. In the real world, parents and pupils can usually partially order the schools on offer to them without being able to rank all schools absolutely. In that sense the criticism that school choice does not operate properly when parents do not have complete information about all possible alternatives is as foolish as suggesting that adding a bad school to the neighbourhood of a good school increases choice.

8
Utility and Functionings

Approaches to utility

Utilitarian economists use the term 'utility' carefully, but as was mentioned above there are two distinct views of it: the 'satisfaction/happiness' view and the 'desire-fulfilment' view. The happiness approach goes back to Bentham and has been used extensively by Marshall (1890), Pigou (1920) and others. The desire-based approach was pioneered by Sidgwick and developed by Ramsey (1926), Harsanyi (1976), Hare (1981), Mirrlees (1982) and others:

> A plausible case can be made for taking either happiness, or desire-fulfilment ... as guides to a person's well-being. It would be odd to claim that a person broken down by pain and misery is doing very well, and no less peculiar to think of a person whose desires are systematically violated as achieving a high level of well-being. The issue is not whether either of these views have some plausibility – they both clearly do. The real question is whether either happiness or desire-fulfilment provides an adequate approach to well-being in general, and not just in rather special cases.
>
> (Sen, 1985a: 17–18)

A more modern approach to utility – Sen calls it a 'real-valued' approach – views utility as the numerical representation of choice. If a student's 'choice function' – in other words, how the student makes specific choices from his or her set of feasible options – is consistent (Richter, 1971; Sen, 1971; Suzumura, 1983), then the student's choice function can be represented by one binary relation and all the choices can be seen as maximization according to that binary relation. That binary relation is frequently seen as 'utility' in the literature, following an approach that goes back at least to the origin of the 'revealed preference' school.

(Ibid.: 18)

Whether a binary relation of choice reflects well-being depends on the motivations that underlie choice and on various other strategic consider-ations (Hennipman, 1976, 1982). As Sen (1985a) says, there is 'an enor-mous difference between choosing tea or coffee according to one's taste' (ibid.: 19), and choosing a particular school, upon which a student's entire future may depend. Applying Sen's approach to the field of school choice leads to the realisation that the assumption that the binary relation under-lying choice (if the choice is consistent enough to yield a binary represen-tation) is necessarily only a student's ordering of his or her own well-being. It is a 'heroic simplification', as Sen calls it – students do not have the option of being someone else or living at another time (Harsanyi, 1976; Borglin, 1982) – and it does not easily accommodate interpersonal com-parisons (Jorgenson & Slesnick, 1984a, 1984b; Jorgenson *et al.*, 1980; Jorgenson *et al.*, 1983). In fact, it may be that the whole concept of using school choice as a measure of student well-being is a fallacy:

> The choice-approach to well-being is ... really a non-starter. But the other two, more classical ... views of utility – happiness and desire-fulfilment – are indeed serious candidates for serving as the basis of a theory of well-being. One difficulty that has to be faced by either of these approaches is the cogency ... of the other. If happiness is impor-tant for well-being, can desire-fulfilment irrespective of happiness be a plausible approach to well-being? If the fulfilment of desires is cen-tral to well-being, can happiness irrespective of desire-fulfilment be a sensible approach to well-being? It is not hard to construct examples in which total reliance on one or the other, but not both, ... produces a view of utility and well-being which is immediately objectionable.
>
> (Sen, 1985a: 20)

This particular problem, according to Sen, 'points to an embarrassment of riches within the utilitarian tradition'. The more serious problems lie elsewhere; namely, in the poverty of the entire utility-based approach. Both views of utility have the twin characteristics of, on the one hand, being fully grounded in the mental attitude of the person (and thus neglecting circumstance), and on the other hand avoiding any direct reference to the person's own valuation. Sen terms the former a 'physical-condition neglect' and the latter a 'valuation neglect'. Adapting this to education, students who are poorly instructed, lack confidence or have unrecognised learning disabilities can still be very happy and have a high level of desire-fulfilment as long as they have learnt to avoid unrealistic ambitions and be resigned to their lot. The physical circumstances of students are not taken into account in either (happiness or desire-fulfilment) utility view of well-being, except insofar as the circumstances are *indirectly* covered by their mental attitudes of happiness or desire. This neglect is

> fortified by the lack of interest of these two perspectives in the person's own valuation as to what kind of a life would be worthwhile. Valuing is not the same thing as desiring, and the strength of desire is influenced by considerations of realism in one's circumstances. Nor is valuing invariably reflected by the amount of pain if the valued object is not obtained.
>
> (Ibid.: 21)

Considerations of feasibility and practical possibility 'enter into what we dare to desire and what we are pained not to get'. Students' mental reactions to what they actually get and what they can sensibly expect involves compromises with reality. Adapting Sen's work to education suggests that the limitations of a utility-based approach to student well-being are particularly serious when the concern is to examine how ranking differs from student to student, rather than how different possibilities rank for each individual. For example, if a student *wants* to attend a vocational college rather than a selective school, and if he or she reckons to be *happier* at the former, then the well-being of the student is clear: it is greater having made the choice to go to the vocational college. But what happens when and if desire and happiness are the result of low expectations, since 'people adapt their preferences and choices according to what they think is possible for them' (Walker, 2006: 167)? Consider, for example, a student from a deprived background who has learnt not to be ambitious and who is more deprived in terms of quality of schooling and career preparation than another student raised in a well-to-do family, but is nevertheless happier than the more affluent pupil *and* has more desires fulfilled. It is not obvious that the disadvantaged pupil has a higher level of well-being than the affluent one, though that is the assessment of both the happiness and desire-fulfilment views of utility.

Although utilitarian views of well-being suffer from the twin defects of physical-condition neglect and valuation neglect, at least it is not an approach that sees well-being simply as opulence (Sen, 1985a). The shortcoming of viewing well-being as simply reflecting opulence or wealth is one of the reasons for making 'real income comparisons' in terms of market command over services like education. Sen (ibid.: 23) suggests that such an approach is a confusion of well-being with being well-off, and a 'confounding of the *state* of a person with the extent of his or her *possessions*'. The opulence view of well-being may be a useful first approximation (Sen, 1981; Arrow, 1982; Ravallion, 1985), but is at best only one of the factors influencing the well-being:

> The utilitarians – whatever their other limitations might be – have not been prone to commit [the] mistake [of opulence], since their concern with the person, as opposed to commodities, is deep-seated, even if it is a bit off target as far as the features of the person is concerned. ... [In] noting and emphasizing the need [to develop] a better notion of utility ...we must not spurn the insights we get from utilitarian moral philosophy, even as we reject utilitarianism.
>
> (Sen, 1985a: 23–4)

Functionings

Another way of judging the well-being of a student is as an index of his or her functionings, which in turn is what he or she succeeds in doing with his or her education. The commodity that is schooling has many desirable characteristic outcomes, of which education is one. Education in turn can be split into different types, related to academic learning, career development, employability, economic prosperity, and so on. Schooling also has desirable properties like developing social skills and making friends. For any given student, having more schooling increases up to a point his or her ability to function in desirable ways; simply put, it enables him or her to progress to a life more free of economic, social and intellectual deprivation. However, in comparing the functionings of different students – in other words, what different students actually *do* with their educations – it is not enough just to look at the respective *quantities* of schooling enjoyed by them. The 'conversion of commodity-characteristics into personal achievements depends on a variety of personal and social factors' (Sen, 1985a: 25–6), a fact which is often forgotten by governments in their frenetic pursuit of school improvement through greater choice.

Educational functionings – what students achieve with their schooling – depend on such factors as intelligence, the presence or absence of learning disorders, ambition, perseverance, age, sex, commitment, parental interest, the physical learning environment and so on. In the case of developing social skills, functionings depend not just on the individual but on interaction with others, and on age, sex, psychological disposition, culture, whether or not a school is mixed, how well students get on with each other and so on.

The utilisation function upon which functionings depend is partly a matter of choice of function from a feasible set of utilisation functions, and choice of commodity from a feasible set of commodities or 'entitlements'. The sum of all these alternative sets from which a student can choose reflects his or her capabilities; 'in other words, the various alternative functioning bundles he or she can achieve through choice' (ibid.: 27).

Sen warns of the importance of distinguishing between 'choice and non-choice factors in the determination of capabilities'. For example, in an education context, a student cannot choose his or her rate of learning. A student with low academic ability may have to be 'reconciled to an unfavourable' set of utilisation functions, but within that set there is almost certainly 'room for better husbandry' (ibid.) through remediation and personal attention. This is why increasing choice for parents and pupils seeking schools is unlikely to result in any great increase in system-wide attainment if it is not accompanied by a raising (or changing) of expectation. Too often, the set of various alternative functionings that can be achieved by students through choice is increased, yet fails to result in greater well-being, because students – especially those from poorer socio-economic circumstances – have become reconciled to under-achievement (or have acquired what is for policymakers an inconvenient set of anti-aspirations) and there are only very basic systems of remediation in place to counter that deficit.

Certainly, there is little evidence that the problem is addressed by school-choice initiatives, which facilitate the transfer of academic pupils from bad schools to good schools, but do little for the poorly attaining pupils left behind. The same questions arise in the choice of commodity sets or entitlements. Students will have some choice within their entitlement sets, but that choice is likely to be limited by circumstance.

Valuing functionings is a legitimate reflection of well-being because how well a student is doing should depend on what kind of being the student is *achieving* and what he or she is succeeding in *doing* (Sen, 1985a). The contrast between the utility view and the functioning view of well-being is best illustrated by the example, given in the previous section, of two students, one from a deprived background attending a poor school who has learnt not to be ambitious, but is nevertheless happier than the other, more affluent student attending a good school. The student from the poorer background also has his desires more fulfilled despite being more deprived in terms of functionings. As Sen points out, the question of valuation is key. 'Being happy with' or 'desiring' is not the same thing as valuing, which is a reflective activity in a way that being happy or desiring is not. A poorly taught student with a learning disorder from a family that does not affirm the value of education, may have learned to come to terms with under-achievement, 'seizing joy in merely coping and wanting no more than what is achievable without much effort' (Sen, 1985a: 29), but these attitudinal shortcomings cannot explain away the sad fact of the student's disadvantage or the fact that the student would most likely welcome the removal of that disadvantage if it were possible. To this extent, the utility-view of well-being is 'fundamentally deficient' as a result of both 'valuation' and 'physical-condition' neglect (ibid.: 29–30).

The functioning view of well-being avoids what Sen (1985a: 30) calls 'premature fixity', by dividing the problem of evaluating well-being into two distinct parts: the specification of functionings and the valuation of functionings. In some situations, when one set of functionings clearly dominates another, the valuation of functionings is non-problematic; in fact, in dealing with the educational well-being of disadvantaged students, such dominance is likely to occur frequently. In other situations, it will *not* be the case that one set of functionings dominates another, so the issue of valuation is more complicated. However, valuation does not need to generate complete orderings:

> The tyranny of 'required completeness' has had a disastrous effect on many problems in economic measurement, ... offering us a false choice between silence and babbling. Natural partial orders are either rejected as incomplete, or forced into arbitrary completeness, raising difficulties that need not have arisen.
>
> (Ibid.: 31)

The evaluation of well-being, in education as in the study of many economic and social relations, is *inherently* partial and incomplete (Majumdar & Sen, 1976; Sen, 1982, 1984a). While one set of functionings may be seen to represent a higher level of well-being than other sets of functionings, it may be impossible to rank the other sets in relation to one other. For example, it is likely to be the case that parents and students know, from instinct or from 'hot' information, that one set of educational functionings on offer at a particular school – in other words, what students achieve with the schooling there and the well-being that results – is superior to another set of functionings available at another school, without knowing or being able to measure the value of all the inferior options relative to one another. Parents in essence want and will choose the best available school, limited by family and other circumstances, irrespective of league tables showing how all the inferior schools rate against one another. And different schools will be the schools of first choice for different families – as research described in the first part of this book has demonstrated – depending on how they judge the relative importance of the various desirable characteristic outcomes of education. Consequently, policymakers should encourage diversity, rather than mimicry, in the schooling system. The more alike schools become, the less well served are those families who need something other than a second-rate replica of a good school somewhere else.

Valuation

Ranking well-being depends on valuing different functionings, which traditional welfare economists see as a purely subjective exercise. Sen rejects this subjectivist position (Nagel, 1980; Scanlon, 1982; Sen, 1985a: 33), one aspect of which is that individuals may rank the same pair of well-beings differently: one student's belief that a particular state of being is higher than another state of being can consistently coexist with a second student's belief in the opposite. Sen holds that there *is* room for the coexistence of different beliefs about states of being. The issue instead is about whether those who claim that the ranking of well-being should be purely objective are *ipso facto* claiming that the ranking of well-being should be complete and unique. This is a question about the nature of rankings themselves, and their completeness and position-dependency. If objectivity is only to demand a partial ordering, rather than completeness – in other words, that school A and school B both deliver higher well-being than school C without ranking school A and school B relatively to each other – then one student's belief that school A is better than school B can be consistent with a second student's belief that school B is higher than school A. Furthermore, if objective judgements *ipso facto* are position-dependent, then it is possible that one student can see school A as better than school B, while another can simultaneously see B better than A. According to Sen:

> The issue of position-dependence is a difficult one ... in the context of moral judgments of states of affairs ... [It] is only when both position-dependence is denied and the completeness of the well-being ranking is required that interpersonal variations must be, of necessity, ruled out, by the ... objectivist view of well-being.
>
> (Sen, 1985a: 34)

Sen's work does not demand an objectivist view – certainly not as it is being adapted here for school choice – but it does limit objectivity in the assessment of well-being and suggests that the objectivist view does not necessarily rule out the possibility of interpersonal variations of well-being rankings. One practical implication of this is that variations between rankers of well-being can exist whether a subjectivist or an objectivist position is taken (ibid.: 35), though this is not to suggest that the issue of subjectivity or objectivity is meaningless even when the practical exercise of ranking well-being turns out to be much the same whichever view is taken:

> It is ... logically possible that the subjective ... activity of valuing ... should go on in just the same way whether there are objective values or not. ... But it does not follow, and it is not true, that there is no difference whatever between these two worlds. In the one there is something that backs up and validates some of the subjective concern which people have for things. [In] the other there is not.
>
> Mackie (1977: 21–2)

The measurement of well-being

According to Sen, views of well-being can be classified according to two distinct criteria. One concerns the interpretation of well-being and the three distinct approaches that have already been considered: utility, opulence and functionings (which Sen favours). The other criterion focuses on the two types of data used for assessing well-being: market purchase data and data from questionnaires.[1]

Traditional analyses of well-being are based on the view that it is best represented by utility and that therefore market purchase data can best assess it. Sen criticises this perspective as being incongruous:

> not only for the dubious nature of the claims of utility to represent well-being, but also for the limited reach of market purchase data in reflecting important aspects of well-being.
>
> (Sen, 1985a: 40)

Only some of the things that form a basis for utility can be bought and sold in the marketplace, especially in education where the equivalent of market purchase data for schools does not take adequate account of the influence of factors such as social deprivation, domestic violence, level of education of parents and so on. However, if market purchase data do not provide a good measure for *utility*, at least they do so for *opulence*. Although two pupils (or their respective parents acting by proxy) might have identical taste in the matter of school choice – in other words, they both might rank commodity sets in exactly the same way – it is possible that one of them has a more favourable utility function than the other:

> Utility comparisons must take note of differences in the utility function (even if 'tastes' are the same), whereas there is no need to do this if we are just comparing the commodity bases of utility, which can be done in a straightforward way when tastes are the same. It is the latter that corresponds to opulence, and thus the commodity information is directly relevant and adequate for assessing opulence in a way it cannot be for assessing utility.
>
> (Ibid.: 41)

In education, most things cannot be bought and sold, however much they are sought by students and parents, so at a minimum, market 'purchase' data need to be supplemented by information gathered from sources relating to non-purchasable things like school ethos, the absence of bullying and the social integration of students in the school. For example, the value that parents attach to such things might be assessed by looking at the fee differential between different private schools with varying characteristics of ethos, anti-bullying measures and models of social integration, even if such indirect information has clear limitations because of differences in motivation and failures of expectation.

The link between utility and market purchase data even in the commercial world is problematic because market purchase data can only reflect what the consumer gets from the marketplace; they take no account of whether the 'consumer' is an individual, a family or a community (Sen, 1985a: 42). In the world of schooling and education, the link is even more tenuous. Market purchase data cannot come close to revealing what is consumed, even in circumstances where the individual student is known to be the consumer. Additionally, there is the problem of division within the family when the family is regarded as the unit of consumption. Individual members of a family do not purchase education themselves. They get it from sharing what has been bought for the community as a whole, which does not pose any great difficulty as long as the divisions within the family take account of differences in need and there is an assumption made of a 'benevolent head' (ibid.). In Becker's approach, for example,

> optimal reallocation results from altruism and voluntary contributions, and the 'group preference function' is identical to that of the altruistic head, even when he does not have sovereign power.
>
> (Becker, 1981: 192)

The problem becomes intractable when the assumption about benevolent leadership of a family or a community *cannot* be made, and when inequality within the family or community is prevalent enough to 'drive a wedge between the prosperity of the family and the commodity command of individual' parents and students (Sen, 1985a: 43). This prompts Sen to raise the question of whether using data to assess utility from direct questionnaires (instead of indirect market purchase data) might not be better:

> Since utility stands for happiness or desire-fulfilment, it is natural to think that the best source of information on this must be the person whose utility is being considered. ... Oddly enough, economics has typically entertained great doubts about direct questioning on these matters, preferring to obtain answers by indirect means such as deducing them from market purchases. ... [The] reasons for these doubts [about questionnaire data] ... are not ultimately persuasive.
>
> (Sen, 1985a: 43)

Gathering data from questionnaires is increasingly used for empirical studies of utility (Van Praag, 1968) and the self-assessment of well-being (Kapteyn & Van Praag, 1976; Scitovsky, 1976; Van Praag, 1977; Van Praag *et al.*, 1980; Van Herwaarden & Kapteyn, 1981; Kapteyn & Wansbeek, 1982; Van Praag *et al.*, 1982), and they often provide a 'more sensible basis for evaluation and comparison than the no question asked format of utility estimation favoured by traditional consumer analyses' (Sen, 1985a: 44). Therefore Sen suggests replacing utility as assessed by market purchase data with, on the one hand, utility assessed by data from questionnaire analyses and on the other, opulence assessed by market purchase data.

In more affluent communities, functionings involving schooling, the development of basic literacy and numeracy skills, avoiding truancy, being ambitious and so on, have less variation from person to person than is the case in poorer communities. However, there are other functionings which do vary a great deal from person to person (Sen, 1985a), like the development of social skills, the ability to make friends and interact with them, and taking part in extra curricular activities at school (Townsend, 1979). Even a simple thing like the ability to go to school without being ashamed of one's background or one's parents is important, even to very successful and confident people. British Prime Minister, Edward Heath, himself the son of a carpenter, poignantly recalls his days at Oxford:

> I had seen snobbery and inequality aplenty between students at Oxford. To have to answer that one's father is a bus driver, or a carpenter, perhaps; to know that one's parents cannot afford to travel to school functions, or to see them there, unhappy and ill at ease, and feel oneself shudder at a rough accent or a 'we was'; to be asked to stay with a school friend and to have to refuse for fear of asking him back to a humble villa; to have no answer to others' stories of travel in the holidays; worst of all, to see one's parents, who had made such sacrifices, grieve because they know one cannot have all the things one's associates have; that is what it [meant to be] a State scholar.
>
> (Heath, 1998: 82)

According to Sen, information concerning functionings of whatever type should be sought from indirect market data, from non-market direct and indirect observations and from direct questionnaires. In some contexts, the indirect route is more sensible for assessing functionings since direct observation and questioning might be insensitive, difficult or invalid. For example, information about the ability to buy school textbooks, computer equipment and school uniforms could more sensibly come from market purchase data. When inequality is prominent within a community, 'market purchase data may be rather remote from individual consumption' (Sen, 1985a: 47), but since observations may be difficult to make and may require an excessive amount of time or resources, market purchase data may well be the best that can be done, 'though it is second-best'.

9
Aggregation and Evaluation

The aggregation of well-being

The assessment of a student's well-being is made in terms of a set of functionings, which is then converted into a scalar measure of well-being through a 'valuation function'. The valuation of the set of functionings may not coincide with that of utility, in any of its interpretations – happiness, desire-fulfilment or choice – and the valuation may be incomplete and take the form of a partial ordering. Sen holds that 'intersection partial ordering' is a sensible attempt at combining alternative views of well-being.

Although the confusion of well-being with utility is, according to Sen, 'deeply problematic', the latter can be relevant and useful in the assessment of the former. Utility in the sense of happiness at school may well be a functioning that is relevant to student well-being, and utility information gleaned from desires and choices can provide evidence for valuation. The most important failing of what Sen calls 'utility calculus' is in the way it deals with comparisons *between* students (Hammond, 1982; Gevers, 1979), not because such comparisons cannot be made, but rather because

> interpersonal comparisons of utility can give a very distorted picture of well-being. The psychological features that are reflected in utility – related to desires, happiness, and so on – have to adjust to unfavourable circumstances, thereby affecting the metric of deprivation and their evidential importance.
>
> (Sen, 1985a: 53)

Sen suggests that since practical comparisons of utility, happiness and desire are difficult to make anyway, and this is particularly true in the case of students, the 'additional difficulty' arising from not relying on utility information is small. He also argues that sets of functionings are themselves of interest in understanding achievements of well-being even when a scalar conversion is impossible, and that partial ordering is of considerable practical use and relevance.

Two critical problems are posed by Sen regarding 'possible misunderstandings of the nature of the valuation problem in the assessment of functionings': the difficulty in avoiding Arrow-type impossibility (Arrow, 1951) in aggregating different valuation judgements for different people; and the difficulty of using the same valuation function in assessing the well-being of different people (Beitz, 1986).

The impossibility problem

Arrow's Impossibility theorem states that when there are three or more choices, no selection or voting system meets all of the following five criteria: non-imposition, monotonicity, independence of irrelevant alternatives, unrestricted domain and non-dictatorship. There is no general way to aggregate preferences without running into some kind of irrationality or unfairness.

- 'Non-imposition' (or 'citizen sovereignty') is the criterion whereby every possible order of preference should be achievable by some set of preferences.
- 'Monotonicity' (or 'positive association of social and individual values') refers to the condition whereby if an individual modifies his or her preference order, then the societal order of preference should never respond by placing that order lower than before. An individual should not be able to hurt an option by ranking it higher.[1]
- 'Independence of irrelevant alternatives' refers to the condition whereby if the welfare function is only applied to a restricted subset of options, the result should be compatible with the outcome for the whole set of options; in other words, changes in individual rankings of irrelevant alternatives (i.e. outside the subset) should have no impact on the societal ranking of the relevant subset. For example, suppose there are three candidates contesting the leadership of the British Labour Party, and suppose one candidate is clearly the frontrunner. According to Arrow's theorem, if one of the two trailing candidates drops out of the race, it might result in the other 'trailing' candidate winning. This seems to many as being unfair, but the point of Arrow's theorem is that these 'unfair' situations cannot be avoided without relaxing some of the five criteria.[2]

- 'Unrestricted domain' (or 'universality') is the criterion whereby the social welfare function should create a deterministic, complete societal order of preference from every possible set of individual orders of preference; in other words, all possible choices should have been ranked relative to one another, the selection mechanism should have processed all possible sets of preferences, and the selection mechanism should give the same result for the same profile of votes every time, without any randomness.

- 'Non-dictatorship' refers to the condition whereby the welfare function does not simply follow the order of preference of a special individual while ignoring all others; in other words, the welfare function is sensitive to the wishes of the many.

Some commentators have suggested that the way out of Arrow's paradox is to weaken the 'independence of irrelevant alternatives' criterion, suggesting that actually it is overly strong and does not hold true in real life. Although this criterion is dropped in majority-rule democracy, dropping it has the disadvantage of encouraging strategic voting and leaving democracy open to manipulation by some voters who get a better result by falsely reporting their orders of preference.

There are other ways out of the paradox. Black (1958), for example, has shown that if there is only one agenda by which preference orders are judged – the so-called single peaked preference – then all five of Arrow's criteria are met by majority-rule democracies. Another way out of the paradox is to limit choice to two alternatives at a time; whenever more than two options are put up for selection, they are paired-off and voted upon. However, the order in which the options are paired strongly influences the outcome, and it fails to meet the 'independence of irrelevant alternatives' criterion and even the Pareto principle.[3]

Other theorists advocate relaxing the rule that choice must create a social preference ordering which satisfies transitivity; in other words, if 'a' is preferred to 'b', and 'b' is preferred to 'c', then 'a' must be preferred to 'c'. Instead, the rule should only require acyclicity; in other words, if 'a' is preferred to 'b', and 'b' is preferred to 'c', then it is *not* the case that 'c' is preferred to 'a'. In this more relaxed acyclicity rule, it is possible for choice to satisfy Arrow's criteria.

Sen has suggested two further alternatives, offering both relaxation of transitivity and the removal of the Pareto principle. He has shown the existence of selection mechanisms that comply with all five of Arrow's criteria but supply only semi-transitive results, and he has demonstrated another interesting result: the Pareto principle is irreconcilable even with very weak liberty (the so-called impossibility of the Paretian Liberal). If there are areas of life in which individuals are decisive regardless of the preferences of others, this is incompatible with the Pareto principle, and Sen has argued that this demonstrates the futility of demanding Pareto optimality in relation to everyday selection mechanisms. Contentiously, Sen's 'impossibility of the Paretian Liberal' principle suggests that *both* the neo-conservative view that the market alone can produce a Pareto-optimal society, and the left-wing view that welfarism rather than consumer freedom should be the mechanism of choice in society, are wrong.[4]

There are several distinct issues that relate to the impossibility problem. Firstly, the Arrow impossibility result can be avoided by the use of a richer information base (Hammond, 1976; Arrow, 1977; d'Aspremont & Gevers, 1977). Secondly, if there is no insistence on completeness or on limiting incompleteness, then having partial orderings provides a method of avoiding impossibility, albeit 'at the cost of being silent on some particular comparisons' (Sen, 1985a: 55). Thirdly, and perhaps most importantly, the problem of getting a common valuation function – complete or partial – for judging the well-being of different individuals is a different exercise from that of judging their preferences. For example, if two students have identical valuation functions in terms of school choice, then the 'common standard problem' is trivially resolved, but the 'social choice problem' of the Arrow-type still persists since the two might rank their social states differently (despite sharing the same view of individual educational well-being). This is not to say that the issue of different views of valuation can easily be resolved, but the differences are limited. Deriving a common standard of well-being is a very different exercise from the interpersonal aggregation of rankings of social states.

The problem of using the same valuation function

Utility, whether interpreted as happiness or desire-fulfilment, has what Sen calls 'independent descriptive content', whereas well-being is just the value of achieved functionings. It might be possible to redefine utility so that it has no independent descriptive content, but this would 'cut it off' from its 'traditional meaning and importance' (Sen, 1985a: 57). Happiness and desire exist in their own right and the utility function establishes a connection between commodities and utility.

Not every student has the same valuation of different functionings, so when they do differ there is likely to be disagreement as to the appropriate valuations; and it is impossible to use one valuation function for one student and another for a second student, and then make 'inter-utility-functional' comparisons about the relative well-being of the two students:

> Inter-utility-functional comparisons make sense only because utility has descriptive content of its own, and it is sensible to ask whether one person is happier than another, or has more desire-fulfilment, despite the two persons having two different utility functions.
>
> (Ibid.: 58)

Sen suggests that the problem of valuation of well-being is similar to that of opulence. If some have a higher command over commodities than others, then they can sensibly be seen as more opulent, though not necessarily happier or having greater well-being, since the relationship varies between commodity possession and functionings. Well-being, like opulence, can be decided by assessing functionings.

The evaluation of advantage

Educational well-being is the assessment of the particular achievements of a student; the kind of educational life he or she succeeds in having. Advantage is not the same thing – it takes account the opportunities offered by chance to the student, of which only one may be chosen at any given time – so the assessment of advantage must therefore be an evaluation of the set of *potential* achievements of a student and not just his or her *actual* achievements. If a student's advantage is being considered and not just his or her well-being, the evaluation of functionings is only 'part of the story' (Sen, 1985a: 59).

One of the problems with evaluating advantage in education is that school choice mostly operates under uncertainty, where the chooser picks a set of feasibilities, from which 'nature' or 'chance' then chooses one particular element. For example, a pupil or parent chooses a school and chance then chooses the other classmates and hence the learning atmosphere of the class for the next three-to-five years. At other times, albeit rarely in education, there is no uncertainty: the chooser picks both the set and then the particular element from the set (Kannai & Peleg, 1984).

As Sen points out, theory suggests that adding an inferior (as judged by the chooser) element to an existing set of feasibilities makes a set worse off when choice is operating under uncertainty, since a pupil might be given the inferior element by chance when chance makes its selection. However, if the intention is only to assess a pupil's opportunities, then adding an inferior element need not make the set worse. Whatever could be chosen earlier can still be chosen, as long as there is no uncertainty; that is to say, as long as nature has no hand in the final choosing.

To what extent does this apply to choice in schooling? If a government widens choice for poorer pupils by allowing them freedom to choose schools outside their particular catchment areas say; if that wider choice includes inferior schools and the final decision is made under uncertainty, which is mostly the case in reality, then pupils are worse off since the risk of going to a bad school has increased. It can be seen that what private schooling does is lower the risk from uncertainty by reducing the number of additional inferior elements in the set of possibilities, which also has more elements. Nothing can remove uncertainty completely, of course, because nature will always have a part to play in the later stages of selection, but insofar as it is possible in a free society, private schooling controls for the variables that most concern aspiring middle-class parents about public schools: indiscipline, large classes, lack of motivation among students from lower socio-economic families, the absence of a religious or cultural ethos and so on.

The value of a student's set of functionings – the student's capability set (or more casually, 'capability') – can be given by the value of its best element. In this view, greater choice is valued only because it allows a superior (as judged by the chooser) element to be chosen, and where it does not, the widening of the set is of no value. Sen (1985a: 61) calls this approach, which assigns to a set the value of its best element, 'elementary evaluation'.[5] It is an approach that can be criticised on several fronts. Firstly, choosing may not be possible when the elements in the capability set are not fully ordered. Partial ordering demands some modification to the elementary evaluation process, such as comparing two capability sets by checking whether there is an element in one set which is better than every element in the other set. This second possible evaluation procedure is slightly different from the original elementary evaluation procedure when the ordering is incomplete. When the ordering is complete, the ranking of a set according to its greatest value – the simple evaluation procedure – coincides with the ranking yielded by the modified procedure (namely, the comparison of two capability sets by checking whether there is an element in one set which is better than every element in the other set). Sen calls this modified approach 'elementary *capability* evaluation', which subsumes the earlier simple 'elementary evaluation'.

The second difficulty with elementary evaluation arises from what is meant and understood by 'freedom'. It may not be adequate to consider what it is that students succeed in doing; it may be that consideration should also be given to what students *could have done*. Consider the situation in which a set from which a student can choose a school gets smaller, but still includes its best element. In terms of achievement, the student's position might be unaffected, assuming the student chooses the best element each time, but the freedom enjoyed by the student has been reduced. In the same way, if the government or a local authority reduces school choice for a community (as part of a school closure programme say) to a very small set of options which still includes the optimal choice, parents and students may or may not perceive their freedom reduced. Perhaps it is the case, hinted at in the Preface, that choice in schooling for a community amounts simply to having a choice between at least two good schools. Sen suggests that a way of dealing with problems like this is to make evaluation take account of the *extent* of choice, in addition to using the value of the best element in the capability set; that is to say, to consider the *number* of elements in the choice set as a reflection of the *extent* of choice, as well as their 'quality'.

A different approach to the problem of freedom is to incorporate 'acts of choosing as among the doings and beings' (Sen, 1985a: 70) in the functioning set and then using elementary evaluation (i.e. assigning to the capability set the value of its best element). The quality of education a student enjoys is not just a matter of what he or she achieves, but also of what options the student had available. A 'good education' is not one in which the student is forced into a good school or onto a good training course, but is also about having genuine choice. Thus Sen helps us close the theoretical gap between well-being and advantage, though as he admits, it is still legitimate to ask about the *extent* of the choice offered in a capability set, having taken note of the acts of choosing.

The final problem is in 'futures'. No matter what evaluation is used, whether it is simple elementary evaluation, dominance evaluation or elementary capability evaluation, and irrespective of what view of freedom parents and students take, it is impossible for students or parents to know how they will rank their school choices in the future, or how they will feel retrospectively about their present rankings:

> Some problems can be avoided by choosing axioms differently. ... The substantive content of the axioms are motivated by 'uncertainty of future tastes'. In the context of some choice problems, we may have to choose first one 'opportunity set' from a class of such sets, and then at a future date choose an element from the opportunity set that was chosen earlier. If we already knew our complete future preference, then ...'elementary evaluation' of the sets would [be] non-problematic. But future rankings may be unknown, and we are not in a position to do an 'elementary evaluation' today in line with fully known future preference.
>
> (Sen, 1985a: 65)

10
Asset-Mapping

Sen's capability framework is essentially a mechanism for determining quality of life. It represents what people can achieve and be, and has very little to do with wealth or possessions, but is about the freedom people have to choose the life paths they value (Sen, 1992, 1999). His approach to evaluating well-being has much in common with the approach some low-income communities have adopted in rebuilding themselves, a successful example of which is described by Jasek-Rysdahl (2001)[1] from outside the field of education, but which schools facing challenging circumstances might profitably use as a route to improvement. It focuses on mapping the capability-enabling assets (Kretzmann & McKnight 1993; McKnight 1995) of stakeholders and using them for improvement. The aim is to create a 'capacity inventory' (Jasek-Rysdahl, 2001: 314) of the capabilities, talents and skills possessed by stakeholders – in the case of schools: students, teachers, parents and others – which they are willing to share with others.[2] If used, such an approach to school improvement, which borrows heavily from Nussbaum's (2000) notions of 'basic', 'internal' and 'combined' capabilities,[3] could form part of a more general movement towards self-reliance and self-confidence, and developing stronger *internal* social relationships in school communities.

To compile a capacity inventory, schools should conduct surveys asking stakeholders about the skills, talents and time they are prepared to make available to the organisation, so that an inventory of resources is produced that can be used to improve the quality of provision and which can help stakeholders realise that they have many internal resources to call upon without feeling that they have to go to outsiders for help. Not every 'failing' school is failing because its leadership and teachers are incompetent, much as policymakers would like us to accept the view that the only solution to school under-performance is to fire and re-hire teachers and parachute in a new headteacher previously successful elsewhere. Some schools serve very underprivileged catchment areas wherein many of the capabilities of parents and other stakeholders in the local community – which in better-performing schools are taken for granted – are under-utilised. Failing schools (which are defined here as schools that lower stakeholder capability) and schools serving 'failing' communities operate under constraints that limit opportunity at every turn. In successful schools, the capability assets of teachers, students, parents, local community and religious leaders, local businesses and so on, infuse the life of the school in a way that breeds confidence and success. Teachers and students at failing schools, by contrast, are told that their escape can only be predicated on *external* help, which in turn breeds dependency and dysfunction. There is no compelling evidence that failing schools turned around by sudden cash injections and new externally imposed leadership are any more viable in the long term than their previous incarnations, but there *is* evidence that schools and communities who turn *themselves* around stay the course.

While Sen's capabilities approach to understanding quality of life is seldom mentioned in community and school regeneration activities, there is a definite link between the two. The inventory of resources resulting from an asset survey is a measure of the capability set of the school that generates it (although skills and talents are crude representations of capabilities) and by studying these sets, a more complete understanding (than is possible by relying solely on information from official sources like school inspections) can be obtained of the quality of life in the school. Material resources should not be ignored either, nor should stakeholders shy away from examining how they are distributed. Walker (2006) quotes Robeyns (2004) in regarding material resources like teacher-time, classroom allocation and the use of ICT equipment as 'capability inputs', and how these are differentially accessed and converted 'into valued capabilities' and opportunities goes to the heart of Sen's approach:

> Are girls, or Black children, or disabled children, or mature learners equally able to convert resources into valued educational opportunities, and are they recognized socially and subjectively as having equal claims on such resources and opportunities? ... . [Sen points out] that 'equalizing ownership of resources ... need not equalize the substantive freedoms enjoyed by different persons, since there can be significant variations in the conversion of resources and primary goods into freedoms' (1992: 33).
>
> (Walker, 2006: 167)

Freedom and agency in school communities

Building school communities as a way of increasing the well-being of those who 'live' in them entails devolving more control to schools. Decision-making by (central or centralised local) government fiat does not offer enough incentive for teachers and others to get involved within schools or between schools and their external stakeholders. It creates a disinterested professional bureaucracy only to 'deal with' school under-performance and its associated problems, and encourages a cult of individualism in schools. According to Jasek-Rysdahl, a similar situation exists in community-building in the United Kingdom and the United States (Bellah *et al.*, 1992; Etzioni, 1993, 1996). For schools, competition and league tables have discouraged schools from cooperation (Kelly, 2001) and the culture of the hero-teacher or hero-school is at least a partial explanation for low system-wide attainment in the United Kingdom.

Just as some parents and pupils choose schools to avoid ethno-cultural diversity, so diversity creates tensions within staff rooms and within school communities. Newcomers arrive at a school with different values and in the case of the children of newly arrived immigrants, with different languages. They do not always want to surrender these cultural norms and indeed were they to do so, it would probably weaken the benefit of their presence to the host society. However, when they retain their old ways of doing, it is frequently met with hostility from those already established in the school, who feel threatened (Jasek-Rysdahl, 2001). The belief among those working to rebuild school communities, like the IQEA (Improving the Quality of Education for All)[4] organisation, is that strong school communities are influences for improvement, providing the structure necessary to support and increase well-being.

As has been discussed already, Sen's understanding of well-being focuses on functionings and capabilities, which terms he uses to describe a standard of living different from utility-based and commodity-based theory. His approach suggests that well-being should concentrate on choice and opportunity, and be based on the idea that well-being is a measure of the life one leads and the degree of choice one has. Functionings describe current *realised* life conditions, unlike capabilities, which are opportunity-based. Functionings are 'aspects of living' or 'states of being' (Sugden, 1993): the 'realised physical and mental states'; the life conditions resulting from choices already made (Sen, 1993); the variables that reflect the current condition of life (Jasek-Rysdahl, 2001: 315). For students, having a certain level of qualification and achievement, being socially mobile, being happy and having a sense of fulfilment, being self-actualised and intellectually nourished, being free from bullying, having the respect of one's classmates and so on, are examples of educational functionings.

Well-being in education is a complex thing. When students and their parents consider their quality of life, they consider many things: their happiness, their current social relationships, their future prospects and so on. Quality of life is more than mere utility or income. An adaptation of Sen's work to education would suggest that to obtain a proper measure of a student's quality of life, his or her set of capabilities should be considered. Capabilities are available life options (Jasek-Rysdahl, 2001) from which a person can choose, taking account of his or her freedom to choose them. Capabilities are the different combinations of functionings that can be achieved, and the capabilities set is the set of all possible functionings available; the set of possible functionings from which a student can choose. The student with the most choices – in other words, the student with the largest set of possible functionings – has the 'best' quality of life. Capabilities include the freedom to choose a particular school, the freedom to choose particular subjects and courses, freedom from poor teaching, the freedom to associate with like-minded peers, the freedom to choose a particular career and so on. Consider for example a student with three secondary school choices in his or her locality. The student has three possible functionings and this set of choices is the pupil's capabilities set in this area of his or her life. Assuming the student eventually chooses one of the schools on offer, the chosen school then becomes the realised functioning; the one particular state of living that is chosen by the student from the capabilities set.

As was noted in earlier chapters, Sen defines capabilities as positive or negative freedoms, but acknowledges that these can be difficult concepts to pin down (Sen, 1984b, 1991, 1992). Freedom generally can be defined as how little one is constrained by authority. Negative freedom, which Sen (1992: 87) admits has a 'special significance' for his capability approach, is then how much one is *allowed* to do – a measure of the lack of external constraint imposed by others – and positive freedom is how much one is *able* to do.[5] Negative freedom has intrinsic as well as instrumental importance (Sen, 1985b). The student with three secondary schools from which to choose might still not be free in a positive sense. For example, the choice of one particular school might require a substantial reorganisation of the student's part-time work commitments and such a student might lack the wherewithal to ignore these; or perhaps the student's particular school of choice requires his or her parents to have a second car. A student in such a situation has negative freedom in that no one is working to prevent him or her from choosing any of the three schools, but the student lacks positive freedom in that he or she cannot in reality have the school he or she wants because of practical constraints. Research on the regeneration of disadvantaged communities suggests that this is most likely to be the case among ambitious students from poorer backgrounds, just as it is among ambitious adults. Jasek-Rysdahl (2001) quotes research from the United States, which finds for example that poorer neighbourhoods have fewer bus routes to centres of employment and have the worst childcare facilities (Entin *et al.*, 1998). This naturally impacts on the educational well-being of students from those communities, despite the movement to offer such students greater choice in schooling. Offering greater school choice does not necessarily increase well-being if adequate external support and enabling structures are not present to overcome the inertia of disadvantage. For example, the *No Child Left Behind* programme in the United States offers students the opportunity to transfer from low-performing schools to high-performing ones. Yet research by Mickelson and Southworth (2005) suggests that a significant proportion of students in such circumstances – 92 per cent in the case study in question – do *not* exercise their option to 'exit from their low-performing schools', which illustrates how

> larger social, economic and political contexts constrain the implementation of standards-based reforms in general and, in particular, the limitations of the transfer option for improving academic achievement and educational equity.
>
> (Mickelson & Southworth, 2005: 249)

Barriers that limit positive freedoms clearly must be removed if school choice is to have its desired impact on student well-being (Sen, 1992: 149). A district-wide case study in England by Parsons and Welsh (2006) supports these findings: pro-choice education policies tend to discriminate against deprived groups and exacerbate differences in recruitment and attainment between schools. Greater school choice may increase 'consumer' satisfaction, but there are curtailments to that when schools adopt negative constraints, such as religious affiliation and academic ability, which inhibit open access and curb the ability of parents to exercise choice. Some consumers, of course, are naturally better equipped to make choices than others, so there are winners and losers, among schools as much as among families. A fair local system of provision needs to recognise the need for choice and the right to individual freedom, but balance that with adequate support and enabling services (Parsons & Welsh, 2006). Policymakers should therefore concentrate on issues like developing school admissions procedures and transport infrastructures that individualise need to a greater extent than they do currently, while remaining cost effective when taking account of the socio-economic benefits of better schooling.

Sen's work focuses on positive freedom (Sen, 1987, 1992; Qizilbash, 1996) by connecting the idea of capabilities to empowerment and agency. The suggested emphasis in adapting his work to education is on giving students the tools to make choices and to achieve; and for advocates of greater school choice, to incorporate the notion of agency into the application of capabilities. Agency is acting to bring about change and is 'central to recognising people as responsible' beings who have the freedom to act or not to act (Sen, 1999: 18–20) in ways that sometimes 'transcend and conflict with personal well-being' (Clark, 2005: 5). In education, agency relates well to capabilities because a student can only make a choice and act responsibly if he or she has choices to make. As Jasek-Rysdahl (2001: 317) succinctly puts it:

> [Sen] shifted [the theory] from just looking at conditions of living to the ability to make choices about conditions of living.

The relationship between capability and agency is core to an understanding of how policymaking effects change in education. Agency is the 'ability to pursue goals that one values' (Walker, 2006: 165), so its absence among students is bound to lead to underachievement and disempowerment. The British government, among others, sees education as significant not just because it increases prosperity and reduces economic deprivation, but because it empowers minorities and the disadvantaged in society and opens up new capabilities sets for them (Abadian, 1996; Sen, 1999). Borrowing from Jasek-Rysdahl's (2001) work on community building in the United States, this relationship between agency and capability is likely to prove important in schools' efforts at improvement, especially for schools serving low-income neighbourhoods where there is the additional burden of needing to improve the community surrounding the school as well as the school itself.

Deficiency and empowering assessments

Asset-mapping, as a method by which a school can improve, is basically a survey of the physical and intellectual capital assets of stakeholders, compiled by canvassing teachers, students, school managers, local community groups and businesses to find out what they can and are willing to offer the school. In that sense, it presupposes an acceptance by the wider community that the school's welfare is *its* concern, but whenever and wherever that is the case, the community probably knows best how to improve the lot of those living and being educated therein (Jasek-Rysdahl, 2001: 319). There is no obvious reason why school improvement should differ from community building in this respect. No matter how asset-poor a school's stakeholders are, they do have abilities and talents to offer, and each time a stakeholder spends the currency of his or her assets, the community is stronger for it and the person more empowered and more powerful.

If research on community building is anything to go by – for example, research by Kretzmann and McKnight (1993) – an approach that focuses on individual stakeholder capacity to rebuild schools is likely to be more effective than one that focuses on the needs of failing schools or schools facing challenging circumstances. In the latter case of a failing school, a database is typically compiled that describes what is deficient, including records of poor teaching, recruitment difficulties, measures of teacher and student absenteeism, examination failure and so on. This data is then used as evidence of the shortcomings of the school and to support external inspectors and professionals who are imported to 'solve' the problem that is the school. Governors, teachers, parents and students are apprised of the extent of the problem, but the focus is not on what stakeholders can do and achieve, rather how they are constrained in what they can do and achieve (Peirce & Steinbach, 1987). It is a 'deficiency assessment' model (Jasek-Rysdahl, 2001).

The message from community-building research is that a more effective way to deal with a school's problems might be to develop an inventory of the *positive* capabilities of stakeholders; to 'shift the focus away from needs and deficiencies, to the abilities and potential of individuals' (Jasek-Rysdahl, 2001: 320) who make up the school community. Such a model is based on 'empowering assessment', which can mobilise rather than suppress a school community (Kretzmann & McKnight, 1993; McKnight, 1995). For example, the inventory developed by Kretzmann and McKnight (1993) in the United States involves stakeholder questionnaires about assets and skills, and when compiled can be separated into four information parts: General Capabilities, Community Capabilities, Social Entrepreneurship and Personal Information. A similar one adapted for use in schools might look like this:

- General Capabilities information focuses on the capabilities that stakeholders have which are not necessarily developed in the school or by teaching, but which nevertheless may be of use to the school.

These may include experience with youth clubs, in sports or pastimes like Bridge or Chess, in music and drama societies, in off-curriculum languages, and so forth.

- Community Capabilities are about stakeholder involvement in local and national organisations outside the school, which might be valuable in aiding the school in its drive to improve.

- Information about Social Entrepreneurship capabilities, interests and experiences is a database on the entrepreneurial doings of the school's stakeholders. The thinking here is that there is much a school in difficulties can learn from commercial organisations that have overcome difficulties, and that such inspiration is more likely to have a positive impact if supplied from within than from 'gurus' moving into the school for an in-service day at the end of the year. For example, a school governor might be on the board of a local cooperative or credit union.

- Personal Information is an over-arching database of non-confidential personal information, which identifies individuals and their capabilities, from inside and outside the school, so that those talents can be called on to help the school as and when they are needed.

The notion of making inventories of soft and hard assets and applying them to school improvement has much in common with Sen's capability approach in economics, which focuses on 'measuring the level of choice people have and then using that information to guide policy to increase choice' (Jasek-Rysdahl, 2001: 321). In community building, research shows that the best way for poor communities to change is for residents of the community to take charge (Kretzmann & McKnight, 1993). It could be thus in schools too; students, parents, teachers, managers, governors and the wider community taking charge of school improvement. At it is most basic, this involves finding out what capabilities stakeholders have – the sets of possible functionings available to them – so that they can be mobilised on behalf of the school. Unfortunately, data sets from asset-mapping exercises have a short shelf-life because poor schools serving low-income neighbourhoods have a high turnover of stakeholders: teachers leave for less challenging pastures and parents are not as long engaged with the schooling system. In addition, asset surveys cannot be done on a large enough scale to draw general conclusions regarding well-being in *all* failing schools, or be made standard enough to make comparisons possible between different schools or different local authorities. What asset surveys *can* do is offer schools a better understanding of their own capabilities, which they can then employ to improve conditions and self-esteem.

The mere fact of participating in inventory-making processes adds to stakeholder empowerment and increases choice. It creates a larger set of functionings and therefore greater well-being. The process is empowering because attention is shifted away from deficiencies and outsiders, to possibilities and insiders, who are thereby encouraged to become agents of change (Jasek-Rysdahl, 2001: 325) and not just clients. Capability frameworks also shift the attention of policymakers away from aggregated outcomes to the processes that affect those outcomes. Asset-mapping allows for a greater level of detail regarding the capabilities of stakeholders than mere inputs to choice (ibid.), and in failing schools the data collected is close to the concept of Sen's capabilities because the inventories are *direct* measures of what teachers and students are *able to do*. The result is that school communities have a better understanding of their own internal ability to effect change and a broader view of their increasing capabilities, all of which enables internal stakeholders to achieve a higher level of functioning, which after all is the whole point of improvement.

Notes

1 School choice: An overview

1. Milton Friedman was the first major economist to call for a system of public education that afforded parents discretion in selecting schools for their children. His proposals centred around the idea of government-funded voucher programmes allowing parents to opt out of the public system and instead send their children to private schools (Rapp, 2000).

2. From 1600 students in 1997–8 to 6000 students in 1998–9. In 2001–2, about 11,000 Milwaukee students used vouchers to attend approximately 100 private schools. Seventy per cent of these voucher students attended parochial, mainly Catholic, schools. Vouchers are given to families with incomes at or below 175 per cent of the poverty level. An analysis of the families participating in the scheme found that 'the people using the vouchers are mostly black and Hispanic and very poor' (Thevenot, 2003). Students in the scheme out-performed their non-participating peers by 11 per cent in mathematics and 6 per cent in reading (Greene *et al.*, 1999).

3. Cleveland has some of the worst public schools in the United States. In 1996, it set up a voucher scheme allowing children from poor families to leave the city's failing schools and use vouchers to attend suburban public schools, independent schools and Charter Schools. Priority is given to families with income below 200 per cent of the federal poverty level. There are means-tested scholarships of up to 90 per cent of fees for the poorest students, and special needs students have all their additional costs covered. Research has shown a 15 per cent advantage for participating students over non-participating students in mathematics and a 7 per cent advantage in reading (McElwee, 2005: 23).

4. Private schools that take vouchers are not allowed to select on any basis: ability, past behaviour or religious affiliation. *Per capita* spending in US private schools is about half *per capita* spending in public schools, and in voucher schools it is even lower because the very expensive elite private schools do not participate in the scheme (Brighouse, 2003).

5. It received 20,000 applications for 1300 scholarships.

6. Herbert (2000) suggests that school league tables are part of an increasing tendency towards the evaluation of competitiveness (Walford, 1996). They were originally designed to provide parents with factual information and to stimulate a quasi-market in schooling, but they have failed adequately to take account of the social background or 'context' of pupils at schools, even though research indicates a strong link between it and educational attainment. Gray (1993) holds that about half of pupils' examination performance can in fact be attributed to social background (Herbert, 2000), though 'school factors' do have some impact (Reynolds & Cuttance, 1992; Reynolds *et al.*, 1996).

7. Research in the United Kingdom by Worpole (1999) shows that the average length of trips to and from schools has increased from 2.1 to 2.7 miles over the course of the 1990s, and that the greater need for families to use cars for schooling further exacerbates the educational divide between the have and the have-nots (Gorard *et al.*, 2002).

8. Supporters of greater school choice point to the United States as an example of privatisation working, but the US public education system is more expensive, less efficient and more unequal than most other countries. The regulatory and tax systems are much more business-friendly than in Europe, but even so there is still no evidence that commercial sector intervention has been more successful than state intervention. Commercial companies involved in education provision do not necessarily make a profit either. The Edison Company, for example, posted losses of $49 million in 1999 and did not then expect to break even for seven more years (Brighouse, 2003: 41).

9. Critics of choice have expressed concern about the participant attrition rates in this research.

10. Home schooling is often the preferred escape route for disaffected parents. It is a sub-form of private education and is enjoying increased popularity in the United States, where between 2 and 3 percent of pupils – more than one million – are home-schooled. It is perceived as an increasingly legitimate alternative, no longer dominated by religious fundamentalists (Arai, 2000; Stevens, 2001), which includes non-religious parents looking for a way to focus humanely on the unique needs of their children. Viewed by supporters as representing the right to choose without espousing neo-liberal market ideology (Aurini & Davies, 2005), and by opponents (Apple, 2000; Riegel, 2001) as destructive of the democratic public school system, it was until quite recently (1993) illegal (Aurini & Davies, 2005).

11. In the United Kingdom, approximately one in three primary schools and one in six secondary schools are faith schools, but of these only 33 are Jewish, four Muslim and two Sikh (Cush, 2005: 436). There are 107 *private* Muslim schools. The ratio of Christian children to places in Christian schools is approximately 3:1, that for Muslim children in Muslim schools is approximately 185:1 (McElwee, 2005).

12. There are complex variables at work that are difficult to disaggregate in any analysis. For one, not all schools segregated along religious lines are faith schools; they only reflect the ethnic composition of the communities they serve, with all the economic, social class and cultural predispositions that it entails.

13. There are other differences too: non-religious private school parents are more likely to be divorced, separated or single compared with religious private school parents.

14. Level of parental education is likely to be linked to parental language competence, which in turn may affect the way parents communicate with their children (Eccles & Davis-Kean, 2005: 202).

15. Families with two parents tend to have higher socio-economic status than single-parent families, which allows them to invest more in education, financially, socially and emotionally (Chiu & Ho, 2006).

16. The Alum Rock project was a voucher experiment in California from 1972 to 1977, funded by the federal government but condemned by the National Educational Association (Kirkpatrick, 1990). Initially, 96 per cent of teachers said the voucher programme enabled them to exercise innovative ideas more frequently, 95 per cent of local parents liked the idea of having a choice of schools and 75 per cent of parents thought their children would receive a better education as a result of the programme. These very high percentages declined slightly over the course of the project, but remained firmly in positive territory, and the project was really only criticised for its low participation rate (Kirkpatrick, 1990).

17. According to Rapp (2000: 37), choice programmes benefit not just participating students, but other students in the local area.

18. Hoxby (1996) also found that collective bargaining by teacher unions reduces educational output.

19. One possible explanation is that 'the mere threat of choice is enough to deter shirking'. Between 1987 and 1991, school choice programmes spread rapidly across the United States and the average public school teacher's preparation time increased from 6.8 to 7.9 hours (per week, though this is not noted by Rapp). By 1994, this had risen to over 8.5 hours (Rapp, 2000: 58).

20. Parents are on a slightly different footing here from taxpayers, though both are stakeholders in education and schooling. For parents, schools create human capital for their children, enhancing their future life prospects. Taxpayers, on the other hand, have an interest in the quality of education primarily because of investment in assets, and in a sense they assign to teachers and administrators the responsibility for managing such assets (Rapp, 2000). Some commentators have argued that there is no agency problem in teaching, that it is not a typical profession because teachers, as a result of their 'vocationalism' and idealism, have no incentive to shirk (Shulman & Sykes, 1983), but this is by no means universally accepted.

21. Rapp (2000: 41) notes, 'Administrators complain that firing teachers for poor performance is nearly impossible, as each dismissal brings high legal costs. In New York, the average disciplinary proceeding against a tenured teacher costs $176,000.'

22. That is, teachers' utility depends negatively on the work effort they expend and positively on the approval of their supervisors. Teachers do not compete to have large classes, so Rapp's model does not include student number as a determinant of teacher utility. (Rapp, 2000: 43).

23. Thus the minus sign in equation (1.3).

24. Some Charter Schools also focus on minority pupils from urban areas, though they generally enrol a wider cross-section of pupils distributed more evenly across the income scale than schools with voucher pupils.

25. Small and rural schools in the United States account for approximately 30 per cent of public school students, and 30 per cent of US public schools are in rural communities with fewer than 2500 inhabitants.

26. In 2005, there were 41 Islamic primary schools with demand for three or four times that number (Van Kessel, 2004).

27. 'Other researchers have come to different conclusions (Gibson & Asthana, 1999, 2000; Lauder *et al.*, 1999; Noden, 2000). In reviewing their evidence

we are not convinced that we have to adjust the general thrust of our arguments.' (Fitz, Taylor & Gorard, 2002: 126)

28. Roughly one-third of schools in the Netherlands are Catholic, one-third Protestant and one-third non-religious. There are in excess of a dozen additional types and almost all are financed by the government. The percentage of private schools is very small (unlike the United Kingdom), but many are only accessible to better-off parents.

29. The southern part of the country is overwhelmingly Catholic and the northern part is overwhelmingly Protestant.

30. Research by Gorard *et al.* (2002) illustrates exactly how tricky ascribing school closure to failure can be. For example, school closures and amalgamations can increase the size of remaining schools in an area. In Brent, for example, in 1989, there were 18 schools and by 1999 this had fallen to 13. This coincided with a rise in the number of students in full-time secondary education there, so superficially, there appears to have been an enormous increase in the popularity of schools in Brent, which was not the case. Furthermore, not all closed schools were in decline when they were closed, and other schools only went into decline after their closure was announced (p. 373). 'Once an LEA has decided to close schools, they often incrementally reduce a school's intake by not admitting a new year of pupils. The effect of this is to make the school fall in size irrespective of any other factors' (p. 376).

2 School choice and transition

1. In particular, the Sex Discrimination Act 1975, the Race Relations Act 1976, the Race Relations (Amendment) Act 2000, the Disability Discrimination Act 1995 and the Special Educational Needs and Disability Act 2001.

2. The Adjudicator found that admissions criteria which favour families with links to a school are unfair because they discriminate against children new to an area, and furthermore are contrary to the Race Relations Act 1976 and the Race Relations (Amendment) Act 2000.

3. A typical set of admissions criteria for a Roman Catholic school might be (in decreasing order of importance): Roman Catholic children baptised into and practising their faith whose parents can produce a letter of support from a priest; other Roman Catholic children baptised into the faith; other Christian children whose parents wish them to attend the school; non-Christian children whose parents wish them to attend the school.

4. The 1998 School Standards and Framework Act defines 'ability' but does not define 'aptitude'. However, the 1999 Code of Practice on admissions states that a pupil 'with aptitude' is one who would benefit from teaching in a specialist subject because they have demonstrated a particular capacity to succeed in that subject.

5. The first three academies were opened in 2002. At the start of 2007, there were 27 and a further 73 were planned. The UK government's stated aim is to see 200 academies up and running by 2010, but the House of Commons Public Accounts Committee and several Members of Parliament have raised questions about value for money. Ministers estimate that each school costs about £20 million to set up, but the National Audit Office reveals that Bexley

Business Academy in southeast London and the Unity City Academy in Middlesborough, for example, cost more than five times that amount. Nevertheless, and despite the 'cash for peerages' scandal, wherein sponsoring businessmen were allegedly offered peerages in return for support, DfES officials say that individuals and companies are still coming forward as sponsors [Source: Daily Telegraph, 11th Nov. 2006. *Blair pushes for more city academies to seal legacy*, by C. Hope & B. Carlin], though the negative publicity is clearly putting off some companies (like GEMS and Edison) [Source: Daily Telegraph, 10th Feb 2007. *Blow to academies programme as US sponsor pulls out*, by G. Paton].

6. A psychodynamic approach, based on work by Klein (1963), can be used to understand the tendency of pupils to idealise and demonise schools. Both are related to a concept of the self as developing out of unconscious defences against anxiety. Disliked parts of a pupil's self are projected onto demonised schools (and their pupils and teachers), while other schools are idealised in what Klein calls a 'paranoid-schizoid' fashion.

7. It should be pointed out that Ireland is unusual in its school profile because of its large number of single-sex schools, attended by 42 per cent of students (Lynch & Lodge, 2002).

8. Power (2006) makes the point that much of the research on markets displays misogynistic tendencies 'as though the blame for social and educational inequalities can now be laid at the door of ... middle-class mothers'.

3 School choice and globalisation

1. A full account of the William Tyndale affair and its fallout can be found in Riley (1998).

2. Dale (1989) has identified the Technical and Vocational Education Initiative (TVEI) in the United Kingdom as an example of a structural policy – in other words, a strategy to pre-define the goals and the means of achieving them – that signalled the change from a reactive to an active mode of educational policy-making (Bonal, 2003: 163).

3. Though meritocracy has had its scathing parody in Michael Young's (1961) *The Rise of the Meritocracy* (Harmondsworth, Penguin).

4. Such Conservative policies, particularly the decision to charge foreign students for education in Britain, caused the then Prime Minister, Margaret Thatcher, to be refused an honorary doctorate from her *alma mater*, Oxford University; an unprecedented rebuke for a sitting UK Prime Minister. Boris Johnson (2006) maintains that a close study of the record reveals that the Conservatives were in fact implementing a policy conceived by Shirley Williams as education secretary in the previous Labour government.

5. Education Action Zones (usually) involved partnerships between several secondary schools and their feeder primary schools. They were scrapped after the 2001 election on the grounds that the private sector had not invested enough money. In EAZs, innovation was encouraged through smaller classes, pay incentives for teachers and a relaxation of the strict requirements of the national curriculum (Power & Whitty, 1999). There were no Education Action Zones in Scotland. Instead there were publicly funded 'New Community Schools' modelled on Full-Service Schools in the United States (Paterson, 2003).

6. Initially, Specialist Schools may choose from 12 specialisms – technology, sports and the performing arts being the most popular – but they may apply later for an additional specialism and get an additional £60 *per capita* in government funding.

7. In 2002, there were nearly 50 such companies operating in the United States. They ran more than 417 public schools in 24 states (Molnar, 2006: 625), 320 of which were Charter Schools.

8. Leading sponsors include: Oracle, the software company; HSBC, the high-street bank (sponsoring schools that teach Mandarin and Portugese, and providing a governor for each school it sponsors); Sir Peter Green, owner of retail chains British Home Stores and Arcadia; Sir Peter Lampl, through his Sutton Trust; and Vosper Thornycroft, the shipbuilder.

9. During the Conservative years (1979–97) spending increased by 1.5 per cent per annum in real terms over that time (Emmerson & Frayne, 2001). The figures under Labour are disputed; they depend on whether one calculates real-term total spend, per capita spend, revenue per capita spend or percentage GDP spend. McElwee (2005: 15) estimates that spending between 1997 and 1999 remained at Conservative government levels, but since 2000 has increased in real terms to around 5 per cent per annum. Likewise, Nelson and Forsyth (2007) claim that the education budget has increased 52 per cent over the decade from 1997, though others would put the figure lower (Patterson, 2003).

10. In 2001, 75 per cent of the 15–19 age group participated in some form of education and training in the United Kingdom, compared for example with 90 per cent in Belgium and Germany (Pring, 2005b: 77).

11. In 2002–3, the Adult Learning Inspectorate judged 46 per cent of work-based learning provision to be inadequate, which astonishingly was a considerable improvement on the previous inspection (Adult Learning Inspectorate, 2003; Pring, 2005b: 78).

12. Burnheim (1985) sees demarchy as an alternative to governance by the nation state, and something particularly appropriate for very complex societies.

13. This last issue is one of the great unanswered questions in school effectiveness research: while ability grouping does not appear to have a strong or uniform impact on student progress, there appears to be a complex set of interactions at work between it, teacher attitude and the curriculum itself.

4   School choice and marketisation

1. Disputes between WTO-member states are settled by special dispute panels, with GATS taking precedence over national laws.

2. As Green (1990) points out in his comparative study of education systems in the United Kingdom, France and the United States, the United Kingdom lagged behind other countries in the development of vocational education and training at this time. In France, for example, elite vocational training in polytechnics was established at the end of the eighteenth century, a century before the United Kingdom. Japan was similarly more advanced (Rosenbrock, 1977).

3. For example, between 1984 and 2001 the percentage of students who did *not* attend their designated school jumped from 28 per cent to 48 per cent at the elementary level (where choice programmes begin), from 39 per cent to

54 per cent at the junior high level, and from 49 per cent to 62 per cent at the senior high school level (Taylor & Woollard, 2003: 620). However, it should be pointed out that 18 per cent of the student population live in neighbourhoods without a local school, so there is some 'mobility from necessity' to be taken into account (ibid.: 634).

4. Taylor's (2001) research used the home postcodes of pupils enrolling in schools across six local authorities in the United Kingdom, in a variety of geographical settings, representing more than 34,000 pupils and nearly 200 secondary schools. Assuming that pupils would, without open enrolment, have attended their nearest school, a method of calculating gains and losses between schools was developed which produced interesting and innovative matrices of gains and losses from school admissions data.

5. These results from Belfield (2003) remained constant even when the responding sample was restricted to those who actually voted in the 1997 UK general election, which was about two-thirds of the whole sample.

6. As Belfield (2003) points out, these results are consistent with earlier research from the United States by Wyckoff (1984) and Lankford (1985).

7. Belfield (2003: 163) interprets this income-neutrality as indicating that neither competition nor selection is thought to have much influence on the tax burden.

8. These are, according to Brighouse (2003), the two preferred vehicles for delivering privatisation in the United Kingdom.

9. An audit in 2001 of Edison's contract with Pennsylvania concluded that the contract was awarded without proper regard to state procurement law and there have been questions about its *educational* effectiveness ever since. Critics have alleged that there has been little by way of innovation and that claims about better-than-average pupil performance are ill founded (Molnar, 2006). In May 2003, the company revealed to the US Securities and Exchange Commission that it was in default on loans totalling nearly $60 million, after which it was taken private by its founder.

5 School choice, competition and performance

1. In their defence, the schools claimed that the Department of Trade and Industry had failed in its duty to inform the schools that their practice of collating data on fee structure had become illegal when the Competition Act (1998) came into force in March 2001. Previously and for a long time, schools had been exempt from competition law.

2. The General Certificate of Secondary Education (GCSE) is the UK school-leaving examination, taken by 16 year olds after five years of compulsory secondary education. Grading is on an eight-point scale, from 'A*' through 'G'. Unlike other countries, the school leaving examination in the UK is not used for university entrance; academic students remain in school for another two years for Advanced ('A-Level') study, which forms the basis for progression to Higher Education. Vocational education and training also happens post-GCSE.

3. Anyway, according to Gorard and Taylor (2002: 10), 'this period involved so many other changes' in education that it would be 'difficult to unpick the threads of each'. These changes included the introduction of coursework to GCSE and the abolition (in 1987) of norm referencing ('allocating grades in

proportion to the entry cohort', which is 'unfair in a system in which not all subjects are taken by the same candidates') in favour of criterion referencing ('allocating grades in terms of skills and competencies').

4. 'Possible confounds to this natural experiment' are 'changes in the gendered nature of fee-paying provision, the relative size of the sectors, differential entry policies, the impact of the Assisted Places Scheme, and other factors' (Gorard & Taylor, 2002: 11–12).

5. Albeit with a 'starting-gun effect', which created an initial surge in social segregation as 'more savvy' parents responded more quickly to the post-1988 market.

6. Noden's (2000) data was based on nearly 4000 secondary schools in 128 of the then 132 Local Education Authorities in England.

7. 'Suspicious' because cooperation is thought to limit choice and end in unholy collusion, where schools conspire 'to subvert the competitive process by agreeing to market-sharing practices' (Davies *et al.*, 2002: 91).

8. For example, it is not possible for public schools to compete on price or profit.

9. Data for the study was collected from over 3000 schools in six LEAs, selected 'to provide a variety of local contexts'. The schools were divided into Approximate Areas of Competition, defined as discrete and non-overlapping groups of schools that served distinct communities and were therefore in competition with each other. Account was taken of the size and relative location of urban areas and road links between them that could affect competition access.

Since schools have generally been improving in the United Kingdom since 1993, other explanatory variables were controlled for in Levacic's (2004) research: whether or not a school was denominational, selective, single sex or had a sixth form; the number and percentage of school types in the area and their spare capacity; the number of students on roll; the percentage (and change over time in the percentage) of pupils eligible for free school meals; and the percentage of pupils obtaining five or more good grades at GCSE in the first year (1991) of the data. Schools starting from a lower baseline of examination results perhaps have more incentive and more scope for improvement (Levacic, 2004: 186).

6   Actualising choice in schools and communities

1. Oplatka (2004: 153) reminds us that the institutional perspective is not without its critics either (Hoy & Miskel, 1996; Tolbert & Zucker, 1996). For one thing, isomorphism tends to be partial rather than total due to the different responses to educational policies provoked in decision-makers, and different internal political arrangements in schools.

2. In that sense, normative conformity is a consequence of being a professional, although Adler (1997) suggests that educational diversity depends in part on distinctive teaching and learning strategies.

3. Youdell's (2004) research is a small-scale ethnographic study undertaken in an Australian (Sydney) secondary school.

4. Of course, there are differences of opinion over what constitutes the public interest and how best to achieve it, and these have shifted over time (Gewirtz & Ball, 2000).

5. Although this finding may have been influenced in the Woods and Woods (2005) research by the fact that many of the participants were grounded in a local government culture before they went to work for the commercial company, and were known to the headteachers who participated.
6. This was measured by the percentage of students entitled to free school meals, students with special educational needs and students whose first language was not English.
7. Fitz, Taylor and Gorard (2002) accept that others disagree with this conclusion (Gibson & Asthana, 1999; Lauder *et al.*, 1999; Gibson & Asthana, 2000; Noden, 2000).
8. This right was first established in the 1980 Education Act.
9. Fitz, Taylor and Gorard (2002) found, for example, that two religious schools in Hammersmith and Fulham had only 36 per cent and 9 per cent respectively of local children as pupils.
10. The view that pupil performance is largely unrelated to school characteristics other than the quality of the pupils therein (Coleman *et al.*, 1966) has been challenged by other research (Card & Krueger, 1992) which suggests that school inputs such as class size and teachers' conditions of service are also important to pupil attainment.
11. The example given by Gleeson and Keep (2004) is telling. In the United Kingdom, employers have generally abandoned work-based apprenticeship schemes in favour of Further Education colleges delivering 'intermediate and technician level skills'.
12. The Workplace Employee Relations Survey (Cully *et al.*, 1998) suggests that only two-fifths of the British workforce is covered by any form of collective bargaining and even this is normally restricted to a limited range of issues. In the private sector, the figure is less than a quarter of the workforce (Cully *et al.*, 1999: 241–2). Regulation of the labour market is (relatively speaking) very weak in the United Kingdom (Gleeson & Keep, 2004: 51).
13. The recommendations of the Dearing report on Higher Education (1997), suggesting that future funding of Higher Education needed to be shared by employers, 'sank without trace'. 'Employers were wholly unenthusiastic and the state [was] unwilling to pursue the issue' (Gleeson & Keep, 2004: 53).

7 Well-being and capability

1. Education is an outcome: the knowledge and development resulting from schooling. Schooling is a process: the developmental process of instructing and habituating students to learning. In the case of public schooling, it is the practical implementation of government education policy.
2. *Criticisms of the capability approach*
   Clark's (2005) lucid and scholarly exposition of Sen's capability approach, which also contains a useful historical account of its genesis, highlights a number of criticisms. Some appear to have been recognised by Sen himself at the time of his development of capability; others emerged as Sen and others progressed the approach; still more seem to result from a fundamental divergence of philosophical views among different academics working in the field of capabilities, loosely defined. To sum up, these criticisms centre on universality, listing,

evaluation, information, indoctrination, over-optimism, negative freedom, the richness of personality, means and ends, and obligations and duties.

1. *The capability approach is insufficient for all evaluative purposes*

   It is acknowledged, not least by Sen (1999, 2005) himself, that the capability approach alone cannot provide a complete theory of justice and development for all people in all contexts. Note needs to be taken of other principles such as personal liberty, economic growth and efficiency (Clark, 2005: 5).

2. *The capability approach does not provide a list of capabilities*

   The capability approach has been criticised for failing to provide an objective universal list of 'important' capabilities (Nussbaum, 1988; Qizilbash, 1998), though others have argued that Sen goes *too far* in insisting that certain capabilities (such as literacy say) *are* universally valuable (Sugden, 1993). However, according to Clarke (2005), this 'listing criticism' misrepresents Sen's actual position. Sen deliberately avoids advocating a definitive list of capabilities because he holds that the selection and relative importance of capabilities depends on personal values (Sen, 1993; Clark, 2002).

3. *The capability approach has a problem comparing and valuing well-being*

   This criticism questions the 'usefulness of the capability approach' in making comparisons between the well-being of individuals especially in circumstances where there is disagreement about the valuation of capabilities and their relative importance (Beitz, 1986). Notwithstanding, Clarke (2005: 6) points out that Sen remains 'optimistic about achieving' broad consensus among people about capability evaluation, suggesting that in practice most individuals rank capabilities in a fairly similar order (Sen, 1985a). This view is supported by Clark's (2002) own research, which found that most people 'share a common vision' of capability that is 'not fundamentally at odds with the capabilities advocated by' theoreticians (Clark, 2005: 8).

4. *The informational requirements of the capability approach are too high*

   The 'informational requirements' (Clark, 2005: 6) of the capability approach can be, as Clark (ibid.) puts it, 'extremely high' (Alkire, 2002). Evaluation depends on collecting and analysing large amounts of data on many different functionings, and in some cases the 'relevant social indicators' are unavailable and there are issues about the non-observable nature of information on choice-making (Clark, 2005: 6).

5. *The problem of cultural indoctrination*

   According to Clark (2005: 8), the capability approach may (like the utility approach) be vulnerable to 'the problem of adaptive preferences and cultural indoctrination' (Nussbaum, 1988; Sumner, 1996), though the evidence to date suggests that this has *not* 'distorted responses to questions about the selection and value of capabilities (Clark, 2002; Qizilbash & Clark, 2005)'.

6. *The capability approach is too idealistic*

   Critics have suggested that Sen's notions of deliberative democracy and public action are overly optimistic, as they underplay the impact of political power and 'may lead to decisions that undermine capabilities or worsen the position of the poor' (Clark, 2005: 8).

7. *The capability approach relies too little on negative freedom*

Here, Sen's capability approach is accused of 'underplaying the importance of negative freedom' (Qizilbash, 1996), which features more prominently in other versions of capability that 'distinguish *internal* capabilities from the external conditions required to achieve them' (Clark, 2005: 9). Clark (ibid.) points out that Sen (1992) does acknowledge the special significance of negative freedom in his approach and argues that 'capability failure can stem from the violation of personal rights as well as from the absence of positive freedoms' (Clark, 2005: 9). In contrast to some theorists like Nussbaum 'who tend to shun personal liberty, Sen (1985a) argues that negative freedom has intrinsic as well as instrumental significance' (ibid.).

8. *The capability approach needs a richer interpretation of human personality*

Gasper (2002, 2004) has argued for a 'richer conception of human personality' that incorporates a 'variety of human values' and motives for action extending 'beyond Sen's (1977) classic distinction between acts of sympathy (feelings for other people)' and acts of 'commitment (goals beyond personal well-being)' (Clark, 2005: 10).

9. *The problem of means and ends*

Critics have suggested that Sen is too circumspect about identifying the means of securing substantive freedoms (Qizilbash, 1996: 161) and the role of capabilities in 'facilitating social change and promoting economic activity' (Clark, 2005:10).

10. *The capability approach needs a theory of obligations and duties*

Clark (2005: 11) writes 'Some commentators have suggested that the capability approach requires a complementary theory of obligations and duties (Gasper, 2004); others have pointed to the possible tension between the goal of basic capability *equality* on the one hand and the objective of (overall) capability *expansion* on the other (Alkire, 2002: 177–8).' In public policy terms, the effect of this is to raise concern that the capability approach is deficient in the way it assumes that *democratic* processes are sufficient to bring about significant societal change (Stewart & Deneulin, 2002; Fukuda-Parr, 2003).

3. Others like Ramsey (1926) were sceptical of this congruence and emphasised the greater relevance of the 'desire' interpretation of utility: *[We] seek things which we want, which may be our own or other people's pleasure, or anything else whatever, and our actions are such as we think most likely to realize these goods* (ibid.: 75).

4. The perceived link between higher education and economic prosperity is at the heart of the United Kingdom widening its participation policy. The government's target is that 50 per cent of 18–30 year olds will participate in higher education by the year 2010 (DfES, 2003b). For an insightful, research-informed critique of this policy, the reader is referred to Watts and Bridges (2006).

8   Utility and functionings

1. A third form, 'non-market observations of personal states', is not considered here (Sen, 1985a: 39, 45–6).

9 Aggregation and evaluation

1. Another version of Arrow's theorem replaces the 'non-imposition' and 'monotonicity' criteria with the criterion of 'Pareto efficiency', which stipulates that if every individual prefers a certain option to another, then so should society. This version of the theorem is stronger – in other words, has weaker conditions – since 'monotonicity', 'non-imposition', and 'independence of irrelevant alternatives' together imply 'Pareto efficiency', whereas 'Pareto efficiency', 'non-imposition', and 'independence of irrelevant alternatives' together do not imply 'monotonicity'.
2. The Gibbard–Satterthwaite theorem, an attempt at weakening the conditions of Arrow's paradox, replaced the 'independence of irrelevant alternatives' criterion with a criterion of non-manipulability, only to reveal the same impossibility.
3. The Pareto principle, also known as 'the vital few and the useful many' principle, states that for many phenomena, 80 per cent of consequences stem from 20 per cent of causes; in other words, that most of the results in any situation are determined by small number of causes. The principle was first suggested by Joseph Juran in the 1950s. It is unrelated to the concept of 'Pareto *efficiency*'. (If an economic system is said to be 'Pareto efficient', no individual can be made better off without another being made worse off. It is commonly accepted that outcomes that are not Pareto efficient should be avoided, and therefore Pareto efficiency is an important criterion for evaluating economic and political policies. It can be shown that under certain idealised (but not real-life) conditions, such as perfectly competitive markets with negligible transaction costs, a free market can lead to Pareto efficiency.)
4. Sen's admirers are keen to distinguish his individualism from that of neo-liberal advocates of choice, though Sen himself is not so preoccupied. Walker (2006: 165–6) eloquently highlights the subtleties: that Sen's capability approach is 'ethically individualistic', unlike the neo-liberal approach, which is 'ontologically individualist'. Sen, she points out (correctly), does not 'view individuals and their opportunities in isolated terms'.
5. Another method of evaluation, which Sen terms 'dominance evaluation', incorporates the idea of dominance: the pair-wise comparison of the elements of two sets. Consider two sets of capabilities with at least as many elements in the first as in the second. Consider now a subset of the first set such that it has *exactly* as many elements as the second. If there is a one-to-one correspondence from the subset to the second set, such that every element of the subset is at least as good as the corresponding element in the second set, then the first set can be regarded as being *at least as good* as the second set (Sen, 1985a: 68, 1993).

10 Asset-mapping

1. Jasek-Rysdahl (2001) describes a Sen-like capabilities approach in low-income neighbourhoods in California to improve the quality of life for residents.
2. There are several lists of capabilities extant in the literature, though none of them relate specifically to school choice or to school improvement and many

use the term more broadly than Sen, who deliberately avoided compiling one (Sen, 1999, 2004). Commonly, they seek to avoid what William Beveridge described in 1942 as the UK's 'five giants': disease, want, squalor, idleness and ignorance. For most, education is but one item on a list of quality-of-life capabilities that have emerged from socio-philosophical theory. The eminent Aristotlian philosopher Martha Nussbaum (2000) suggests the following list: life; physical health and bodily integrity; affiliation; imagination, feeling and thought; emotions; control of the environment; the use of reason; and play. Narayan and Petesch (2002) suggest the following: physical health and bodily integrity; material wealth; emotions; respect and dignity; affiliation; cultural identity; imagination; information and education; organisation; political representation and accountability. Alkire's (2002) list comprises of the following: knowledge, work, relationships and empowerment. Walker (2006), with reference specifically to schooling in South Africa, includes: autonomy; instrumental and intrinsic knowledge; social relations and friendship; respect, recognition, self-confidence and self-esteem; aspiration and motivation; voice; physical health and bodily integrity; and emotions.

A composite list, subject to ongoing revision, might look like this: physical and mental health (Robeyns, 2003); material well-being (Rawls, 1971) and social mobility; physical security (Sen, 1999) and integrity (Nussbaum, 1990, 1995, 2000); emotional security and imagination (Nussbaum, 1990, 1995, 2000); respect (Rawls, 1971; Sennett, 2003) and recognition (Sen, 1999; Walker, 2006); socialisation and affiliation (Nussbaum, 2000); a sense of place, time and culture; flourishing (Nussbaum, 1988, 1990); travel and leisure (Nussbaum, 2000); spirituality (Clark, 2002; Robeyns, 2003); liberty and emancipation (Marx, 1844); political engagement and parrhesia (Sen, 1999); control of environment (Nussbaum, 1990, 1995, 2000); gainful employment (Clark, 2002; Watts & Bridges, 2006); and education, knowledge and information (Sen, 1984a; Alkire, 2002; Robeyns, 2003).

3. *Basic* capabilities are the innate predispositions and facilities of people to develop more advanced capabilities. They are latent talents from which, following interaction with the environment, *internal* capabilities and mature states of being are produced. These in turn combine with environmental influences to produce *combined* capabilities (Nussbaum, 2000).

4. Improving the Quality of Education for All (IQEA) was founded in Cambridge University's School of Education by West, Ainscow, Hopkins and Southworth. It is now run as a private company by Clarke, West and Ainscow and has a high international profile in the field of school improvement, with exclusive (at the time of writing) school improvement contracts in China and elsewhere.

5. The distinction between positive and negative freedom was noted by Immanuel Kant (1724–1804) and by John Stuart Mill (1806–1873), but more extensively developed by Isaiah Berlin (1958). Berlin's work was critical of these concepts, which Sen (1999) later regarded as cornerstones of his work.

References and Further Reading

References

Abadian, S. (1996) Women's autonomy and its impact on fertility, *World Development*, 24(12), 1793–809.

Adler, M. (1997) Looking backwards to the future: parental choice and education policy, *British Educational Research Journal*, 23(3), 297–313.

Adler, M., Petch, A. & Tweedie, J. (1989) *Parental Choice and Educational Policy* (Edinburgh, Edinburgh University Press).

Adnett, N. & Davies, P. (1999) Schooling quasi-markets: reconciling economic and sociological analyses, *British Journal of Educational Studies*, 47(3), 221–34.

—— (2000) Competition and curriculum diversity in local schooling markets: theory and evidence, *Journal of Education Policy*, 15(2), 157–67.

—— (2003) Schooling reforms in England: from quasi-markets to co-opetition? *Journal of Education Policy*, 18(4), 393–406.

Adult Learning Inspectorate (2003) *Chief Inspector's Annual Report* 2002–3 (London, DfES).

Ahonen, S. (2000) What happens to the common school in the market? *Journal of Curriculum Studies*, 32(4), 483–94.

Ailwood, J. (2000) Time, space and mobility in a globalizing world: what's in it for young children? *Discourse*, 21(1), 105–11.

Ainley, P. (2004) The new 'market-state' and education, *Journal of Education Policy*, 19(4), 497–514.

Ainley, P. & Corney, M. (1990) *Training for the Future, the Rise and Fall of the Manpower Services Commission* (London, Cassell).

Akerlof, G. (1983) Loyalty filters, *American Economic Review*, 73 (March), 54–62.

Alberta (1988) *School Act: Statutes of Alberta* (Edmonton, Queen's Printer for Alberta).

Alkire, S. (2002) *Valuing Freedoms: Sen's Capability Approach and Poverty Reduction* (Oxford, Oxford University Press).

Allat, P. (1993) Becoming privileged: the role of family processes, in: I. Bates & G. Riseborough (Eds) *Youth and Inequality* (Buckingham, Open University Press).

Ambler, J. (1997) Who benefits from educational choice? Some evidence from Europe, in: E. Cohn (Ed.) *Market Approaches to Education* (Oxford, Elsevier Science).

Angus, L. (1994) Sociological analysis and educational management: the social context of the self-managing school, *British Journal of Sociology of Education*, 15(1), 79–92.

—— (2004) Globalization and educational change: bringing about the reshaping and renorming of practice. *Journal of Education Policy*, 19(1), 23–41.

Anthony, A. (1998) What about the workers? *The Observer*, 13 December.

Anyon, J. (1997) *Ghetto Schooling: A Political Economy of Urban Educational Reform* (New York, Teachers College Press).

Appadurai, A (1996) *Modernity at Large: Cultural Dimensions of Globalization* (Minneapolis, University of Minnesota Press).

Apple, M. (2000) Away with all teachers: the cultural politics of home schooling, *International Studies in Sociology of Education*, 10(1), 61–80.

—— (2001) *Educating the 'Right' Way: Markets, Standards, God and Inequality* (London, RoutledgeFalmer).

Arai, B. (2000) Changing motives for homeschooling in Canada, *Canadian Journal of Education*, 25(3), 204–17.

Armey, R.K. & Jefferson, W.J. (1991) Should school choice be included in Federal education reform? *Congressional Digest*, 70, 298–313.

Armstrong, P., Glynn, A. & Harrison, J. (1984) *Capitalism since World War II: The Making and the Break-up of the Great Boom* (London, Fontana).

Arrow, K.J. (1951) *Social Choice and Individual Values* (New York, Wiley).

—— (1977) Extended sympathy and the possibility of social choice, *American Economic Review*, 67, 219–25.

—— (1982) Why people go hungry, *New York Review of Books*, 29, 15 July.

—— (1984) The economics of agency, in: J.W. Pratt & R.J. Zeckhauser (Eds) *Principals and Agents: The Structure of Business* (Boston, MA, Harvard Business School Press).

Ashton, D. & Sung, J. (1997) Education, skill formation and economic development: the Singaporean approach, in: A.H. Halsey, H. Lauder, P. Brown & A.S. Wells (Eds) *Education, Economy, Society* (Oxford, Oxford University Press).

Atkinson, A. & Gregg, P. (2004) *Selective Education: Who Benefits from Grammar Schools* (Bristol, Autumn bulletin from the Centre for Market & Public Organisation).

Aurini, J. & Davies, S. (2005) Choice without markets: homeschooling in the context of private education, *British Journal of Sociology in Education*, 26(4), 461–74.

Bacchi, C. (2000) Policy as discourse: what does it mean? Where does it get us? *Discourse*, 21(1), 45–57.

Back, L., Cohen, P. & Keith, M. (1999) *Between Home and Belonging: Critical Ethnographies of Race, Place and Identity, Finding The Way Home Working Papers 2* (London, CNER).

Bagley, C. (1996) Black and white unite or flight? The racialised dimension of schooling and parental choice, *British Educational Research Journal*, 22(5), 569–80.

—— (2006) School choice and competition: a public-market in education revisited, *Oxford Review of Education*, 32(3), 347–62.

Bagley, C. & Woods, P. (1998) Rejecting schools: towards a fuller understanding of the process of parental choice, *Belfast, BERA Annual Conference*.

Bagley, C., Woods, P.A. & Woods, G. (2001) Implementation of school choice policy: interpretation and response by parents of students with special educational needs, *British Educational Research Journal*, 27(3), 287–311.

Bagley, C., Woods, P.A. & Glatter, R. (2001) Rejecting schools: towards a fuller understanding of the process of parental choice, *School Leadership & Management*, 21(3), 309–25.

Ball, S.J. (1981) *Beachside Comprehensive* (Cambridge, Cambridge University Press).

Ball, S.J. (1990) *Politics and Policymaking in Education* (London, Routledge).

Ball, S.J. (1994) *Education Reform: A Critical and Post-Structural Approach* (Buckingham, Open University Press).

Ball, S. (2003a) *Class Strategies and the Education Market: The Middle Classes and Social Advantage* (London, RoutledgeFalmer).

—— (2003b) The risks of social reproduction: the middle class and education markets, *London Review of Education*, 1(3), 163–75.

Ball, S.J., Bowe, R. & Gewirtz, S. (1995) Circuits of schooling: a sociological explo-ration of parental choice of school in social class contexts, *The Sociological Review*, 43(1), 52–78.

—— (1996) School choice, social class and distinction: the realization of social advantage in education, *Journal of Education Policy*, 11(1), 89–112.

Ball, S. & Vincent, C. (1998) 'I heard it on the grapevine': 'hot' knowledge and school choice, *British Journal of Sociology of Education*, 19(3), 377–95.

—— (2001) New class relations in education: the strategies of the 'fearful' middle-classes, in: J. Demaine (Ed.), *Sociology of Education Today* (London, Palgrave Macmillan).

Bamber, C. (1990) Public school choice: will we be ready? *Education Digest*, 55, 19–22.

Barbanel, J. (1992) Is school choice a real choice? *New York Times*, 16 November.

Barbelet, J.M. (1998) *Emotion, Social Theory and Social Structure: A Macrosociological Approach* (Cambridge, Cambridge University Press).

Barnes, T., Momen, A., Ryan, C. & Watson, J. (1998) 'New start' under New Labour? A case study of the new settlement of education and training, *Education and Social Justice*, 1(1), 22–8.

Barrow, M. (1996) The reform of school funding: some case-study lessons, *Environment and Planning C*, 14, 351–66.

—— (1998) Financing of Schools: a national or local quasi-market? in: W. Bartlett, J.A. Roberts & J. Le Grand (Eds) *A Revolution in Social Policy: Quasi-Market Reform in the 1990s* (Bristol, The Policy Press).

Barton, D. (1995) *The Myth of Separation* (Aledo, TX, Wallbuilders).

Bass, B. (1985) *Leadership and Performance beyond Expectations* (Cambridge, MA, Harvard University Press).

Basu, K. (1984) *The Less Developed Economy: A Critique of Contemporary Theory* (Oxford, Blackwell).

Bauch, P.A. & Goldring, E.B. (1995) Parent involvement and school responsive-ness: facilitating the home-school connection in schools of choice, *Education Evaluation and Policy Analysis*, 17(1), 1–21.

Bauman, Z. (1998) *Globalization: The Human Consequences* (Cambridge, Polity Press).

Beck, J. (1999) Makeover or takeover? The strange death of educational auto-nomy in neo-liberal England, *British Journal of Sociology of Education*, 20(2), 223–38.

Beck, U. (1999) *World Risk Society* (Cambridge, Polity).

—— (2000) Risk society revisited: theory, politics and research programmes, in: B. Adams, U. Beck & J. Van Loon (Eds) *The Risk Society and Beyond: Critical Issues for Social Theory* (London, Sage).

Beck, U. & Beck-Gernsheim, E. (2002) *Individualization* (London, Sage).

Becker, G.S. (1981) *A Treatise on the Family* (Cambridge, MA, Harvard University Press).

Beitz, C.R. (1986) Amartya Sen's resources, values and development, *Economics and Philosophy*, 2(2), 282–91.

Belfield, C.R. & Levin, H.M. (2001) The effects of competition on educational outcomes: a review for the US, *Review of Educational Research*, 72(2), 279–341.

Belfield, C. (2003) Political preferences and the privatization of education: Evidence From The UK, *Education Economics*, 11(2), 155–68.

Bell, K. & West, A. (2003) Specialist schools: an exploration of competition and co-operation, *Educational Studies*, 29, 273–89.

Bellah, R.N., Madsen, R., Sullivan, W.M., Swindler, A. & Tipton, S. (1992) *The Good Society* (New York, Vintage Books).

Berki, B. (1999) Parental choice in danger, *Times Educational Supplement*, 23 April.

Bernal, J.L. (2005) Parental choice, social class and market forces: the consequences of privatization of public services in education, *Journal of Education Policy*, 20(6), 779–92.

Besen, S. & Farrell, J. (1994) Choosing how to compete: strategies and tactics in standardization, *Journal of Economic Perspectives*, 8(2), 117–31.

Bienefeld, S. (2001) *The World Trade Organisation (WTO) and the General Agreement on Trade in Services (GATS): An Introduction* (National Union of Students in Europe, ESIB). http://www.esib.org/commodification/documents/ [Accessed: 12/3/06].

Bishop, J. (1997) The effects of national standards and curriculum-based exams on achievement. *American Economic Review*, 87(2), 260–4.

Black, D. (1958). *The Theory of Committees and Elections* (Cambridge, Cambridge University Press,).

Blair, M. (1994) Black teachers, black students and education markets, *Cambridge Journal of Education*, 24(2), 277–91.

Blunkett, D. (1999) *Tackling social exclusion: empowering people and communities for a better future, Speech, 16 June* (London, DfEE).

Bobbitt, P. (2002) *The Shield of Achilles: War, Peace and the Course of History* (London, Allen Lane).

Bonal, X. (2003) The Neoliberal educational agenda and the legitimation crisis: old and new state strategies. *British Journal of Sociology of Education*, 24(2), 159–75.

Borglin, A. (1982) States and persons: on the interpretation of some fundamental concepts in the theory of justice as fairness, *Journal of Public Economics*, 18, 85–104.

Bosetti, L. (1998) *Canada's charter schools: initial report* (Kelowna, BC, Society for the Advancement of Excellence in Education).

—— (2000) Alberta charter schools: paradox and promises, *Alberta Journal of Educational Research*, 46(2), 179–90.

—— (2001) Can markets save our schools? The Alberta charter school experience, in: C. Hepburn (Ed.) *Can Markets Save Our Schools?* (Vancouver, BC, Fraser Institute).

—— (2004) Determinants of school choice: understanding how parents choose elementary schools in Alberta, *Journal of Education Policy*, 19(4), 387–405.

Bottery, M. (1992) *The Ethics of Educational Management* (London, Cassell).

—— (1994) *Lessons for Schools: A Comparison of Business and Educational Management* (London, Cassell).

—— (1998) *Professionals and Policy* (London, Cassell).

—— (2001) Globalisation and the UK competition state: no room for transformational leadership in education? *School Leadership & Management*, 21(2), 199–218.

Bottery, M. & Wright, N. (2000) *Teachers and the State – Towards a Directed Profession* (London, Routledge).

Boulding, K. (1973) *Challenge to Leadership, Managing in a Changing World* (New York, The Free Press).

Bourdieu, P. (1986a) *Distinction: A Social Critique of the Judgement of Taste* (London, Routledge).

—— (1986b) Forms of capital, in: J. Richardson (Ed.) *Handbook of Theory and Research for the Sociology of Education* (New York, Greenwood Press).

Bourdieu, P. & Passeron, C. (1992) *Reproduction in Education, Society and Culture* (London, Sage).

Bourdieu, P. & Wacquant, L. (1992) *An Invitation to Reflexive Sociology* (Chicago, IL, University of Chicago Press).

Bowe, R., Ball, S. & Gewirtz, S. (1994) 'Parental choice'. Consumption and social theory: the operation of micro-markets in education, *British Journal of Educational Studies*, 42(1), 38–52.

Bowe, R., Gewirtz, S. & Ball, S. (1994) Captured by the discourse? Issues and concerns in researching 'parental choice', *British Journal of Sociology of Education*, 15, 63–78.

Boyles, D. (1998) *American Education and Corporations: The Free Market Goes to School* (New York, Garland).

Bradley, S., Crouchley, R., Millington, J. & Taylor, J. (2000) Testing for quasi-market forces in secondary education, *Oxford Bulletin of Economics and Statistics*, 62(3), 357–90.

Bradley, S., Johnes, G. & Millington, J. (2001) The effect of competition on the efficiency of secondary schools in England, *European Journal of Operational Research*, 135, 545–68.

Bradley, S. & Taylor, J. (2000) *The effect of the quasi-market on the efficiency-equity trade-off in the secondary school sector, [Discussion Paper EC9/00]* (Lancaster, Lancaster University Management School).

Brandenburger, A. & Nalebuff, B. (1997) *Co-opetition* (London, Harper Collins Business).

Brecher, J. (1993) Global village or global pillage, *The Nation*, 6 December.

Brennan, J. & Shah, T. (2003) *Access to What? Converting Educational Opportunity into Employment Opportunity* (Milton Keynes, Open University Press).

Bridges, D. (1994) Parents: customers or partners, in: D. Bridges & T. McLaughlin (Eds) *Education and the Market Place* (London, Falmer Press).

Bridges, D. & McLaughlin, T. (1994) Education and the market place: an introduction, in: D. Bridges & T. McLaughlin (Eds) *Education and the Market Place* (London, Falmer Press).

Brighouse, H. (1998) Why states should fund schools, *British Journal of Educational Studies* 46(1), 138–51.

—— (2003) Against Privatizing Schools in the United Kingdom, *London Review of Education*, 1(1), 35–45.

Brimelow, P. (1985) Competition for public schools, in: B. Gross & R. Gross (Eds) *The Great School Debate: which way for American education?* (New York, Simon & Schuster).

Broadfoot, P. (2001) Empowerment or performativity? Assessment policy in the late twentieth century, in: R. Phillips & J. Furlong (Eds) *Education, Reform and the State: Twenty-Five Years of Politics, Policy and Practice* (London, RoutledgeFalmer).

Broccolichi, S. & Van Zanten, A. (2000) School competition and pupil flight in the urban periphery, *Journal of Education Policy*, 15(1), 51–60.

Brown, B. (1992) Why government' s run schools, *Economics of Education Review*, 11(4), 287–300.

Brown, F. (1992) The Dutch experience with school choice: implications for American education, in: P.W. Cookson (Ed.) *The Choice Controversy* (Newbury Park, CA, Corwin).

Brown, P. & Lauder, H. (1997) Education, globalization and economic development, in: A.H. Halsey, H. Lauder, P. Brown & A.S. Wells (Eds) *Education, Economy, Society*, 172–92 (Oxford, Oxford University Press).

Buchanan, J. & Tullock, G. (1962) *The Calculus of Consent: Logical Foundations of a Constitutional Democracy* (Ann Arbor, University of Michigan Press).

Bulkley, K. (2005) Understanding the charter school concept in legislation: the cases of Arizona, Michigan and Georgia, *International Journal of Qualitative Studies in Education*, 18(4), 527–54.

Burnheim (1985) *Is Democracy Possible?* (Cambridge, Cambridge University Press).

Burtless, G. (1993) Current proposals for school reform: an economist's assessment, in: R. Thornton & A. O'Brien (Eds) *The Economic Consequences of American Education* (Greenwich, CT, JAI Press).

Bush, T., Coleman, M. & Glover, D. (1993) *Managing Autonomous Schools* (London, Paul Chapman).

Butler, T. (1995) The debate over the middle-classes, in: T. Butler & M. Savage (Eds), *Social Change and the Middle Classes* (London, University College Press).

Butler, T. & Robson, G. (2003) Plotting the middle classes: gentrification and circuits of education in London, *Housing Studies*, 18(1), 5–28.

Califano, J. & Bennett, W. (2000) The need for school choice, *The Atlanta Journal-Constitution*, 30 July, G1.

Carnoy, M. (1995) Structural adjustment and the changing face of education, *International Labour Review*, 134(6), 653–73.

Card, D. & Krueger, A. (1992) Does school quality matter? *Journal of Political Economy*, 100(1), 1–40.

Carr, W. & Hartnett, A. (1996) *Education and the Struggle for Democracy* (Buckingham, Open University Press).

Carroll, S. & Walford, G. (1997) The child's voice in school choice, *Educational Management and Administration*, 25, 169–80.

Case, R.B. (1996) Incompatible with Christian teaching, *Christian Social Action*, 9, 7–9.

Castells, M. (1996) *The Rise of the Network Society: The Information Age: Economy, Society and Culture* (Oxford, Blackwell).

Cherlin, A., Furstenburg, F., Chase-Lansdale, P., Kiernan, K., Robins, P., Morrison, D. & Teitler, J. (1991) Longitudinal studies of effects of divorce on children in Great Britain and the United States, *Science*, 252, 1386–9.

Cheshire, P. & Sheppard, S. (2003) *Capitalised in the Housing Market or How We Pay for Free Schools: The Impact of Supply Constraints and Uncertainty* (London, London School of Economics).

Chiu, M.M. & Ho, E.S.C. (2006) Family effects on student achievement in Hong Kong, *Asia Pacific Journal of Education*, 26(1), 21–35.

Chubb, J. & Hill, P. (1991) Can public schools survive? *US News and World Report*, 9 December.

Chubb, J. & Moe, T. (1988) Politics, markets and the organization of schools, *American Political Science Review*, 82(4), 1065–87.

—— (1990) *Politics, Markets, and America's Schools* (Washington, DC, Brookings Institution).

—— (1992) Why markets are good for education, in: P.R. Kane (Ed.) *Independent Schools, Independent Thinkers* (San Francisco, CA, Jossey-Bass).

Clark, D.A. (2002) *Visions of Development: A Study of Human Values* (Cheltenham, Edward Elgar).

—— (2005) *The Capability Approach: Its Development, Critiques and Recent Advances, GPRG-WPS-032* (Manchester, Global Poverty Research Group). http:// www.gprg.org/pubs/workingpapers/pdfs/gprg-wps-032.pdf [Accessed: 23/1/07].

Clark, D.A. (2005) The capability approach: Its development, critiques and recent advances [GPRG-WPS-032] (Manchester, ESRC Global Poverty Research Group).

Clarke, J., Cochrane, A. & McLaughlin, E. (Eds) (1994) *Managing Social Policy* (London, Sage).

Clarke, J. & Newman, J. (1997) *The managerial state: power, politics and ideology in the remaking of social welfare* (London, Sage).

Cohen, S. (1990, reprinted in 2001) *The Indian Army: Its Contribution to the Development of a Nation* (New Delhi, Oxford University Press).

Coldron, J. & Boulton, P. (1991) 'Happiness' as a criterion of parents' choice of school, *Journal of Education Policy*, 6, 169–78.

Coleman, J.S. (1988) Social capital in the creation of human capital, *American Journal of Sociology*, 94, 95–120.

Coleman, J. (1992) Some points on choice in education, *Sociology of Education*, 65(2), 260–2.

Coleman, J., Campbell, E., Hobson, C., McPartland, J., Mood, A., Weinfeld F., & York, R. (1966) *Equality of Educational Opportunity* (Washington, DC, National Center for Educational Statistics).

Coleman, J., Hoffer, T. & Kilgore, S. (1982) *High School Achievement: Public, Private and Catholic Schools Compared* (New York, Basic Books).

Collins, J. (2005) Schooling for faith, citizenship and social mobility: Catholic secondary education in New Zealand, 1924–1944, *Journal of Educational Administration and History*, 37(2), 157–72.

Colopy, K.W. & Tarr, H.C. (1994) *Minnesota's Public School Options* (Washington, DC, Policy Studies Associates).

Confederation of British Industry (CBI) (1989) *Towards a Skills Revolution – A Youth Charter* (London, CBI).

Connolly, P. & Neill, J. (2001) Constructions of locality and gender and their impact on the educational aspirations of working-class children, *International Studies in Sociology of Education*, 11, 107–29.

Connors, L. (2000) Schools in Australia: a hard act to follow, in: P. Karmel (Ed.) *School Resourcing: Models and Practices in Changing Times* (Canberra, Australian College of Education).

Consumers International (2001) *The General Agreement on Trade in Services: an impact assessment by Consumers International* (London, Consumers International).

Conway, S. (1997) The reproduction of exclusion and disadvantage: symbolic violence and social class inequalities in 'parental choice' of secondary education, *Sociological Research On-line*, 2(4). http://www.socresonline.org.uk/2/4/4.html [Accessed: 25/1/07].

Considine, M. (1988) The corporate management framework as administrative science; a critique, *Australian Journal of Public Administration*, 37(1), 4–18.

Cookson, P.W. (1994) *School Choice: The Struggle for the Soul of American Education* (New Haven, CT, Yale University Press).

Cotterell, J. (1986) The adjustment of early adolescent youngsters to secondary school: some Australian findings, in: B. Youngman (Ed.) *Mid-School Transfer* (Slough, National Foundation for Educational Research).

Crocker, D. (1992) Functioning and capabilities: the foundation of Sen's and Nussbaum's development ethic, *Political Theory*, 20(4), 584–612.

Crocker, J., Major, B. & Steele, C. (1998) Social stigma, in: D.T. Gilbert, S.T. Fiske & G. Lindzey (Eds) *Handbook of Social Psychology*, 4th edition (Boston, MA, McGraw-Hill).

Crooks, S. (1999) Ordering risk, in: D. Lupton (Ed.) *Risk and Sociocultural Theory* (Cambridge, Cambridge University Press).

Crozier, G. (2000) *Parents and Schools: Partners or Protagonists?* (Stoke, Trentham Press).

Cully, M., O'Reilly, A., Millward, N., Forth, J., Woodland, S., Dix, G. & Bryson, A. (1998) *Workplace Employee Relations Survey: First findings* (London, Dti) http://www.dti.gov.uk/files/file11678.pdf [Accessed: 27/5/2007].

Cully, M., Woodland, S., O'Reilly, A. & Dix, G. (1999) *Britain at Work* (London, Routledge).

Culpepper, P. D. & Finegold, D. (Eds) (1999) *The German Skills Machine – Sustaining Comparative Advantage in a Global Economy* (Oxford, Berghahn Books).

Cush, D. (2005) Review essay: The faith schools debate, *British Journal of Sociology of Education*, 26(3), 435–42.

Dahl, R. (1999) Can international organisations be democratic? A sceptics view, in: I. Shapiro & C. Hacker-Gordon (Eds) *Democracy's Edges* (Cambridge, Cambridge University Press).

Dale, R. (1989) *The State and Education Policy* (Buckingham, Open University Press).

—— (1998) Globalisation: a new world for comparative education? in: J. Schreiwer (Ed.) *Discourse Formation in Comparative Education* (Berlin, Peter Lang).

—— (1999) Specifying globalisation effects on national policy: focus on the mechanisms, *Journal of Education Policy*, 14(1), 1–17.

—— (2000) Globalization and education: demonstrating a 'common world educational culture' or locating a 'globally structured education agenda'? *Educational Theory*, 50(4), 427–48.

D'Aspremont, C. & Gevers, L. (1977) Equity and informational basis of collective choice, *Review of Economic Studies*, 44 (June), 199–209. http://ideas.repec.org/a/bla/restud/=v44y1977i2p199-209.html [Accessed: 25/1/07].

Davey, J. & Dwyer, M. (1984) *Meeting Needs in the Community: A Discussion Paper on School Service* (Wellington, New Zealand Planning Council).

David, M., Davies, J., Edwards, R., Reay, D. & Standing, K. (1997) Choice within constraints: mothers and schooling, *Gender and Education*, 9(4), 397–410.

David, M., West, A. & Ribbens, J. (1994) *Mother's Intuition? Choosing Secondary Schools* (London, Falmer).

Davies, G. (1986) *A First Year Tutorial Handbook* (Oxford, Blackwell).

Davies, P. & Adnett, N. (1999) *Market Forces and School Curriculum, Working Paper No: 99.1* (Staffordshire, Centre for Economics and Business Education Staffordshire University Business School). ftp://all.repec.org/RePEc/wuk/ stafwp/WP991.DOC [Accessed: 21/1/07].

Davies, P., Adnett, N. & Mangan, J. (2002) Diversity and dynamics of competition: analysis and evidence from two local schooling markets, *Oxford Review of Education*, 28(1), 91–107.

Davis-Kean, P. (2005) The influence of parent education and family income on child achievement: the indirect role of parental expectations and the home environment, *Journal of Family Psychology*, 19(2), 294–304.

Day, C., Harris, A., Hadfield, M., Tolley, H. & Beresford, J. (2000) *Leading Schools in Times of Change* (Buckingham, Open University Press).

Dearing, R. (1997) *Higher Education in the Learning Society: Report of the National Committee of Inquiry into Higher Education* (London, HMSO).

Dehli, K. (1996) Travelling tales: education reform and parental 'choice' in post-modern times, *Journal of Education Policy*, 11(1), 75–88.

Delamont, S. (1991) The hit list and other horror stories, *Sociological Review*, 39(2), 238–59.

Denessen, E., Driessena, G. & Sleegers, P. (2005) Segregation by choice? A study of group-specific reasons for school choice, *Journal of Education Policy*, 20(3), 347–68.

Department for Education and Employment (1999) *Code of Practice on School Admissions* (London, DfEE).

Department for Education and Skills (DfES) (2001) *Schools Achieving Success* (Norwich, Stationary Office).

—— (2003a) *Code of Practice on School Admissions* (London, DfES).

—— (2003b) *The Future of Higher Education* (London, HMSO).

DiMaggio, P.J. & Powell, W.W. (1991) *The New Iinstitutionalism in Organisational Analysis* (Chicago, IL, University of Chicago Press).

Dobson, J. & Henthorne, K. (1999) Leavers who don't fare well, *Times Educational Supplement*, 29 October.

Docking, J. (Ed.) (2000) *New Labour's Policies for Schools: Raising the Standard?* (London, David Fulton).

Doerr E. & Menendez, A.J. (1991) *Church Schools and Public Money* (Buffalo, NY, Prometheus).

Dore, C. & Flowerdew, R. (1981) Allocation procedures and the social composition of comprehensive schools, *Manchester Geographer*, 2(1), 47–55.

Douglas, M. (1992) *Risk and Blame: Essays in Cultural Theory* (London, Sage).

Downey, D. (1994) The school performance of children from single-mother and single-father families? *Journal of Family Issues*, 15(1), 129–47.

Downs, A. (1967) *Inside Bureaucracy* (Boston, MA, Little, Brown & Company).

Dreze, J. & Sen, A. (1995) *India: Economic Development and Social Opportunity* (Oxford, Oxford University Press).

Driessen, G. & Bezemer, J. (1999) Background and achievement levels of Islamic schools in the Netherlands: are the reservations justified? *Race Ethnicity and Education*, 2(2), 235–56.

Driessen, G. & Merry, M. (2004) *Islamic Schools in the Netherlands: Expansion or Marginalization?* (Nijmegen, ITS).

Driessen, G. & Van der Slik, F. (2001) Religion, denomination, and education in the Netherlands: cognitive and noncognitive outcomes after an era of secularisation, *Journal for the Scientific Study of Religion*, 40(4), 561–72.

Driscoll, M.E. & Kerchner, C.T. (1999) The implications of social capital for schools, communities, and cities: educational administration as if a sense of place mattered, in: J. Murphy & K.S. Louis (Eds) *Handbook of Research on Educational Administration*, 2nd edition (San Francisco, Jossey-Bass).

Dronkers, J. (1995) The existence of parental choice in the Netherlands, *Educational Policy*, 9(3), 227–43.

Duckworth, K. & Sabates, R. (2005) Effects of mothers' education on parenting: an investigation across three generations, *London Review of Education*, 3(3), 239–64.

Du Gay, P. (1996) *Consumption and Identity at Work* (London, Sage).

Dunleavy, P. (1980) The political implications of sectoral cleavages and the growth of state employment: part 2, cleavages structures and political alignment, *Political Studies*, 28(4), 527–49.

Duru-Bellat, M. & Kieffer, A. (2000) Inequalities in educational opportunities in France: educational expansion, democratization or shifting barriers? *Journal of Education Policy*, 15(3), 333–52.

Eccles, J. & Davis-Kean, P. (2005) Influences of parents' education on their children's educational attainments: the role of parent and child perceptions, *London Review of Education*, 3(3), 191–204.

Echols, F.H. & Willms, J.D. (1995) Reasons for school choice in Scotland, *Journal of Education Policy*, 10(2), 143–56.

Edmonds, R. (1979) Effective schools for the urban poor, *Educational Leadership*, 37(1), 15–24.

Edwards, T. & Whitty, G. (1992) Parental choice and educational reform in Britain and the United States, *British Journal of Educational Studies*, 40(2), 101–17.

Edwards, R., Nicoll, K. & Tait, A. (1999) Migrating metaphors: the globalization of flexibility in policy, *Journal of Education Policy*, 14(6), 619–30.

Ehrenreich, B. (1989) *Fear of Falling: the Inner Life of the Middle Class* (New York, Pantheon).

Elam, S.M., Rose, L.C. & Gallup, A.M. (1996) The 28th Annual Phi Delta Kappa/Gallup Poll of the public's attitudes toward the public schools, *Phi Delta Kappan*, 78(1), 41–59.

Elliott, A. (2002) Beck's sociology of risk: a critical assessment, *Sociology*, 36(2), 293–315.

Elmore, R.E. (1987) Choice in public education, in: W. Boyd & C. Kerchner (Eds) *The Politics of Excellence and Choice in Education [Politics of Education Association (PEA) yearbook]* (Philadelphia, PA, Falmer Press).

Emmerson, C. & Frayne, C. (2001) *Spending on Public Services* (London, Institute of Fiscal Studies).

Ennew, J. (1996) Time for children or time for adults? in: J. Ovortrup, M. Bardy & G. Scritta (Eds) *Childhood Matters: Social Theory, Practice and Politics* (Aldershot, Avebury).

Entin, K., Jasek-Rysdahl, K., Hughes, S., Aly, N., Sumser, J., O'Brien, P., Schmandt, X, Harris, R. & Giventer, L. (1998) *Critical Links: Employment Growth, Unemployment and Welfare-to-Work in Stanislaus County* (Turlock, CA, Center for Public Policy Studies at California State University, Stanislaus).

Esping-Andersen, G. (1993) *Changing Classes* (London, Sage).

Etzioni, A. (1993) *The Spirit of Community: The Reinvention of American Society* (New York, Touchstone).

Etzioni, A. (1996) *The New Golden Rule: Community and Morality in a Democratic Society* (New York, Basic Books).

Falk, R. (1999) *Predatory Globalisation: A Critique* (Cambridge, Polity Press).

Featherstone, M. (1991) *Consumer Culture and Postmodernism* (London, Sage).

Fecho, B. (2001) Toward literacies of engagement: the politics of compliance and school choice, *Journal of Curriculum Studies*, 33(5), 621–30.

Feinstein, L. & Symons, J. (1999) Attainment in secondary school, *Oxford Economic Papers*, 51(2), 300–21.

Felkins, L. (1997, revised in 2001) *Introduction to Public Choice Theory*. http://perspicuity.net/sd/pub-choice.html [Accessed 25/2/2006].

Fidler, B., Russell, S. & Simkins, T. (Eds) (1997) *Choices for Self-Managing Schools* (London, Paul Chapman).

Fielding, M. (Ed.) (2001) *Taking Education Really Seriously* (London, Routledge Falmer).

Fielding, S. (1997) *The Ideologies of New Labour*, Unpublished paper, University of Salford, cited in: L. Paterson (2003) The Three Educational Ideologies of the British Labour Party, 1997–2001, *Oxford Review of Education*, 29(2), 165–86.

Fielding, T. (1995) Migration and middle-class formation in England and Wales 1981–91, in: T. Butler & M. Savage (Eds) *Social Change and the Middle Classes* (London, University College Press).

Finch, L.W. (1989) Choice: claims of success, predictions of failure, *Education Digest*, 55, 12–15, cited in: W. Jeynes (2000) Assessing school choice: a balanced perspective, *Cambridge Journal of Education*, 30(2), 223–41.

Fine, M. (1993) Apparent involvement: reflections on parents, power and urban public schools, *Teachers College Record*, 94, 682–710.

Finkelstein, N. & Grubb, W. (2000) Making sense of education and training markets: lessons from England, *American Educational Research Journal*, 37(3), 601–32.

Finn, P.J. (1999) *Literacy with an Attitude: Educating Working-Class Children in Their Own Self-Interest* (Albany, NY, State University of New York Press).

Fitz, J., Gorard, S. & Taylor, C. (2002) School admissions after the School Standards and Framework Act: bringing the LEAs back in? *Oxford Review of Education*, 28(2–3), 373–93.

Fitz J., Halpin D. & Power S. (1993) *Education in the Market Place: Grant Maintained Schools* (London, Kogan Page).

Fitz J., Halpin D. & Power S. (1997) 'Between a rock and a hard place': diversity, institutional identity and grant-maintained schools, *Oxford Review of Education*, 23(1), 17–30.

Fitz, J., Taylor, C. & Gorard, S. (2002) Local education authorities and the regulation of educational markets: four case studies, *Research Papers in Education*, 17(2), 125–46.

Flatley, J. Connolly, H., Higgins, V., Williams, J., Coldron, J., Stephenson, K., Logie, A. & Smith, N. (2001) *Parents' Experiences of the Process of Choosing a Secondary School* (London, DfES).

Foskett, N. (1998) Schools and marketization, *Educational Management and Administration*, 26, 197–210.

Foskett, N. & Hemsley-Brown, J. (2001) *Choosing Futures: Young People's Decision-Making in Education, Training and Careers Markets* (London, RoutledgeFalmer).

Forster, P. (1992) Whose choice is it anyway? *Managing Schools Today*, 1, 36–7.

Friedman, M. & Friedman, R. (1980) *Free to Choose* (Harmondsworth, Penguin).

Fukuda-Parr, S. (2003) The human development paradigm: operationalizing Sen's ideas on capabilities, *Feminist Economics*, 9(2–3), 301–17.

Fuller, A. & Unwin, L. (2003) Creating a 'modern apprenticeship': a critique of the UK's multisector, social inclusion approach, *Journal of Education and Work*, 6(1), 5–25.

Fuller, B., Elmore, R. & Orfield, G. (1996) Policy-making in the dark: illuminating the school choice debate, in: B. Fuller, R. Elmore & G. Orfield (Eds) *Who Chooses? Who Loses?* (NY, Teachers College Press).

Gaffney, M. & Smith, A. (2001) An evaluation of New Zealand's targeted individual entitlement scheme, in: C. Hepburn (Ed.) *Can the Market Save our Schools?* (Vancouver, BC, The Fraser Institute).

Galton, M. & Willcock, J. (1983) *Moving From the Primary Classroom* (London, Routledge & Kegan Paul).

Gamble, A. & Wright, T. (Eds) (1999) *The New Social Democracy* (Oxford, Blackwell).

Ganaway, H. (1976) Making sense of school, in: M. Stubbs & S. Delamont (Eds) *Explorations in Classroom Observation* (London, Wiley).

Gardner, R., Cairns, J. & Lawton, D. (Eds) (2005) *Faith Schools: Consensus or Conflict?* (London, RoutledgeFalmer).

Garrod, J. (2003) Faith schools, *Sociology Review*, 12(3), 32–3.

Gasper, D. (2002) Is Sen's capability approach an adequate basis for considering human development? *Review of Political Economy*, 14(4), 435–61.

—— (2004) *The Ethics of Development* (Edinburgh, Edinburgh University Press).

Gates, B. (2005) Faith schools and colleges of education since 1800, in: R. Gardner, J. Cairns & D. Lawton (Eds) (2005) *Faith Schools: Consensus or Conflict?* (London, RoutledgeFalmer).

Gee, J.P. (1996) *Social Linguistics and Literacies: Ideology in Discourses*, 2nd edition (London, Falmer Press).

Geske, T.G. (2003) Review of Gill, B.P., Timpane, P.M., Ross, K.E. & Brewer, D.J. (2001) The new reality of school choice: rhetoric versus reality: what we know and what we need to know about vouchers and charter schools (Santa Monica, CA, Rand) *School Effectiveness and School Improvement*, 14(1), 111–8.

Gevers, L. (1979) On interpersonal comparability and social welfare orderings, *Econometrica*, 47(1), 75–90.

Gewirtz, S. (2002) *The Managerial School: Post-Welfarism and Social Justice in Education* (London, Routledge).

Gewirtz, S. & Ball, S. (2000) From 'welfarism' to 'new managerialism': shifting discourses of school headship in the education marketplace *Discourse*, 21(3), 253–68.

Gewirtz, S., Ball, S. & Bowe, R. (1994) Parents, privilege and the education market place, *Research Papers in Education*, 9(1), 3–29.

Gewirtz, S., Ball, S.J. & Bowe, R. (1995) *Markets, Choice and Equity in Education* (Buckingham, Open University Press).

Gibson, A. & Asthana, S. (1999) *Local Markets and the Polarization of Schools in England and Wales* (Exeter University, Department of Geography).

Gibson, A. & Asthana, S. (2000) What's in a number? Commentary on Gorard and Fitz's 'Investigating the determinants of segregation between schools', *Research Papers in Education*, 15(2), 133–53. [See also: Gorard, S. (2000) Here we go again: a reply to 'What's in a number?' by Gibson and Asthana, *Research Papers in Education*, 15(2), 155–62.]

Giddens, A. (1991) *Modernity and Self-Identity: Self and Society in the Late Modern Age* (Cambridge, Polity Press).

Giddens, A. (1998) Risk society: the context of British politics, in: J. Franklin (Ed.) *The Politics of Risk Society* (Cambridge, Polity Press).

Gill, B.P., Timpane, P.M., Ross, K.E. & Brewer, D.J. (2001) *The New Reality of School Choice: Rhetoric Versus Reality: What We Know and What We Need to Know about Vouchers and Charter Schools.* (Santa Monica, CA, Rand).

Gillborn, D. (1997) Racism and reform: new ethnicities/old inequalities? *British Educational Research Journal,* 23(3), 345–60.

Gillborn, D. & Youdell, D. (2000) *Rationing Education: Policy, Practice, Reform and Equity* (Buckingham, Open University Press).

Gipps, C. (1993) Policy-making and the use and misuse of evidence, in: C. Chitty & B. Simon (Eds) *Education Answers Back* (London, Lawrence & Wishart).

Glatter, R., Johnson, D. & Woods, P.A. (1993) Marketing, choice and responses in education, in: M. Smith & H. Busher (Eds) *Managing Schools in an Uncertain Environment: Resources, Marketing and Power* (Sheffield, BELMAS).

Glatter, R. & Woods, P. (1994) The impact of competition and choice on parents and schooling, in: W. Bartlett, C. Propper, D. Wilson & J. Le Grand (Eds) *Quasi-Markets in the Welfare State: The Emerging Findings* (Bristol, SAUS Publications).

Glatter, R., Woods, P. & Bagley, C. (1997) Diversity, differentiation and hierarchy. School choice and parental preferences, in: R. Glatter, P. Woods & C. Bagley (Eds), *Choice and Diversity in Schooling: Perspectives and Prospects* (London, Routledge).

Glazer, N. (1983) The future under tuition tax credits, in: T. James & H. Levin (Eds) *Public Dollars for Private Schools: The Case of Tuition Tax Credits* (Philadelphia, PA, Temple University Press).

Gleeson, D. & Keep, E. (2004) Voice without accountability: the changing relationship between employers, the state and education in England, *Oxford Review of Education,* 30(1), 37–63.

Glenn, C.L. (1989) *Choice of Schools in Six Nations* (Washington, DC, US Department of Education).

Glenn, C. & De Groof, J. (2002) *Finding the Right Balance: Freedom, Autonomy and Accountability in Education* (Utrecht, Lemma).

Goddard, A. (1998) Pay reflects school ties, *Times Higher Education Supplement,* 30 October.

Goffman, E. (1963) *Stigma: Notes on the Management of Spoiled Identity* (Harmondsworth, Penguin).

Gokulsing, K.M. (2006) Without prejudice: and exploration of religious diversity, secularism and citizenship in England (with particular reference to the state funding of Muslim faith schools and multiculturalism, *Journal of Education Policy,* 21(4), 459–70.

—— (1999) School choice: an examination of the empirical evidence on achievement, parental decision making and equity, *Educational Researcher,* 28(9), 16–25.

—— (2000) School choice: do we know enough? *Educational Researcher,* 29(8), 21–2.

Goldhaber, D., Brewer, D. & Anderson, D. (1999) A three-way error component analysis of educational productivity, *Education Economics,* 7(3), 199–208.

Goldhaber, D. & Eide, E. (2002) What do we know (and need to know) about the impact of school choice reforms on disadvantaged students? *Harvard Educational Review,* 72(2), 157–76.

Goldring, E. (1991) Parents motives for choosing a privatized public school system: an Israeli example, *Educational Policy*, 5(4), 412–26.

Goldthorpe, J. (1996) Class analysis and the reorientation of class theory: the case of persisting differentials in educational attainment, *British Journal of Sociology*, 47(3), 481–505.

Gorard, S. (1996) Three steps to 'heaven'? The family and school choice, *Educational Review*, 48(3), 237–52.

Gorard, S. (1997) *School Choice in an Established Market* (Aldershot, Ashgate).

Gorard, S. (1999) 'Well. That about wraps it up for school choice research': a state of the art review, *School Leadership and Management*, 19(18), 25–47.

Gorard, S. (2000) *Education and Social Justice* (Cardiff, University of Wales Press).

Gorard, S. & Fitz, J. (1998a) The more things change … the missing impact of marketisation? *British Journal of Sociology of Education*, 19(3), 365–76.

Gorard, S. & Fitz, J. (1998b) Under starters' orders: the established market, the Cardiff study and the Smithfield project, *International Studies in the Sociology of Education*, 8(3), 299–314.

Gorard, S. & Fitz, J. (2000a) Investigating the determinants of segregation between schools, *Research Papers in Education*, 15(2), 115–32.

Gorard, S. & Fitz, J. (2000b) Markets and stratification: a view from England and Wales, *Educational Policy*, 14(3), 405–28.

Gorard, S. & Taylor, C. (2001) The composition of specialist schools in England: track record and future prospect, *School Leadership and Management*, 21(4), 365–81.

Gorard, S. & Taylor, C. (2002) Market forces and standards in education: a preliminary consideration, *British Journal of Sociology of Education*, 23(1), 5–18.

Gorard, S., Taylor, C. & Fitz, J. (2002) Does school choice lead to 'spirals of decline'? *Journal of Education Policy*, 17(3), 367–84.

Gorard, S., Taylor, C. & Fitz, J. (2003) *Schools, Markets and Choice Policies* (London, RoutledgeFalmer).

Gouvias, D. & Vitsilakis-Soroniatis, C. (2005) Student employment and parental influences on educational and occupational aspirations of Greek adolescents, *Journal of Education and Work*, 18(4), 421–49.

Grace, G. (1994) Education is a public good: on the need to resist the domination of economic science, in: D. Bridges & T.H. McLaughlin (Eds) *Education and the Marketplace* (London, Falmer Press).

Grace, G (1995) *School Leadership: Beyond Education Management: An Essay in Policy Scholarship* (London, Falmer).

—— (2002) *Catholic Schools: Mission, Markets and Morality* (London, RoutledgeFalmer).

Gray, J. (1993) The quality of schooling: frameworks for judgement, in: M. Preedy (Ed.) *Managing the Effective School* (London, Paul Chapman).

Green, A. (1990) *The Rise of Educational Systems in England, France and the USA* (London, Macmillan).

Green, A. (1997) *Education, Globalisation and the Nation State* (New York, St. Martin's).

—— (1999) Education and globalisation in Europe and East Asia: convergent and divergent trends, *Journal of Policy Studies*, 14(1), 55–72.

Greene, J. (2001) A survey of results from voucher experiments: where we are and what we know, in: C. Hepburn (Ed.) *Can Markets Save Our Schools?* (Vancouver, BC, The Fraser Institute).

Greene, J., Peterson, P. & Du, J. (1999) The effectiveness of school choice in Milwaukee: the Milwaukee experiment, *Education and Urban Society*, 31(2), 190–213.

Guile, D. (2002) Skill and work experience in the European knowledge economy, *Journal of Education and Work*, 15(3), 251–76.

Gunter, H. (2001) Modernising headteachers as leaders: an analysis of the NPQH, in: M. Fielding (Ed.) *Taking Education Really Seriously* (London, RoutledgeFalmer).

Habermas, J. (1984) What does a legitimation crisis mean today? Legitimation problems in late capitalism, in: W. Connolly (Ed.) *Legitimacy and the State* (Oxford, Basil Backwell).

Hackett, G. (2000) Children still class bound, *The Times Educational Supplement*, 21 April, p. 11.

Halpin, D., Power, S. & Fitz, J. (1997) Opting into the past? Grant maintained schools and the reinvention of tradition, in: R. Glatter, P. Woods & C. Bagley (Eds) *Choice and Diversity in Schooling: Perspectives and Prospects* (London, Routledge).

Halsey, A.H. (1995) *Change in British Society* (Oxford, Oxford University Press).

Hammond, P.J. (1976) Equity, Arrow's conditions and Rawls's difference principle, *Econometrica*, 44, 793–804.

—— (1982) Utilitarianism, uncertainty and information, in: A. Sen & B. Williams (Eds) *Utilitarianism and beyond* (Cambridge, Cambridge University Press).

Hammond, T. & Dennison, B. (1995) School choice in less populated areas, *Educational Management and Administration*, 23(2), 104–13.

Hannan, D., Smyth, E., McCullagh, J., O'Leary, L. & McMahon, D. (1996) *Coeducation and Gender Equality* (Dublin, Oak Tree Press).

Hanushek, E. A. (1998) Conclusions and controversies about the effectiveness of schools, *Federal Reserve Bank of New York Economic Policy Review*, 4(1), 11–27. http://www.newyorkfed.org/research/epr/98v04n1/9803hanu.pdf [Accessed: 15/12/06].

Hardin, R. (1982) *Collective Action* (Baltimore, Johns Hopkins University Press).

Harding, N. (2006) Ethnic and social class similarities and differences in mothers' beliefs about kindergarten preparation, *Race, Ethnicity and Education*, 9(2), 223–37.

Hardy, J. & Vieler-Porter, C. (1990) Race, schooling and the 1988 Education Reform Act, in: M. Flude & M. Hammer (Eds) *The Education Reform Act, 1988: Its Origins and Implications*, 173–85 (London, Falmer Press).

Hare, R.M. (1981) *Moral Thinking: Its Levels, Method and Point* (Oxford, Clarendon).

Hargreaves, A., Earl, L. & Ryan, J. (1996) *Schooling for Change: Reinventing Education for Early Adolescents* (London, Falmer Press).

Harsanyi, J. (1976) *Essays in Ethics, Social Behaviour, and Scientific Explanation* (Dordrecht, Reidel).

Hatcher, R. (1994) Market relationships and the management of teachers, *British Journal of Sociology of Education*, 15(1), 41–61.

—— (1998) Class differentiation in education: rational choices? *British Journal of Education*, 19(1), 5–24.

—— (2006) Privatization and sponsorship: the re-agenting of the school system in England, *Journal of Education Policy*, 21(5), 599–619.

Hatcher, R. & Hirtt, N. (1999) The business agenda behind Labour's education policy, in: M. Allen, C. Benn, C. Chitty, M. Cole, R. Hatcher, N. Hirtt & G. Rikowski

(Eds) *Business, Business, Business: New Labour's Education Policy* (London, Tufnell Press).

Heath, A. (2006) Never mind the sleaze, look how pupils benefit, *Spectator*, 16 September.

Heath, E. (1998) *The Autobiography of Edward Heath: The Course of My Life* (London, Hodder & Stoughton).

Held, D. (1999) The transformation of political community: rethinking democracy in the context of globalisation, in: I. Shapiro & C. Hacker-Gordon (Eds) *Democracy's Edges* (Cambridge, Cambridge University Press).

Held, D., McGrew, A., Goldblatt, D. & Perraton, J. (1999) *Global Transformations* (Cambridge, Polity Press).

Henderson, V., Mieszkowski, P. & Sauvageau, Y. (1976) *Peer Group Effects and Educational Production Functions* (Ottawa, Economic Council of Canada).

Henig, J.R. (1994) *Rethinking School Choice: Limits of the Market Metaphor* (Princeton, NJ, Princeton University Press).

Hennipman, P. (1976) Pareto optimality: value judgement or analytical tool, in: J.S. Cramer, A. Heertje, & P. Venekamp (Eds) *Relevance and Precision: From Quantitative Analysis to Economic Policy : Essays in Honour of Pieter de Wolff* (Amsterdam, North-Holland).

Hennipman, P. (1982) Wicksell and Pareto: Their relationship in the theory of public finance, *History and Political Economy*, 14(1), 37–64.

Henry, M., Lingard, B., Rizvi, F. & Taylor, S. (1999) Working with/against globalisation in education, *Journal of Education Policy*, 14(1), 85–97.

Herbert, D. (2000) School choice in the local environment: headteachers as gatekeepers on an uneven playing field, *School Leadership & Management*, 20(1), 79–97.

Hesketh, A. & Knight, P. (1998) Secondary school prospectuses and educational markets, *Cambridge Journal of Education*, 28(1), 21–35.

Hirschman, A. (1970) *Exit, Voice, and Loyalty: Responses to Decline in Firms, Organizations, and States* (Cambridge, Harvard University Press).

Hirschman, A. (1982) *Shifting Involvements* (Princeton, NJ, Princeton University Press).

Hirst, P. & Thompson, G. (1996) *Globalization in Question: The International Economy and the Possibility of Governance* (Cambridge, Polity Press).

Hodgson, A. & Spours, K. (1999) *New Labour's Educational Agenda* (London, Kogan Page).

Hoffer, T., Greeley, A. & Coleman, J. (1985) Achievement growth in public and Catholic schools, *Sociology of Education*, 58(2), 74–97.

Holmes, G., DeSimone, J. & Rupp, N. (2003) *Does School Choice Increase School Quality?* (Cambridge, MA, National Bureau of Economic Research Working Papers, 9683).

Honig, B. (1993) Why privatizing public education is a bad idea, in: P.R. Kane (Ed.) *Independent Schools, Independent Thinkers* (San Francisco, CA, Jossey-Bass).

Hook, S. (1999) Failing schools and dying cities, *Times Educational Supplement*, 7 May.

Howell, W., Wolf, P., Campbell, D. & Peterson, P. (2002) School vouchers and academic performance: results from three randomized field trials, *Journal of Policy Analysis and Management*, 21(2), 191–217.

Howson, J. (2000) Solid state, *Times Educational Supplement*, 14 July.

Hoxby, C.M. (1994) *Does competition among public schools benefit students and tax-payers? National Bureau of Economic Research Working Paper 4979* (Cambridge, MA, National Bureau of Economic Research).

—— (1995) *Is there an equity efficiency trade-off in school finance? Tiebout and a theory of the local public goods producer, National Bureau of Economic Research Working Paper 5265* (Cambridge, MA, National Bureau of Economic Research).

Hoy, K.H. & Miskel, C.G. (1996) *Educational Administration: Theory, Research and Practice* (New York, Allyn & Bacon).

Huddleston, P. & Unwin, L. (2002) *Teaching and Learning in Further Education* (London, RoutledgeFalmer).

Hughes, M., Wikeley, F. & Nash, T. (1994) *Parents and Their Children's Schools* (Oxford, Blackwell).

Hunter, J.B. (1991) Which school? A study of parents' choice of secondary school, *Educational Research*, 33(1), 31–41.

Hustler, D., Stronach, I. & West, A. (2000) Editorial: Is New Labour Delivering the Goods? *British Educational Research Journal*, 26(4), 435–39.

Hutton, W. (1999) New Keynesianism and New Labour, in: A. Gamble & T. Wright (Eds) *The New Social Democracy* (Oxford, Blackwell).

Jackson, R. (Ed.) (2003) Should the state fund faith based schools? A review of the arguments, *British Journal of Religious Education*, 25(2), 89–102.

Jackson, C. & Bisset, M. (2005) Gender and school choice: factors influencing parents when choosing single-sex or co-educational independent schools for their children, *Cambridge Journal of Education*, 35(2), 195–211.

Jackson, C. & Warin, J. (2000) The importance of gender as aspect of identity formation at key transition points in compulsory education, *British Educational Research Journal*, 26(3), 375–91.

James, T. & Levin, H.M. (1983) Introduction, in: T. James & H.M. Levin (Eds) *Public Dollars for Private Schools: The Case of Tuition Tax Credits* (Philadelphia, PA, Temple University Press).

James, C. & Phillips, P. (1995) The practice of educational marketing in schools, *Educational Management and Administration*, 23(2), 75–88.

—— (1997) Markets and marketing, in: B. Fidler, S. Russell & T. Simkins (Eds) *Choices for Self-Managing Schools* (London, Paul Chapman).

Jasek-Rysdahl, K. (2001) Applying Sen's capabilities framework to neighbourhoods: using local asset maps to deepen our understanding of well-being, *Review of Social Economy*, 59(3), 313–29.

Jencks, C., Smith, M., Ackland, H., Bane, M., Cohen, D., Gintis, H., Heyns, B. & Micholson, S. (1972) *Inequality: A Reassessment of the Effect of Family and Schooling in America* (New York, Basic Books).

Jenkins, E. (1973) *New York Times*, 29 May.

Jenson, D.N. (1983) Constitutional and legal implications of tuition tax credits, in: T. James & H.M. Levin (Eds) *Public Dollars for Private Schools: The Case of Tuition Tax Credits* (Philadelphia, PA, Temple University Press).

Jeynes, W. (2000) Assessing school choice: a balanced perspective, *Cambridge Journal of Education*, 30(2), 223–41.

Jimerson, L. (2005) Placism in NCLB – How rural children are left behind, *Equity & Excellence in Education*, 38(3), 211–19. http://www.ingentaconnect.com/content/routledg/ueee/2005/00000038/00000003/art00006 [Accessed: 13/11/06].

Johnson, B. (2006) Thatcher's legacy to us, *Cherwell*, March 3. http://www.cherwell.org/oped/comment/thatchers_legacy_to_us [Accessed: 16/4/2006].

Jorgenson, D.W. & Slesnick, D.T. (1984a) Inequality in the distribution of individual welfare, in: R.L. Basmann & G.F. Rhodes (Eds) *Advances in Econometrics (Volume 3). Economics Inequality: Measurement and Policy* (Greenwich, JAI Press).

Jorgenson, D.W. & Slesnick, D.T. (1984b) Aggregate consumer behaviour and the measurement of inequality, *Review of Economic Studies*, 51, 369–92.

Jorgenson, D.W., Lau, L.J. & Stoker, T.M. (1980) Welfare comparison under exact aggregation, *American Economic Review*, 70(2), 268–72.

Jorgenson, D.W., Slesnick, D.T. & Stoker, T.M. (1983) *Exact aggregation over individuals and commodities, Discussion paper 1005* (Cambridge, MA, Harvard Institute of Economic Research).

Kannai, Y. & Peleg, B. (1984) A note on the extension of an order on a set to the power set, *Journal of Economic Theory*, 32, 172–5.

Kapteyn, A. & Van Praag, B.M.S. (1976) A new approach to the construction of family equivalent scales, *European Economic Review*, 7, 313–35.

Kapteyn, A. & Wansbeek, T.S. (1982) Empirical evidence of preference formation, *Journal of Economic Psychology*, 2(2), 137–54.

Karsten, S. (1994) Policy on ethnic segregation in a system of choice: the case of the Netherlands, *Journal of Education Policy*, 9(3), 211–25.

Katz, M. & Shapiro, C. (1994) Systems competition and network effects, *Journal of Economic Perspectives*, 8(2), 93–115.

Keep, E. & Payne, J. (2002) Policy interventions for a vibrant work-based route – or when policy hits reality's fan (again), in: K. Evans, P. Hodkinson & L. Unwin (Eds) *Working to Learn* (London, Kogan Page).

Kelly, A. (2001) *Benchmarking for School Improvement* (London, Routledge Falmer).

—— (2003) *Decision Making Using Game Theory* (Cambridge, Cambridge University Press).

—— (2004) *The Intellectual Capital of Schools* (Dordrect, Kluwer Academic Press).

Kenway, J. & Bullen, E. (2001) *Consuming Children* (Buckingham, Open University Press).

Kerr, D. (2001) *Elect the Ambassador: Building Democracy in a Globalised World* (Annandale, NSW, Pluto Press).

Kiernan, K. (1992) The impact of family disruption in childhood on transition made in young adult life, *Population Studies*, 46(2), 213–34.

Kirkpatrick, D.W. (1990) *Choice in Schooling* (Chicago, IL, Loyola University Press).

Kogan, M. (1990) Education policy and values, in: I. McNay & J. Ozga (Eds) *Policy-Making in Education: The Breakdown of Consensus*, (Oxford, Pergamon Press).

Kohn, A. (Ed.) (1997) *Education Inc.: Turning Learning into a Business* (Portsmouth, NH, Heinemann).

Kozol, J. (1991) *Savage Inequalities: Children in America's Schools* (New York, Harper Perennial).

Kretzmann, J.P. & McKnight, J.L. (1993) *Building Communities from the Inside Out: A Path Toward Finding and Mobilizing a Community's Assets* (Evanston, IL, Institute for Policy Research).

Kuehn, L. (2001a) *Globalization, Trade Agreements and Education: Trade Deals Prevent Governments from Protecting Education* (National Union of Students in Europe (ESIB), Committee on Commodification). http://www.esib.org/commodification/documents/ [Accessed: 12/6/05].

—— (2001b) *Keep Public Education Out of Trade Agreements* (National Union of Students in Europe (ESIB), Committee on Commodification). http://www.esib. org/commodification/documents/ [Accessed: 12/6/05].

Kymlicka, W. (1998) *Finding Our Way: Rethinking Ethnocultural Relations in Canada* (Toronto, Oxford University Press).

Lankford, H.R. (1985) Preferences of citizens for public expenditures on elementary and secondary education. *Journal of Econometrics*, 27(1), 1–20.

Lauder, H., Hughes, D., Watson, S., Waslander, S., Thrupp, M., Strathdee, R., Simiyu, I., Depuis, A., McGlinn, J. & Hamlin, J. (1999) *Trading in Futures: Why Markets in Education Don't Work* (Buckingham, Open University Press).

Leblond, D. & Trincaz, J. (1999) Pluriculturality in the French and British education systems: cross perspectives, *Education and Social Justice*, 1(3), 16–24.

Lee, J. (1987) Pride and prejudice: teachers, class and an inner city infants school, in: M. Lawn & G. Grace (Eds) *Teachers: The Culture and Politics of Work* (Lewes, UK, Falmer Press).

Lee, V. (1993) Educational choice: the stratifying effects of selecting schools and courses, *Educational Policy*, 7(2), 125–48.

Lee, M.J. (1993) *Consumer Culture Reborn* (London, Routledge).

Lee, V. & Bryk, A. (1993) *Catholic Schools and the Common Good* (Cambridge, MA, Harvard University Press).

Legge, K. (1989) Human resource management: a critical analysis, in: J. Storey (Ed.) *New Perspectives in Human Resources Management* (London, Routledge).

Leithwood, K., Jantzi, D. & Steinbach, R. (1999) *Changing Leadership for Changing Times* (Buckingham, Open University Press).

Levacic, R. (1995) *Local Management of Schools: Analysis and Practice* (Buckingham, Open University Press).

—— (1998) Local management of schools in England: results after six years. *Journal of Education Policy*, 13(3), 331–50.

—— (2004) Competition and the performance of English secondary schools: further evidence, *Education Economics*, 12(2), 177–93.

Levacic, R. & Hardman, J. (1998) Competing for resources: the impact of social disadvantage and other factors on English secondary schools' financial performance, *Oxford Review of Education*, 24(3), 303–28.

Levin, B. (2001) *Reforming Education: From Origins to Outcomes* (London, RoutledgeFalmer).

Levin, H. (1991) The economics of educational choice, *Economics of Education Review* 10(2), 137–58.

—— (2000) *A comprehensive framework for evaluating educational vouchers, Occasional Paper No. 5* (New York, National Centre for the Study of Privatization in Education, Teachers College, Columbia University).

Levin, H. (2001) Forum: for-profit schools, *Education Matters More*, Spring. Cited in: Molnar, J. (2006) The commercial transformation of public education, Journal of Education Policy, 21(5), 621–40.

—— (2002) A comprehensive framework for evaluating educational vouchers, *Educational Evaluation and Policy Analysis*, 24(3), 159–74.

Levin, B. & Riffel, J. (1997), School system responses to external change: implications for school choice, in: R. Glatter, P. Woods & C. Bagley (Eds) *Choice and Diversity in Schooling: Perspectives and Prospects* (London, Routledge).

Lightfoot, S.L. (1977) Family-school interactions: the cultural image of mothers and teachers, *Signs*, 3(2), 395–408.

Lingard, R. (2000) It is and it isn't: vernacular globalization, educational policy and restructuring, in: N. Burbules & C. Torres (Eds) *Globalization and Education: Critical Perspectives* (London, Routledge).

Lubienski, C. (2005) School choice as a civil right: district responses to competition and equal educational opportunity, *Equity & Excellence in Education*, 38, 331–41.

Lucey, H. & Reay, D. (2000) Identities in transition: anxiety and excitement in the move to secondary school, *Oxford Review of Education*, 26(2), 191–205.

—— (2002) A market in waste: psychic and structural dimensions of school-choice policy in the UK and children's narratives on 'demonized' schools. *Discourse*, 23(3), 253–66.

Luke, C. (1999) What next? Toddler netizens, playstation thumb, techno-literacies, *Contemporary Issues in Early Childhood*, 1(1), 95–100.

Lupton, D. and Tullock, J. (2002) Risk is part of your life: risk epistemologies among a group of Australians, *Sociology*, 36(2), 317–34.

Lynch, K. (1989) The ethos of girls' schools: an analysis of differences between male and female schools, *Social Studies*, 10, 11–81.

Lynch, K. & Lodge, A. (1999) The status of children, in: K. Lynch (Ed.) *Equality in Education* (Dublin, Gill & Macmillan).

—— (2002) *Equality and Power in Education* (London, RoutledgeFalmer).

Lynch, K. & Moran, M. (2006) Markets, schools and the convertibility of economic capital: the complex dynamics of class choice, *British Journal of Sociology of Education*, 27(2), 221–35.

MacEwan, A. (1999) *Neo-Liberalism or Democracy? Economic Strategy, Markets, and Alternatives for the Twenty-First Century* (London, Zed Books).

Mackie, J.L. (1977) *Ethics: Inventing Right and Wrong* (Harmondsworth, Penguin).

Maddaus, J. (1990) Parental choice of school: what parents think and do, *Review of Research in Education*, 16, 267–95.

Maguire, M., Ball, S.J. & McCrae, S. (1999) Promotion, persuasion and class-taste: marketing (in) the UK post-compulsory sector, *British Journal of Sociology of Education*, 20(3) 291–308.

Majumdar, M. & Sen, A.K. (1976) A note on representing partial ordering, *Review of Economic Studies*, 43(3), 543–5.

Marginson, S. (1997) *Educating Australia: Government, Economy and Citizen since 1960* (Cambridge, Cambridge University Press).

Marginson, S. (1999) After globalisation: emerging politics of education, *Journal of Education Policy*, 14(1), 19–31.

Marginson, S. (2002) Nation-building universities in a global environment: the case of Australia, *Higher Education*, 43(3), 409–28.

Margolis, H. (1982) *Selfishness, Altruism and Rationality* (Cambridge, Cambridge University Press).

Marsden, T., Harrison, M. & Flynn, A. (1998) Creating competitive space: exploring the social and political maintenance of retail power, *Environment and Planning A*, 30(3), 481–98.

Marshall, A. (1890, reprinted in 1920) *Principles of Economics*, 8th edition (London, Macmillan). http://www.econlib.org/library/Marshall/marP.html [Accessed: 23/10/06].

Martin, M. & Burke, D.B. (1990) What's best for children in the schools-of-choice movement? *Educational Policy*, 4, 73–92.

Martin, J., Ranson, S. & Vincent, C. (2000) *'Little Polities': Schools, Governance and Parental Participation, Exploring Parental Voice in Schools, Project report* (Birmingham, University of Birmingham).

Marx, K. (1844, reprinted in 1977) *Economic and Philosophic Manuscript* (London, Lawrence & Wishart).

Massey, D. (1995) Reflections on gender and geography, in: T. Butler & M. Savage (Eds) *Social Change and the Middle Classes* (London, University College Press).

Matthewsa, J. & Sidhub, R. (2005) Desperately seeking the global subject: international education, citizenship and cosmopolitanism, *Globalisation, Societies and Education*, 3(1), 49–66.

McArthur, E., Colopy, K.W. & Schlaline, B. (1995) *Use of School Choice Educational Policy Issues: Statistical Perspectives* (Washington, DC, National Center for Educational Statistics).

McElwee, M. (Ed.) (2005) *Choice and Freedom for All: Education Policies for the Next Ten Years* (London, Bow Group).

McGinn, N. F. (1997) The impact of globalization on national education systems, *Prospects*, 27(1), 41–54.

McKnight, J. (1995) *The Careless Society: Community and Its Counterfeits* (New York, Basic Books).

McLanahan, S. & Sandefur, G. (1994) *Growing up With a Single Parent: What Hurts, What Helps* (Cambridge, MA, Harvard University Press).

McMurtry, J. (1991) Education and the market model, *Journal of Philosophy of Education*, 25(2), 209–17.

McQuaig, L. (2001) *All You Can Eat: Greed, Lust, and the New Capitalism* (Toronto, Penguin).

Measor, L. & Woods, P. (1984) *Changing Schools: Pupil Perspectives on Transfer to a Comprehensive* (Milton Keynes, Open University Press).

Medoff, J. & Harless, A. (1996) *The Indebted Society: Anatomy of an Ongoing Disaster* (Boston, MA, Little, Brown & Company).

Meier, D.W. (1992a) Myths, lies, and public schools, *The Nation*, 21 September.

—— (1992b) Choices: a strategy for educational reform, in: P.R. Kane (Ed.) *Independent Schools, Independent Thinkers* (San Francisco, CA, Jossey-Bass).

Meyer, J.W. & Rowan, B. (1977) Institutionalised organizations: formal structure as myth and ceremony, *American Journal of Sociology*, 83(2), 340–63.

—— (1978) The structure of educational organizations, in: M.W. Meyer (Ed.) *Environments and Organizations* (San Francisco, CA, Jossey-Bass).

Meyer, J.W., Scott, W.R. & Deal, T.E. (1992) Institutional and technical sources of organizational structure: explaining the structure of educational organizations, in: J.W. Meyer & W.R. Scott (Eds) *Organizational Environments: Ritual and Rationality* (Newbury Park, CA, Sage Publications).

Mickelson, R.A. & Southworth, S. (2005) When opting out is not a choice: implications for NCLB's transfer option from Charlotte, North Carolina, *Equity & Excellence in Education*, 38(3), 249–63.

Milne, A., Myers, D., Rosenthal, A. & Ginsburg, A. (1986) Single parents, working mothers, and the educational achievement of school children, *Sociology of Education*, 59(3), 125–39.

Mirrlees, J.A. (1982) The economic uses of utilitarianism, in: A. Sen & B. Williams (Eds) *Utilitarianism and Beyond* (Cambridge, Cambridge University Press).

Molnar, A. (2006) The commercial transformation of public education, *Journal of Education Policy*, 21(5), 621–40.

Moore, D.R. & Davenport, S. (1989a) High school choice and students at risk, *Education Digest*, 55, 7–10.

Moore, D.R. & Davenport, S. (1989b) Cheated again: school choice and students at risk, *School Administrator*, 46(7), 12–15.

—— (1989c) High school choice and students at risk, *Equity and Choice*, 5(1), 5–10.

Morgan, V., Dunn, S., Cairns, E. & Fraser, G. (1993) How do parents choose a school for their child? An example of the exercise of parental choice, *Educational Research*, 35(2), 139–48.

Morris, G. (1994) Local education authorities and the market place, in: D. Bridges & T. McLaughlin (Eds) *Education and the Market Place* (London, Falmer Press).

Mortimore, P. (2001) Globalisation, effectiveness and improvement, *School Effectiveness and School Improvement*, 12(1), 229–49.

Mortimore, P., Gopinathan, S., Leo, E., Myers, K., Stoll, L., & Mortimore, J. (2000) *The Culture of Change: Case Studies of Improving Schools in Singapore and London* (London, Institute of Education).

Mortimore, P., Sammons, P., Stoll, L., Lewis, D. & Ecob, R. (1988, reprinted in 1995) *School Matters: The Junior Years* (London, Open Books). [Reprinted 1995: London, Paul Chapman].

Moynihan, D.P. (1989) What the Congress can do when the Court is wrong, in: E.M. Gaffney (Ed.) *Private Schools and the Public Good* (Notre Dame, IN, Notre Dame University Press).

Murphy, J. (1990) Class inequality in education, in: I. McNay & J. Ozga (Eds) *Policy-making in Education: The Breakdown of Consensus* (Oxford, Pergamon Press).

Nagel, T. (1980) The limits of objectivity, in: S. McMurin (Ed.) *Tanner Lectures on Human Values* (Cambridge, Cambridge University Press).

Naismith, D. (1994) In defense of the educational voucher, in: D. Bridges & T. McLaughlin (Eds) *Education and the Market Place* (London, Falmer Press).

Naisbett, J. & Aburdene, P. (1988) *Mega-Trends 2000* (London, Sidgwick & Jackson).

Narayan, D. & Petesch, P. (2002) *Voices of the Poor from Many Lands* (Washington, The World Bank).

Nathan, J. (1990) School choice in Minnesota, *Religion and Public Education*, 17, 345–54, cited in: W. Jeynes (2000) Assessing school choice: a balanced perspective, *Cambridge Journal of Education*, 30(2), 223–41.

Nathan, J. & Ysseldyke, J. (1994) What Minnesota learned about school choice, *Phi Delta Kappan*, 75(9), 682–88.

National Union of Students in Europe (ESIB), Committee on commodification (2001) *Commodification of Education Introductory Information* [Information sheet/ CoCo/BM41] http://www.esib.org/commodification/documents/ [Accessed: 9/6/05].

National Center for Education Statistics (1996) *Digest of Education Statistics 1996* (Washington, DC, US Department of Education, Office of Educational Research and Improvement).

—— (1997) *The Condition of Education 1997* (Washington, DC, US Department of Education, Office of Educational Research and Improvement).

Naughton, P. (1998) Time for change: a study of primary to second level schooling transition, *Irish Educational Studies*, 17, 312–26.

Newman, J. (1998) Managerialism and social welfare, in: G. Hughes & G. Lewis (Eds) *Unsettling Welfare: The Reconstruction of Social Policy* (London, Routledge).

Newman, J. & Clarke, J. (1995) Going about our business? the managerialization of public service, in: J. Clarke, A. Cochrane & E. McLoughlin (Eds) *Managing Social Policy* (London, Sage).

Nisbet, J. & Entwhistle, N. (1969) *The Transition to Secondary Education* (London, University of London Press).

Niskanen, W.A. (1973) Bureaucracy: Servant or Master? (London, Institute of Economic Affairs).

Noden, P. (2000) Rediscovering the impact of marketisation: dimensions of social segregation in England's secondary schools, 1994–99, *British Journal of Sociology of Education*, 21(3), 371–90.

Noden, P., West, A., David, M. & Edge, A. (1998) Choices and destinations at transfer to secondary schools in London, *Journal of Education Policy*, 13(2), 221–36.

Noyes, A. (2004) Learning landscapes, *British Educational Research Journal*, 30(1), 27–41.

Noyes, A. (2006) School transfer and the diffraction of learning trajectories, *Research papers in Education*, 21(1), 43–62.

Nussbaum, M. (1988) Nature, function and capability: Aristotle on political distribution, *Oxford Studies in Ancient Philosophy*, Supplementary Volume, 145–84.

—— (1990) Aristotelian social democracy, in: B. Douglas, G. Mara & H. Richardson (Eds) *Liberalism and the Good* (New York, Routledge).

—— (1995) Human capabilities, female human beings, in: M. Nussbaum & J. Glover (Eds) *Women, Culture and Development* (Oxford, Clarendon Press).

—— (1996) Patriotism and cosmopolitanism, in: J. Cohen (Ed.) *For Love of Country: Debating the Limits of Patriotism* (Boston, Beacon Press).

—— (2000) *Women and Human Development: The Capabilities Approach* (Cambridge, Cambridge University Press).

O'Brien, M. (2001) *A Study of Student Transfer from Primary to Second-Level Schooling: Pupils', Parents' and Teachers' Perspectives* (Dublin, Department of Education & Science).

—— (2003) Girls and transition to second-level schooling in Ireland: 'moving on' and 'moving out', *Gender and Education*, 15(3), 249–67.

Offe, C. (1984) *Contradictions of the Welfare State* (London, Hutchinson).

—— (1985) *Disorganized Capitalism* (Oxford, Polity Press).

Office for Standards in Education (OFSTED) (1999) *The Annual Report of Her Majesty's Chief Inspector of Schools* (London, The Stationery Office).

Ogawa, R.T. & Dutton, J.S. (1994) Parental choice in education: examining the underlying assumptions, *Urban Education*, 29(3), 270–9.

Ohmae, K. (1995) *The End of the Nation State* (New York, Free Press).

Olasky, M.N. (1988) *Prodigal Press: The Anti-Christian Bias of the American News Media* (Westchester, IL, Crossway Books).

Olssen, M. (2004) Neoliberalism, globalisation, democracy: challenges for education. *Globalisation, Societies and Education*, 2(2), 231–75.

Oplatka, I. (2002) The emergence of educational marketing: lessons from the experiences of Israeli principals, *Comparative Education Review*, 46(2), 211–33.

—— (2004) The characteristics of the school organization and the constraints on market ideology in education: an institutional view, *Journal of Education Policy*. 19(2), 143–61.

Oplatka, I., Hemsley-Brown, J. & Foskett, N.H. (2002) The voice of teachers in marketing their school: personal perspectives in competitive environments, *School Leadership and Management*, 22(2), 177–96.

Oppenheim, C. (2001) Enabling participation? New Labour's welfare-to-work policies, in: S. White (Ed.) *New Labour: The Progressive Future?* (London, Palgrave Macmillan).

O'Reilly, B. (2002) Why Edison doesn't work, *Fortune*, 9 December.

O'Reilly, R. & Bosetti, L. (2000) Charter schools: the search for community, *Peabody Journal of Education*, 75(4), 19–36.

Organisation for Economic Cooperation and Development (OECD), Centre for Educational Research and Innovation (1994) *School: A Matter of Choice* (Paris, OECD).

Ouston, J., Maughan, B. & Mortimore, P. (1979) School influences, in: M. Rutter (Ed.) *Developmental Psychiatry* (London, Heinemann).

Pardey, D. (1991) *Marketing for Schools* (London, Kogan Page).

Parekh, B. (2003) Cosmopolitanism and global citizenship, *Review of International Studies*, 29(1), 3–17. http://journals.cambridge.org/action/displayIssue?jid=RIS&volumeId=29&issueId=01 [Accessed: 3/10/07].

Parkin, F. (1979) *Marxism and Class Theory: A Bourgeois Critique* (London, Tavistock).

Parsons, C. & Welsh, P. (2006) Public sector policies and practice, neo-liberal consumerism and freedom of choice in secondary education: a case study of one area in Kent, *Cambridge Journal of Education*, 36(2), 237–56.

Parsons, E., Chalkley, B. & Jones, A. (2000) School catchments and pupil movements: a case study in parental choice, *Educational Studies*, 26(1), 33–48.

Parsons, W. (1995) *Public Policy* (Cheltenham, Edward Elgar).

Paterson, L. (2003) The three educational ideologies of the British Labour Party, 1997–2001, *Oxford Review of Education*, 29(2), 165–86.

Pearce, D. & Gordon, L. (2005) In the zone: New Zealand's legislation for a system of school choice and its effects, *London Review of Education*, (3)2, 145–57.

Peirce, N.R. & Steinbach, C.F. (1987) *Corrective Capitalism: The Rise of America's Community Development Corporations* (New York, Ford Foundation).

Peltzman, S. (1992) The political economy of the decline of American public education, *Center for the Study of the Economy and the State, Working Paper* 78 (Chicago, IL, CSES).

Perkin, H. (1989) *The Rise of Professional Society: England since 1800* (London, Routledge).

Peterson, P.E., Green, J.P. & Noyes, C. (1996) School choice in Milwaukee, *Public Interest*, 125, 38–56.

Phillips, R. & Harper-Jones, G. (2003) Thematic review: Whatever next? Education policy and New Labour: the first four years, 1997–2001, *British Educational Research Journal*, 29(1), 125–32.

Pigou, A.C. (1920, reprinted in 1952) *Economics of Welfare*, 4th edition (London, Macmillan).

Plank, D.N. & Sykes, G. (1999) How choice changes the education system: a Michigan case study, *International Review of Education*, 45(5–6), 385–416.

Plewis, I. (1999) Educational inequalities and education action zones, in: C. Pantazis & D. Gordon (Eds) *Tackling Inequalities* (Bristol, Policy Press).

Plummer, G. (2000) *Failing Working Class Girls* (Stoke-on-Trent, Trentham).

Pollock, A., Shaoul, J., Rowland, D., & Player, S. (2002) *Public Services and the Private Sector: A Response to the IPPR* (London, Catalyst).

Porter, J. (1999) *Reschooling and the Global Future: Politics, Economics and the English Experience* (Oxford, Symposium Books).

Power, S. (2001) Missing: A sociology of educating the middle class, in: J. Demaine (Ed.) *Sociology of Education Today* (London, Palgrave Macmillan).

—— (2006) Markets and misogyny: educational research on educational choice, *British Journal of Education Studies*, 54(2), 175–88.

Power, S., Halpin, D. & Whitty, G. (1997) Managing the state and the market: 'new' education management in five countries, *British Journal of Educational Studies*, 45(4), 342–62.

Power, S. & Whitty, G. (1999) New Labour's education policy: first, second or third way? *Journal of Education Policy*, 14(5), 535–46.

Powers, J. & Cookson, P. (1999) The politics of school choice research: fact, fiction and statistics, *Educational Policy*, 13(1), 104–22.

Pratt, J.W. & Zeckhauser, R.J. (1984) *Principals and Agents: The Structure of Business* (Boston, MA, Harvard Business School Press).

Pring, R. (2005a) Faith schools: are they justified? in: R. Gardner, J. Cairns & D. Lawton (Eds) (2005) *Faith Schools: Consensus or Conflict?* (London, Routledge-Falmer).

—— (2005b) Labour government policy 14–19, *Oxford Review of Education*, 31(1), 71–85.

Qizilbash, M. (1996) Capabilities, well-being and human development: a survey, *The Journal of Development Studies*, 33(2), 143–62.

—— (1998) The concept of well-being, *Economics and Philosophy*, 14, 51–73.

Qizilbash, M. & Clark, D.A. (2005) The capability approach and fuzzy measures of poverty: an application to the South African context, *Social Indicators Research*, 74(1), 103–39.

Raab, C.D., Munn, P., McAvoy, L., Bailey, L., Arnott, M. & Adler, M. (1997) Devolving the management of schools in Britain, *Educational Administration Quarterly*, 33(2), 140–57.

Ramsey, F.P. (1926) Truth and probability, in: F.P. Ramsey (1978) *Foundations: Essays in Philosophy, Logic, Mathematics and Economics* (London, Routledge).

Ranson, S. (1990) Changing relations between centre and locality in education, in: I. McNay & J. Ozga (Eds) *Policy-Making in Education: The Breakdown of Consensus*, (Oxford, Pergamon Press).

Rapp, G.C. (2000) Agency and choice in education: does school choice enhance the work effort of teachers? *Education Economics*, 8(1), 37–63.

Ravallion, M. (1985) The performance of rice markets in Bangladesh during the 1974 famine, *Economic Journal*, 95, 15—29 http://ideas.repec.org/a/ecj/econjl/v95y1985i377p15-29.html [Accessed: 23/7/06].

Ravitch, D. (1992) The role of private schools in American education, in: P.R. Kane (Ed.) *Independent Schools, Independent Thinkers* (San Francisco, CA, Jossey-Bass).

Rawls, J. (1971) *A Theory of Justice* (Oxford, Clarendon Press).

Reay, D. (1998) Engendering social reproduction: mothers in the educational marketplace, *British Journal of Sociology of Education*, 19(2), 195–209.

Reay, D. & Ball, S. (1997) 'Spoilt for choice': the working classes and education markets, *Oxford Review of Education*, 23(1), 89–101.

—— (1998) 'Making their minds up': family dynamics and school choice, *British Educational Research Journal*, 24, 431–48.

Reay, D. & Lucey, H. (2000) Children, school choice and social differences, *Educational Studies*, 26(1), 83–100.

—— (2003) The limits of choice: children and inner city schooling, *Sociology*, 37, 121–42.

Reeder, D. (1979) A recurring debate: education and industry, in: G. Bernbaum (Ed.) *Schooling in Decline* (London, Macmillan).

Rees, G., Gorard, S., Fevre, R. & Furlong, J. (2000) Participating in the learning society: history, place and biography, in: F. Coffield (Ed.) *Differing Visions of a Learning Society: Research Findings* (Bristol, The Policy Press).

Reid, A. (2002) Public education and democracy: a changing relationship in a globalizing world, *Journal of Education Policy*, 17(5), 571–85.

Reynolds, D., Bollen, R., Creemers, B., Hopkins, D., Stoll, L. & Lagerweij, N. (1996) Making Good Schools: linking school effectiveness and school improvement (London, Routledge).

Reynolds, D. & Cuttance, P. (1992) School Effectiveness (London, Cassell).

Ribchester, C. & Edwards, W.J. (1998) Cooperation in the countryside: small primary school clusters, *Educational Studies*, 24(3), 281–93.

Richter, M.K. (1971) Rational choice, in: J.S. Chipman, L. Hurwicz, M.K. Richter & W.F. Sonnenschein, *Preference, Utility and Demand* (New York, Harcourt).

Riegel, S. (2001) The home schooling movement and the struggle for democratic education, *Studies in Political Economy*, 65 (Summer), 91–125.

Riley, K.A. (1998) *Whose School is it Anyway?* (London, Falmer Press).

Robertson, H. (1998) *No More Teachers, No More Books: The Commercialization of Canada's Schools* (Toronto, McClelland & Stewart).

Robertson, R. (1992) *Globalization, Social Theory and Global Culture* (London, Sage).

Robertson, S. & Dale, R. (2002) Local states of emergency: the contradictions of neo-liberal governance in education in New Zealand, *British Journal of Sociology of Education*, 23(3), 463–82.

Robertson, D. & Symons, J. (2003) Self-selection in the state school system, *Education Economics*, 11(3), 259–72.

Robeyns, I. (2003) Sen's capability approach and gender inequality: selecting relevant capabilities, *Feminist Economics*, 9(2&3), 61–91.

—— (2004) Justice as fairness and the capability approach, *Pavia, Italy, Fourth International Conference on the Capability Approach*.

Robinson, P. & Smithers, A. (1999) Should the sexes be separated for secondary education? comparisons of single-sex and co-educational schools, *Research Papers in Education*, 14(1), 23–49.

Rose, N. (1996) Governing 'advanced' liberal democracies, in: A. Barry, T. Osborne & N. Rose (Eds) *Foucault and Political Reason: Liberalism, Neo-Liberalism and Rationalities of Government* (London, UCL Press).

Roseberg, B. (1989) How do we balance public school choice? *Education Digest*, 55, 7–11.

Rosenbrock, H. (1977) The future of control, *Automatica*, 13, 389–92.

Rudduck, J. (1996) Going to 'the big school': the turbulence of transition, in: J. Rudduck, R. Chaplain & G. Wallace (Eds) *School Improvement: What Can Pupils Tell Us?* (London, David Fulton Publishers).

Ruddock, J., Chaplain, R. & Wallace, G. (Eds) (1996) *School Improvement: What Can Pupils Tell Us* (London, David Fulton).

Rudduck, J., Galton, M. & Gray, J. (1998) Lost in the maze of the new, *Times Education Supplement*, 20 November.

Rutter, M., Maughan, B., Mortimore, P. & Ouston, J. (1979, reprinted in 1995) *Fifteen Thousand Hours: Secondary Schools and Their Effects on Children* (London, Open Books). [Reprinted 1995: London, Paul Chapman].

Safstrom, C.A. (2005) The European knowledge society and the diminishing state control of education: the case of Sweden, *Journal of Education Policy*, 20(5), 583–93.

Saltman, R.B. & Von Otter, C. (1992) *Planned Markets and Public Competition* (Buckingham, Open University Press).

Sammons, P., Hillman, J. & Mortimore, P. (1995) *Key Characteristics of Effective Schools: A Review of School Effectiveness Research* (London, Institute of Education – OFSTED).

Savage, M., Barlow, J., Dickens, P. & Fielding, T. (1992) *Property, Bureaucracy and Culture* (London, Routledge).

Scalia, A. (1989) On making it look easy by doing it wrong, in: E.M. Gaffney (Ed.) *Private Schools and the Public Good* (Notre Dame, IN, Notre Dame University Press).

Scanlon, T.M. (1982) Contractualism and utilitarianism, in: A. Sen & B. Williams (Eds) *Utilitarianism and Beyond* (Cambridge, Cambridge University Press).

Schagen, S., Davies, D., Rudd, P. & Schagen, I. (2002) *The Impact of Specialist and Faith Schools on Performance (Local Government Association Research Report 28)* (Slough, NFER).

Schneider, M., Teske, P., Marschall, M., Mintrom, M. & Roch, C. (1997) Institutional arrangements and the creation of social capital: the effects of public school choice, *American Political Science Review*, 91(1), 82–93.

Schulz, G. (1993) Socioeconomic advantage and achievement motivation: important mediators of academic performance in minority children in urban schools, *Urban Review*, 25(3), 221–32.

Scitovsky, T. (1976) *The Joyless Economy* (Oxford, Oxford University Press).

Scott, W.R. (1995) *Institutions and Organizations* (Thousand Oaks, CA, Sage Publications).

Scott, A. (2000) Risk society or angst society? Two views of risk, consciousness and community, in: B. Adam, U. Beck and J. Van Loon (Eds) *The Risk Society and Beyond: Critical Issues for Social Theory* (London, Sage).

Sedden, T. (2001) Revisiting inequality and education; a reminder of class; a retrieval of politics; a rethinking of governance, *Melbourne Studies in Education*, 42(2), 131–44.

Segal, J. (1985) *Phantasy in Everyday Life* (Harmondsworth, Penguin).

Sen, A.K. (1971) Choice functions and revealed preference, *Review of Economic Studies*, 38 (115), 307–17.

—— (1973) Behaviour and the concept of preference, *Economica*, 40 (159), 241–59.

—— (1977, reprinted in 1982) Rational fools: A critique of the behavioural foundations of economic theory, *Philosophy and Public Affairs*, 6. [Reprinted in 1982 in: *Choice, Welfare and Measurement* (Oxford, Blackwell)].

—— (1981) *Poverty and Famines: An Essay on Entitlement and Deprivation* (Oxford, Clarendon).

—— (1982) Rights and agency, *Philosophy and Public Affairs*, 11, 3–39.

—— (1984a) *Resources, Values and Development* (Oxford, Basil Blackwell).

—— (1984b) The living standard, *Oxford Economic Papers*, 36, 74–90. http://oep.oxfordjournals.org/cgi/reprint/36/supp/74 [Accessed: 19/11/05].

—— (1985a) *Commodities and Capabilities* (Amsterdam, North-Holland).

—— (1985b) Well-being, agency and freedom: the Dewey lectures, *Journal of Philosophy*, 82(4), 169–221.

—— (1987) *The Standard of Living: The Tanner Lectures* (Cambridge, Cambridge University Press).

—— (1991) Welfare, preference and freedom, *Journal of Econometrics*, 50(1&2), 15–29.

—— (1992) *Inequality Reexamined* (Oxford, Clarendon Press).

—— (1993) Capability and well-being, in: M. Nussbaum & A. Sen (Eds) *The Quality of Life* (Oxford, Clarendon Press).

—— (1999) *Development as Freedom* (Oxford, Oxford University Press).

—— (2004) Capabilities, lists and public reason: continuing the conversation, *Feminist Economics*, 10(3), 77–80.

—— (2005) Human Rights and Capabilities, *Journal of Human Development*, 6(2), 151–66.

Sennett, R. (2003) *Respect: The Formation of Character in an Age of Inequality* (London, Penguin Books).

Shah, S. (2006) Educational leadership: an Islamic perspective, *British Educational Research Journal*, 32(3), 363–85.

Shaw, J. (1995) *Education, Gender and Anxiety* (London, Taylor & Francis).

Sheil, C. (Ed.) (2001) *Globalisation: Australian Impacts* (Sydney, University of New South Wales Press).

Sherman, J. (1983) Public finance of private schools: observations from abroad, in: T. James & H.M. Levin (Eds) *Public Dollars for Private Schools: The Case of Tuition Tax Credits* (Philadelphia, PA, Temple University).

Shleifer, A. (1998) State versus private ownership, *Journal of Economic Perspectives*, 12(4), 133–50.

Shulman, L. & Sykes, G. (Eds) (1983) Handbook of Teaching and Policy (New York, Longman).

Simkins, T. (1997) Autonomy and accountability, in: B. Fidler, S. Russell & T. Simkins (Eds) *Choices in Self-managing Schools* (London, Paul Chapman).

Skeggs, B. (1996) *Becoming Respectable: An Ethnography of White Working Class Women* (Cambridge, Polity Press).

—— (1997) Classifying practices: representations, capitals and recognitions, in: P. Mahony & C. Zmroczek (Eds) *Class Matters: Working Class Women's Perspectives on Social Class* (London, Taylor & Francis).

Smedley, D. (1995) Marketing secondary schools to parents some lessons from the research on parental choice, *Educational Management and Administration*, 23(2), 96–103.

Smith, A. (1776, reprinted in 1976) *An Inquiry into the Nature and the Causes of the Wealth of Nations* [Reprinted in: E. Cannon (Ed.) (1976) *The Wealth of Nations* (Chicago, University of Chicago Press)].

Smith, M.J. (1994) Understanding the 'politics of catch-up': the modernisation of the Labour Party, *Political Studies*, 42(4), 708–15. http://www.blackwell-synergy.com/doi/abs/10.1111/1467-856X.00010 [Accessed: 19/1/06].

Smrekar, C. & Goldring, E. (1999) *School Choice in Urban America: Magnet Schools and the Pursuit of Equity* (New York, Teachers College Press).

Soudien, C. (2005) Globalisation and Its Malcontents: In pursuit of the promise of education, *Asia Pacific Journal of Education*, 25(2), 145–58.

Stambach, A. (2001) Consumerism and gender in an era of school choice: a look at US charter schools, *Gender and Education*, 13(2), 199–216.

Stambach, A. & Becker, N.C. (2006) Finding the old in the new: on race and class in US charter school debates, *Race Ethnicity and Education*, 9(2), 159–82.

Standing, K. (1997) Scrimping, saving and schooling: lone mothers and choice in education, *Critical Social Policy*, 17(51), 79–99.

Stasz, C. (1998) Do employers need the skills they want? Evidence from technical work, *Journal of Education and Work*, 10(3), 205–23.

Stevens, M. (2001) *Kingdom of Children: Culture and Controversy in the Home-Schooling Movement* (New Jersey, Princeton University Press).

Stewart, F. & Deneulin, S. (2002) Amartya Sen's contribution to development thinking, *Studies in Comparative International Development*, 37(61), 61–70.

Storey, J. (1992) *Developments in the Management of Human Resources* (Oxford, Blackwell).

Sugden, R. (1993) Welfare, resources, and capabilities: a review of inequality re-examined by Amartya Sen, *Journal of Economic Literature*, XXXI, 1947–62.

Sumner, L.W. (1996) *Welfare, Happiness and Ethics* (Oxford, Clarendon Press).

Suzumura, K. (1983) *Rational Choice, Collective Decisions and Social Welfare* (Cambridge, Cambridge University Press).

Symonds, W. (2000) Edison's Chris Whittle: 'winners of this race are children', *Businessweek*, 7 February.

Szerszynski, B. & Urry, J. (2002) Cultures of cosmopolitanism, *The Sociological Review*, 50(4), 461–81.

Taylor, A. (2001a) 'Fellow travellers' and 'true believers': a case study of religion and politics in Alberta schools, *Journal of Education Policy*, 16(1), 15–37.

—— (2001b) *The Politics of Educational Reform in Alberta* (Toronto, University of Toronto Press).

—— (2003) Position and privilege: 'adding value' to the high school diploma, in: W. Antony & L. Samuelson (Eds) *Power and Resistance* (Halifax, Fernwood).

Taylor, C. (2001) Hierarchies and 'local' markets: the geography of the 'lived' market place in secondary education provision, *Journal of Education Policy*, 16(3), 197–214.

—— (2002) *Geography of the 'New' Education Market Place: Secondary School Choice in England and Wales* (Aldershot, Ashgate).

Taylor, R. (2002) *Britain's World of Work – Myths and Realities* (Swindon, Economic and Social Research Council).

Taylor, C. & Gorard, S. (2001) 'Local schools for local children' and the role of residence in segregation, *Environment and Planning A*, 30(10), 1829–52.

Taylor, A. & Woollard, L. (2003) The risky business of choosing a high school. *Journal of Education Policy*, 18(6), 617–35.

Teelken, C. (1998) Market mechanisms in education: a comparative study of school choice in the Netherlands, England and Scotland (Amsterdam, University of Amsterdam Press).

Teese, R. (2000) *Academic Success and Social Power: Examinations and Inequality* (Melbourne, Melbourne University Press).

Thevenot, B. (2003) Recycled school data yield different results, *Times-Picayune*, 26 March. [Cited in McElwee (2005: 22)].

Thomas, A. & Dennison, B. (1991) Parental or pupil choice – who really decides in urban schools? *Educational Management and Administration*, 19(4), 243–9.

Thomson, P. (2001) The sound of one hand grasping at straws? The struggle for equity and quality in public education, in: C. Bacchi & P. Nursey-Bray (Eds) *Left Directions. Is there a Third Way on Australian Politics?* (Perth, University of Western Australia Press).

Thrupp, M. (1998) Exploring the politics of blame: school inspection and its contestation in New Zealand and England, *Comparative Education*, 34, 195–208.

—— (1999) *Schools Making a Difference: Let's be Realistic!* (Buckingham, Open University Press).

Tikly, L. (1999) Postcolonialism and comparative education, in: C. Soudien & P. Kallaway (Eds) *Education, Equity and Transformation* (Dordrecht, Kluwer Academic Publishers).

Tolbert, P. & Zucker, L. (1996) The institutionalisation of institutional theory, in: S. Clegg, C. Handy & W. Nord (Eds) *Handbook of Organization Studies* (London, Sage).

Tomlinson, S. (1991) Home-school partnerships, in: S. Tomlinson & A. Ross (Eds) *Teachers and Parents* (London, Institute of Public Policy Research).

—— (1997) Diversity, choice and ethnicity: the effects of educational markets on ethnic minorities, *Oxford Review of Education*, 23(1), 63–76.

Tooley, J. (1992) The pink tank on the education reform act, *British Journal of Educational Studies*, 40(4), 335–49.

—— (1993) *A Market-Led Alternative for the Curriculum: Breaking the Code* (London, Institute of Education / Tufnell Press).

—— (1994) In defense of markets in educational provision, in: D. Bridges & T. McLaughlin (Eds) *Education and the Market Place* (London, Falmer Press).

—— (1996) *Education without the State* (London, IEA Education and Training Unit).

—— (2000) *Reclaiming Education* (London, Cassell).

Townsend, P. (1979) *Poverty in the United Kingdon* (Harmondsworth, Penguin).

Tuckman, H. (1998) Competition, commercialization, and the evolution of nonprofit Organizational Structures, *Journal of Policy Analysis and Management*, 17(2), 175–94.

Turner, B.S. (2002) Cosmopolitan virtue, globalisation and patriotism, *Theory, Culture & Society*, 19(1&2), 45–63.

Vandenberghe, V. (1999) Combining market and bureaucratic control in education: an answer to market and bureaucratic failure? *Comparative Education*, 35(3), 271–82.

Van Herwaarden, F.G. & Kapteyn, A. (1981) Empirical comparison of the shape of welfare functions, *European Economic Review*, 15, 261–86.

Van Praag, B.M.S. (1968) *Individual Welfare Functions and Consumer Behaviour* (Amsterdam, North-Holland).

—— (1977) The perception of welfare inequality, *European Economic Review*, 10(2), 189–207.

Van Praag, B.M.S., Goedhart, T. & Kapteyn, A. (1980) The poverty line: A pilot study in Europe, *Review of Economics and Statistics*, 62(3), 461–5. http://www.jstor.org/view/00346535/di953011/95p0329f/0 [Accessed: 12/9/06].

Van Praag, B.M.S., Hagenaars, A.J.M. & Van Weeren, H. (1982) Poverty in Europe, *Journal of Income and Wealth*, 28, 345–59.

Venn, C. (2002) Altered states: post enlightenment cosmopolitanism and trans-modern socialities, *Theory, Culture & Society*, 19(1–2), 65–80.

Vincent, C. (1996) *Parents and Teachers: Power and Participation* (London, Falmer Press).

—— (2000) *Including Parents? Education, Citizenship and Parental Agency*, (Buckingham, Open University Press).

—— (2001) Social class and parental agency, *Journal of Education Policy*, 16(4), 347–64.

Vincent, C. & Martin, J. (2000) School-based parents' groups: a 'politics of voice and representation'? *Journal of Education Policy*, 15(5), 459–80.

Wainwright, H. (2003) *Reclaim the State: Experiments in Popular Democracy* (London, Verso).

Walford, G. (1986) *Life in Public Schools* (London, Methuen).

—— (1996) Diversity and choice in school education: an alternative view, *Oxford Review of Education*, 22(2), 143–54.

—— (2001) Does the market ensure quality? *Westminster Studies in Education*, 24(1), 23–33.

Walker, M. (2006) Towards a capability-based theory of social justice for education policy-making, *Journal of Education Policy*, 21(2), 163–85.

Walkerdine, V. (1999) Violent Boys and precocious girls: regulating childhood at the end of the millennium, *Contemporary Issues in Early Childhood*, 1(1), 3–23.

Walkerdine, V., Walkerdine, H. & Melody, J. (2002) *Growing up Girl: Psychosocial Explorations of Gender and Class* (Basingstoke, Palgrave Macmillan).

Wallace, L. (2004) Freedom as progress: Laura Wallace interviews Nobel Prize-winner Amartya Sen, *Finance & Development*, September pp. 4–7.

Wallace, C. & Chandler, J. (1989) *Some Alternatives in Youth Training: Franchise and Corporatist Models* (Plymouth, Polytechnic South West).

Waslander, S. & Thrupp, M. (1995) Choice, competition and segregation: an empirical analysis of a New Zealand secondary school market, 1990–93, *Journal of Education Policy*, 10(1), 1–26.

Watts, M. & Bridges, D. (2006) The value of non-participation in higher education, *Journal of Education Policy*, 21(3), 267–90.

Weick, K.E. (1976) Educational organizations as loosely coupled systems, *Administrative Science Quarterly*, 21(1), 1–19.

Weiler, H.N. (1989) Why reforms fail: the politics of education in France and the Federal Republic of Germany, *Journal of Curriculum Studies*, 21(4), 433–48.

—— (1990) Curriculum reform and the legitimation of educational objectives: the case of the Federal Republic of Germany, *Oxford Review of Education*, 16(1), 15–27.

Wells, A. (1993) The sociology of school choice: why some win and others lose in the educational marketplace, in: E. Rasell & R. Rothstein (Eds) *School Choice: Examining the Evidence* (Washington, DC, Economic Policy Institute).

—— (2000) *In Search of Uncommon Schools: Charter School Reform in Historical Perspective (Part 3) Charter Schools as Uncommon Schools*. Available online at: http://www.tcrecord.org [Accessed: 18/2/2004].

Wells, A., Lopez, A., Scott, J. & Jellison Holme, J. (1999) Charter schools as post-modern paradox: rethinking social stratification in an age of deregulated choice, *Harvard Educational Review*, 69(2), 172–204.

West, A. (2006) School choice, equity and social justice: the case for more control, *British Journal of Education Studies*, 54(1), 15–33.

West, M. (2001) Reforming teachers' pay: crossing the threshold, in: M. Fielding (Ed.) *Taking Education Really Seriously: Four Years' Hard Labour* (London, Routledge).

West, A., Hind, A. & Pennell, H. (2004) School admissions and 'selection' in comprehensive schools: policy and practice, *Oxford Review of Education*, 30(3), 347–69.

West, A. & Ingram, D. (2001) Making school admissions fairer? Quasi-regulation under New Labour, *Educational Management and Administration*, 29(4), 459–73.

West, A., Noden, P., Edge, A., David, M. & Davies, J. (1998) Choices and expectations at primary and secondary stages in the state and private sectors, *Educational Studies*, 24(1), 45–60.

West, A., Noden, P., Kleinman, M. & Whitehead, C. (2000) *Examining the Impact of the Specialist Schools Programme* (London, DfEE).

West, A. & Pennell, H. (2000) Publishing school examination results in England: incentives and consequences, *Educational Studies*, 26(4), 423–35.

West, A. & Pennell, H. (2003) *Underachievement in Schools* (London, Routledge-Falmer).

West, A., Pennell, H. & Noden, P. (1998) School admissions: increasing equity, accountability and transparency, *British Journal of Educational Studies*, 46(2), 188–200.

White, P., Gorard, S., Fitz, J. & Taylor, C. (2001) Regional and local differences in admission arrangements for schools, *Oxford Review of Education*, 27(3), 317–37.

Whitfield, D. (2001) *Public Services or Corporate Welfare, Rethinking the Nation State in the Global Economy* (London, Pluto).

Whitty, G. (1990) The new right and the national curriculum: state control or market forces? in: M. Flude & M. Hammer (Eds) *The Education Reform Act, 1988: Its Origins and Implications* (London, Falmer Press).

—— (1997) Creating quasi-markets in education: a review of recent research on parental choice and school autonomy in three countries, *Review of Research in Education*, 22, 3–47. [Edited by Michael Apple]

Whitty, G. & Edwards, T. (1998) School choice policies in England and the United States: an exploration of their origins and significance, *Comparative Education*, 34(2), 211–27.

Whitty, G., Power, S. & Halpin, D. (1998) *Devolution and Choice in Education: The School, the State and the Market* (Buckingham, Open University Press).

Willis, P. (1977) *Learning to Labour: How Working-Class Kids Get Working-Class Jobs* (Farnborough, UK, Saxon House).

Willms, D. (1992) *Monitoring School Performance: A Guide for Educators* (London, Falmer Press).

—— (1996) School choice and community segregation: findings from Scotland, in: A. Kerckhoff (Ed.) *Generating Social Stratification: Towards a New Research Agenda* (Oxford, Westview Press).

Willms, J. & Echols, F. (1992) Alert and inert clients: the Scottish experience of parental choice of schools, *Economics of Education Review*, 11(4), 339–50.

Wilson, J.Q. (1996) Against homosexual marriage, *Commentary*, 101, 34–9.

Witte, J.F. (1990) *Choice in American Education* (Charleston, WV, Appalchia Educational Laboratory).

—— (1996) School choice and student performance, in: H.F. Ladd (Ed.) *Holding Schools Accountable: Performance-Based Reform in Education* (Washington, DC, Brookings).

—— (1999) The Milwaukee voucher experiment: the good, the bad, and the ugly, *Phi Delta Kappan*, 81(1), 59–64.

Witte, J.F. & Thorn, C. (1996) Who chooses voucher and interdistrict choice programs in Milwaukee, *American Journal of Education*, 104(3), 186–217.

Wolf, A. (2002) *Does Education Matter? Myths about Education and Economic Growth* (London, Penguin).

Woodhead, C. (2002) *Class War* (London, Little Brown).

Woods, P. (1990) *The Happiest Days: How Pupils Cope with School* (London, Falmer Press).

—— (1992) Empowerment through choice? Towards and understanding of parental choice and school responsiveness, *Educational Management and Administration*, 20(4), 204–11.

—— (1996) Choice, class and effectiveness, *School Effectiveness and School Improvement*, 7(4), 324–41.

Woods, P., Bagley, C. & Glatter, R. (1997) *The Public Market in England: School Responsiveness in a Competitive Climate. Occasional Research Paper 1* (School of Education, Open University).

Woods, P.A., Bagley, C. & Glatter, R. (1998) *School Choice and Competition: Markets in the Public Interest?* (London, Routledge).

Woods, P., Jeffrey, B. & Troman, G. (2001) The impact of New Labour's educational policy on primary schools, in: M. Fielding (Ed.) *Taking Education Really Seriously: Four Years Hard Labour* (London, RoutledgeFalmer).

Woods, G. & Woods, P. (2005) At the hard edge of change: views from secondary head teachers on a public-private partnership, *Journal of Education Policy*, 20(1), 23–38.

World Trade Organisation (1994) *General Agreement on Trade in Services* (Geneva, WTO).

Worpole, K. (1999) Driving forces, *The Guardian*, 8 June.

Wringe, C. (1994) Markets, values and education, in: D. Bridges & T.H. McLaughlin (Eds) *Education and the Market Place* (London, Falmer Press).

Wyckoff, J.H. (1984) The non-excludable publicness of primary and secondary public education, *Journal of Public Economics*, 24(3), 331–51.

Wynne, D. (1998) *Leisure, Lifestyle and the New Middle Class* (London, Routledge).

Yaari, M.E. & Bar-Hillel, M. (1984) On dividing justly, *Social Choice and Welfare*, 1(1), 1–24.

Yeatman, A. (1993) Corporate managerialism and the shift from the welfare to the competition state, *Discourse*, 13(2), 10–17.

Youdell, D. (2004) Engineering school markets, constituting schools and subjectivating students: the bureaucratic, institutional and classroom dimensions of educational triage, *Journal of Education Policy*, 19(4), 407–31.

Youngman, B. (Ed.) (1986) *Mid-School Transfer: Problems and Proposals* (Slough, National Foundation for Educational Research).

Further reading

Abell, P. (1995) The new institutionalism and rational choice theory, in: W.R. Scott & S. Christnesne (Eds) *The Institutional Construction of Organizations* (Thousand Oaks, CA, Sage Publications).

Adnett, N. (2003) Reforming teachers' pay: incentive payments, collegiate ethos and UK policy, *Cambridge Journal of Economics*, 27(1), 145–57.

—— (2004) Private-sector provision of schooling: an economic assessment, *Comparative Education*, 40(3), 385–99.

Adnett, N., Bougheas, S. & Davies, P. (2002) Market-based reforms of public schooling: some unpleasant dynamics, *Economics of Education Review*, 21(4), 323–30.

Adnett, N. & Davies, P. (2002) *Markets for Schooling: An Economic Analysis* (London, Routledge).

Aggleton, P. & Whitty, G. (1985) Rebels without a cause? Socialisation and subcultural style among the children of the new middle-classes, *Sociology of Education*, 58(1), 60–72.

Alkire, S. & Black, R. (1997) A practical reasoning theory of development ethics: furthering the capabilities approach, *Journal of International Development*, 9(2), 263–79.

Alwin, D.F. (1976). Socioeconomic background, colleges, and post-collegiate achievements, in: W. Sewell, R. Hauser & D. Featherman (Eds) *Schooling and Achievement in American Society*. (New York, Academic Press).

Alwin, D.F. & Otto, L.B. (1977) High school context effects on aspirations, *Sociology of Education*, 50(4), 259–73.

Anyon, J. (1980) Social class and the hidden curriculum of work, *Journal of Education*, 162(2), 67–92.

—— (1981) Social class and school knowledge, *Curriculum Inquiry*, 11(1), 3–42.

Appleton, S., Sives, A. & Morgan, W.J. (2006) The impact of international teacher migration on schooling in developing countries – the case of Southern Africa, *Globalisation, Societies and Education*, 4(1), 121–42.

Arnot, M., Ruddock, J. & Gray, J. (1998) *Recent Research on Gender and Educational Performance* (London, The Stationery Office).

Atkinson, A.B. (1983) *Social Justice and Public Policy* (Cambridge, MA, MIT Press).

Audit Commission (1996) *Trading Places: The Supply and Allocation of School Places* (London, The Audit Commission).

Avis, J., Bloomer, M., Esland, G., Gleeson, D. & Hodkinson, P. (1996) *Knowledge and Nationhood* (London, Cassell).

Ball, S.J. (1993) Education markets, choice and social class: the market as a class strategy in the UK and the USA, *British Journal of Sociology of Education*, 14(1), 3–19.

—— (1997) Performativity and fragmentation in 'postmodern schooling', in: J. Carter (Ed.) *Postmodernity and the Fragmentation of Welfare: A Contemporary Social Policy* (London, Routledge).

Ball, S.J., Bowe, R. & Gewirtz, S. (1996) Circuits of schooling: a sociological explanation or parental choice in social class contexts, *Sociological Review*, 43(1), 52–78.

Beck, U. (1992) *Risk Society: Towards A New Modernity* (Newbury Park, CA, Sage).

Bekhradnia, B. (2003) *Widening Participation and Fair Access: An Overview of the Evidence*. (London, Higher Education Policy Institute).

Bekhradnia, B. & Thompson, J. (2002) *Who Does Best at University?* (London, HEFCE).

Benn, C. & Chitty, C. (1996) *Thirty Years On: Is Comprehensive Education Alive and Well or Struggling to Survive?* (London, David Fulton).

Berlin, I. (1958, reprinted in 1982) *Two Concepts of Liberty* (Oxford, Clarendon Press). [Originally given as an inaugural lecture in Oxford. Reprinted in: I. Berlin (1982) *Four Essays on Liberty* (Oxford, Oxford University Press)].

Betts, J.R. (1996) Is there a link between school inputs and earnings? Fresh scrutiny of an old literature, in: G. Burtless (Ed.) *Does Money Matter? The Effect of School Resources on Student Achievement and Adult Success* (Washington, DC, Brookings Institution).

Blackorby, C., Donaldson, D. & Weymark, J. (1984) Social choice with interpersonal utility comparisons: a diagrammatic introduction, *International Economic Review*, 25(2), 327–56.

Blair, J.P. & Staley, S. (1995) Quality competition and public schools: further evidence. *Economics of Education Review*, 14(2), 193–8.

Borland, M.V. & Howsen, R.M. (1992) Student academic achievement and the degree of market concentration in education, *Economics of Education Review*, 11(1), 31–9.

Bowe, R. & Ball, S.J. with Gold, A. (1992) *Reforming Education and Changing Schools: Case Studies in Policy Sociology* (London, Routledge).

Boyd, L.W. & Walberg, H.J. (Eds) (1990) *Choice in Education: Potential and Problems* (Berkeley, CA, McCutchan Publishing).

Bradley, S. & Taylor, J. (2002) The effect of the quasi-market on the efficiency of the secondary school sector, *Bulletin of Economic Research*, 54(3), 295–314.

Brighouse, H. (2000) *School Choice and Social Justice* (Oxford, Oxford University Press).

Bredo, O., Foersom, T. & Laursen, P.F. (1993) Students' choice: a model. *Higher Education Review*, 26(1), 64–72.

British Humanist Association (2001) *Religious Schools: The Case Against* (London, British Humanist Association).

Bryman, A. (1992) *Charisma and Leadership in Organizations* (London, Sage).

Burns, J.M. (1978) *Leadership* (New York, Harper and Row).

Burton, N. & Brundrett, M. (2000) The first year of Beacon School status: maintaining excellence and sharing success, *School Leadership & Management*, 20(4), 489–98.

Butler, T. & Savage, M. (1995) *Social Change and the Middle Classes* (London, UCL Press).

Caire, K.M. (2002) The truth about vouchers, *Educational Leadership*, 59(7), 38–42.

Carnoy, M. (2000) School choice? Or is it privatization? *Educational Researcher*, 29(7), 15–20.

Chitty, C. (1989) *Towards a New Education System: The Victory of the New Right?* (London, Falmer).

Clark, D.A. & Qizilbash, M. (2005) *Core Poverty, Basic Capabilities and Vagueness: An Application to the South African Context*, GPRG-WPS-026 (Manchester, Global Poverty Research Group). http://www.gprg.org/pubs/workingpapers/pdfs/gprg-wps-026.pdf [Accessed: 17/01/07].

Clune, W. & White, J. (1990) *Choice and Control in American Education* (London, Falmer).

Cohn, E. (1997) *Market Approaches to Education* (Oxford, Pergamon).

Colclough, C. (Ed.) (1997) *Marketizing Education and Health in Developing Countries: Miracle or Mirage?* (Clarendon Press, Oxford).

Colclough, C. & Manor, J. (Eds) (1991) *States or Markets? Neo-Liberalism and the Development Policy Debate* (Oxford, Clarendon Press).

Commission for Racial Equality (1990) *Schools of Faith: Religious Schools in a Multicultural Society* (London, Commission for Racial Equality).

Corbridge, S. (2002) Development as freedom: the spaces of Amartya Sen, *Progress in Development Studies*, 2(3), 183–217.

Cuban, L. & Shipps, D. (Eds) (2000) *Reconstructing the Common Good in Education. Coping with Intractable American dilemmas* (Stanford, Stanford University Press).

Dale, R. (1997) Educational markets and school choice, *British Journal of Sociology of Education*, 18(3), 451–68.

—— (1997) The state and the governance of education: an analysis of the restructuring of the state-education relationship, in: A.H. Halsey, H. Lauder, P. Brown & A.S. Wells, (Eds) *Education: Culture, Economy, Society* (Oxford, Oxford University Press).

David, M.E. (1993) *Parents, Gender and Education Reform* (Cambridge, MA, Polity Press).

—— (1997) Diversity, choice and gender, *Oxford Review of Education*, 23(1), 77–87.

Davies, H. (2002) *A Review of Enterprise and the Economy in Education* (London, DTI).

Davies, P. & Adnett, N. (1999) Quasi-market reforms and vocational schooling in England, *Journal of Education and Work*, 12(2), 139–54.

Dearing Report (1996) *Review of Qualifications for 16 to 19 year olds* (Hayes, Middlesex, SCAA).

Deaton, A. & Muellbauer, J. (1980) *Economics and Consumer Behaviour* (Cambridge, Cambridge University Press).

Department for Education & Employment, (2003) *Youth Cohort Study: Activities and Experiences of 16 Year Olds: England and Wales 2002* (London, DfEE)

Department for Education & Skills (2003) *Every Child Matters* (Nottingham, DfES).

Department of Trade & Industry (1998) *Our Competitive Future: Building the Knowledge Driven Economy* (London, HMSO).

Demaine, J. (Ed.) (1999) *Education Policy and Contemporary Politics* (London, Macmillan).

Desai, M. (1995) Poverty and capability: towards an empirically implementable measure, in: M.Desai *The Selected Essays of Meghnad Desai: Poverty, Famine and Economic Development* (Aldershot, Edward Elgar).

Devine, F. (2004) *Class Practices: How Parents Help their Children to Get Good Jobs* (Cambridge, Cambridge University Press).

Edwards, T. & Whitty, G. (1997) Specialisation and selection in secondary education, *Oxford Review of Education*, 23(1), 5–15.

Evans, W.N., Oates, W.E. & Schwab, R.M. (1992) Measuring peer group effects: a study of teenage behavior, *Journal of Political Economy*, 100(5), 966–91. http://www.jstor.org/view/00223808/di980598/98p00546/0 [Accessed: 13/11/06].

Fields, G.S. (1980) *Poverty, Inequality and Development* (Cambridge, Cambridge University Press).

Fitz, J. & Beers, B. (2002) Education management organisation and the privatisation of public education: a cross-national comparison of the USA and Britain, *Comparative Education*, 38(2), 137–54.

Fowler, F.C. (2003) School choice: silver bullet, social threat or sound policy? *Educational Researcher*, March, 33–9.

Fox, I. (1985) *Private Schools and Public Issues: The Parents' View.* (London, Macmillan).

Franklin, J. (Ed.) (1998) *The Politics of Risk Society* (Cambridge, Polity Press).

Fuller, B. & Elmore, R. (Eds) (1996) *Who Chooses? Who Loses?* (New York, Teachers College Press).

Gasper, D. (1997) Sen's capability approach and Nussbaum's capabilities ethic, *Journal of International Development*, 9(2), 281–302.

Gewirtz, S. (1997) Post-welfarism and the reconstruction of teachers' work in the UK, *Journal of Education Policy*, 12(4), 217–31.

—— (2002) Can managerial means be harnessed to social democratic ends? Critical reflections on New Labour's 'third way' policies for schooling in England, *Prospero: A Journal for New Thinking in Philosophy for Education*, 8(3), 36–47.

Giddens, A. (1994) *Beyond Left and Right* (Stanford, Stanford University Press).

Glatter, R., Woods, P.A. & Bagley, C. (1997) *Choice and Diversity in Schooling: Perspective and Prospects* (London, Routledge).

Gleeson, D. (1990) *The Paradox of Training: Making Progress Out of Crisis* (Milton Keynes, Open University Press).

Glennerster, H. (1991) Quasi-markets for education? *Economic Journal*, 101(408), 1268–76.

Goldring, E. & Hausman, C. (1999) Reasons for parental choice of urban schools, *Journal of Education Policy*, 14(5), 469–90.

Gorard, S., Fitz, J. & Taylor, C. (2001) School choice impacts: what we know? *Educational Researcher*, 30(7), 18–23.

Grace, G. (2002) *Catholic Schools: Mission, Markets and Morality* (London, Routledge).

Green, A. & Vyronides, M. (2005) Ideological tensions in the educational choice practices of modern Green Cypriot parents: the role of social capital, *British Journal of Sociology of Education*, 26(3), 327–42.

Green, D. & Shapiro, I. (1994) Pathologies of Rational Choice Theory (New Haven, CT, Yale University Press).

Halsey, A.H., Lauder, H., Brown, P., & Wells, A.S. (Eds) (1998) *Education: Culture, Economy, Society* (Oxford, Oxford University Press).

Hanushek, E.A. (1986) The economics of schooling: production and efficiency in public schools, *Journal of Economic Literature*, 24(3), 1141–77.

Hanushek, E.A., Rivkin, S.G. & Taylor, L.L. (1994) Aggregation and the estimated effects of school resources, *Review of Economics and Statistics*, 78(4), 611–27.

Haq, M. ul (1995) *Reflections on Human Development* (Oxford, Oxford University Press).

Hare, R.M. (1976) Ethical theory and utilitarianism, in: H.D. Lewis (Ed.) *Contemporary British Philosophy* (London, Allen & Unwin).

Hargreaves, D. (1996) Diversity and choice in school education: a modified libertarian approach, *Oxford Review of Education*, 22(2), 131–41.

Hatcher, R. (2001) Getting down to business: schooling in the globalised economy, *Education and Social Justice*, 3(2), 45–59.

Hatcher, R. & Jones, K. (2005) Researching resistance: campaigns against academies in England, *British Journal of Education Studies*, 54(3), 329–51.

Hawthorn, G. (Ed.) (1987) *The Standard of Living* (Cambridge, Cambridge University Press).

Hayes, M.A. & Gearon, L. (Eds) (2002) *Contemporary Catholic Education* (Leominster, Gracewing).

Held, D. (1995) *Democracy and the Global Order: from modern state to cosmopolitan governance* (Cambridge, Cambridge University Press).

Held, D. & McGrew, A. (2000) *The Global Transformations Reader: An Introduction to the Globalization Debate* (Cambridge, Polity Press).

Herbert, D. & Thomas, C. (1998) School performance, league tables and social geography, *Applied Geography*, 18(3), 199–223.

Hindness, B. (1987) *Freedom, Equality and the Market: Arguments on Social Policy* (London, Tavistock).

Hirst, P. (2000) Democracy and governance, in: J. Pierre (Ed.) *Debating Governance* (Oxford, Oxford University Press).

—— (2000) Globalization, the nation state and political theory, in: N.O'Sullivan (Ed.) *Political theory in transition* (London, Routledge).

Hodkinson, P., Sparkes, A.C. & Hodkinson, H. (1996) *Triumphs and Tears – Young People, Markets and the Transition from School to Work* (London, David Fulton).

Hyland, T. & Musson, D. (2001) Unpacking the new deal for young people: promise and problems, *Educational Studies*, 27(1), 5–67.

James, E. (1993) Why do different countries choose a different public-private mix of educational services? *Journal of Human Resources*, 28(3), 571–92. http://www.jstor.org/view/0022166x/ap010111/01a00080/0 [Accessed: 2/4/06].

Jessop, B. (2002) *The Future of the Capitalist State* (Cambridge, Polity).

Judge, H. (Ed.) (2001) *The Oxford Review of Education: Special Edition: The State, Schools and Religion*, 27(4), 461–592.

—— (2002) *Faith-Based Schools and the State: Catholics in America, France and England* (Oxford, Symposium).

Kakwani, N.C. (1980) *Income Inequality and Poverty* (New York, Oxford University Press).

Keep, E. (1997) 'There's no such thing as society': some problems with an individual approach to creating a learning society, *Journal of Educational Policy*, 12(6), 457–71.

Keep, E. & Mayhew, K. (1999) The assessment: knowledge, skills and competitiveness, *Oxford Review of Economic Policy*, 15(1), 1–15.

Kelly, A. (1988) Option choice for boys and girls, *Research in Science and Technological Education*, 6(1), 5–23.

Kemshall, H. (2002) *Risk, Social Policy and Welfare* (Buckingham, Open University Press).

Kirzner, I. (1997) *How Markets Work: Disequilibrium, Entrepreneurship and Discovery* (London, Institute of Economic Affairs).

Labour Party (2001) *Realising the Talent of All* (London, Labour Party).

Lamdin, D. & Mintrom, M. (1997) School choice in theory and practice: taking stock and looking ahead. *Education Economics*, 5(3), 211–44.

Langan, M. (Ed.) (1998) *Welfare: Needs, Rights and Risks* (London, Routledge).

Lawn, M. (2001) Borderless education: imagining a European education space in a time of brands and networks, *Discourse*, 22(2), 173–84.

Levacic, R. & Hardman, J. (1999) The performance of grant-maintained schools in England: an experiment in autonomy, *Journal of Education Policy*, 14(2), 185–212.

Levin, H.M. (1997) Educational vouchers: effectiveness, choice and costs, *Journal of Policy Analysis and Management*, 17(3), 373–92.

Lightfoot, S.L. (1975) Families and schools: creative conflict or negative dissonance? *Journal of Research and Development in Education*, 9(1), 34–43.

Lloyd, C. & Payne, J. (2003) The political economy of skill and the limits of educational policy, *Journal of Education Policy*, 18(1), 85–107.

Lockwood, D. (1995) Marking out the middle-class(es), in: T. Butler & M. Savage (Eds) *Social Change and the Middle Classes* (London, University College Press).

Lupton, D. (Ed.) (1999) *Risk and Sociocultural Theory: New Directions and perspectives* (Cambridge, Cambridge University Press).

MacCormick, N. (1999) *Questioning Sovereignty* (Oxford, Clarendon).

Majumdar, M. & Subramanian, S. (2001) Capability failure and group disparities: some evidence from India from the 1980s, *Journal of Development Studies*, 37(5), 104–40.

Marginson, S. (1997) *Markets in Education* (St Leonards, NSW, Allen & Unwin).

Martin, J. & Vincent, C. (1999) Parental voice: an exploration, *International Studies in Sociology of Education*, 9(2), 231–52.

Mayston, D.J. (1996) Educational attainment and resource use: mystery or economic misspecification? *Education Economics*, 4(2), 127–42.

McEwan, P. (2000) The potential impact of large scale voucher programs, *Review of Educational Research*, 70(2), 103–49.

McVicar, M. (1996) Education, in: D. Farnham & S. Horton (Eds) *Managing the New Public Services* (London, Macmillan).

Murray, S.E., Evans, W.N. & Schwab, R.M. (1998) Education-finance reform and the distribution of education resources. *American Economic Review*, 88(4), 789–812.

Neave, G. (1991) *Prometheus Bound: The Changing Relationship between Government and Higher Education in Western Europe* (Oxford, Pergamon).

Nisbet, J.D. & Entwistle, N.J. (1969) *The Transition To Secondary School* (London, London University Press).

Nussbaum, M. (2000) *Women and Human Development: The Capabilities Approach* (Cambridge, Cambridge University Press).

Nussbaum, M.C. (2003) Capabilities as fundamental entitlement: Sen and social justice, *Feminist Economics*, 9(2–3), 33–59.

Office for Standards in Education (OFSTED) (2003) *Access and Attainment in Deprived Urban Areas* (London, The Stationery Office).

O'Malley, P. (1996) Risk and responsibility, in: A. Barry, T. Osborne & N. Rose (Eds) *Foucault and Political Reason: Liberalism, Neo-Liberalism and Rationalities of Government*, (London, UCL Press).

Osmani, S.R. (1982) *Economic Inequality and Group Welfare* (Oxford, Clarendon).

Parker-Jenkins, M., Hartas, D. & Irving, B. (2004) *In Good Faith: Schools, Religion and Public Funding* (Aldershot, Ashgate).

Patrinos, H.A. (2000) Market forces in education, *European Journal of Education*, 35(1), 53–64.

Phillips, R. & Furlong, J. (Eds) (2001) *Education, Reform and the State: Twenty-Five years of politics, policy and practice* (London, RoutledgeFalmer).

Pierson, C. (1998) The new governance of education: the Conservatives and education 1988–1997, *Oxford Review of Education*, 24(1), 131–42.

Pollitt, C. & Bouckaert, G. (2000) *Public Management Reform: A Comparative Analysis* (Oxford: Oxford University Press).

Powell, M. (Ed.) (1999) *New Labour, New Welfare State? The 'Third Way' in British Social Policy* (Bristol, Policy Press).

Power, S., Edwards, T., Whitty, G. & Wigfall, V. (2002) *Education and the Middle Class* (London, RoutledgeFalmer).

Power, S. & Gewirtz, S. (2001) Reading education action zones, *Journal of Education Policy*, 16(1), 39–51.

Rasell, E. & Rothstein, R. (Eds) (1993) *School Choice: Examining the Evidence* (Washington, DC, Economic Policy Institute).

Rasell, E. & Swift, R. (2003) *How Not to be a Hypocrite: School Choice for the Morally Perplexed* (London, RoutledgeFalmer).

Reay, D. (1998) Setting the agenda: the growing impact of market forces in pupil grouping in British secondary schools, *Journal of Curriculum Studies*, 30(5), 545–58.

—— (2001) Finding or losing yourself? Working class relationships to education, *Journal of Education Policy*, 16(4), 333–46.

Reich, R. (2002) *Bridging Liberalism and Multiculturalism in American Education* (Chicago, University of Chicago Press).

Robertson, S. & Dale, R. (2000) Competitive contractualism: a new social settlement in New Zealand education, in: D. Coulby, R. Cowan & C. Jones (Eds) *World Yearbook 2000: Education in Transition* (London, Kogan Page).

Robertson, D. & Symons, J. (2003) Do peer groups matter? Peer group versus schooling effects on academic attainment, *Economica*, 70(1), 31–53.

Rodger, J. (2000) *From a Welfare State to a Welfare Society: the Changing Context of Social Policy in a Postmodern Era* (Basingstoke, Macmillan).

Rowan, B. (1982) Organizational structure and the institutional environment: the case of public schools, *Administrative Science Quarterly*, 27, 259–79.

Saito, M. (2003) Amartya Sen's capability approach to education: a critical exploration, *Journal of Philosophy of Education*, 37(1), 17–33.

Scheerens, J., & Bosker, R.J. (1997) *The Foundations of Educational Effectiveness* (Oxford, Elsevier Science).

Scheerens, J. & Creemers, B.P.M. (1989) Conceptualizing school effectiveness, *International Journal of Educational Research*, 13, 691–706.

Scott, P. (Ed.) (1998) *The Globalization of Higher Education* (Buckingham, Open University Press).

Sen, A. (1979) The welfare basis of real income comparisons: a survey, *Journal of Economic Literature*, 17(1), 1–45. http://www.jstor.org/view/00220515/dm990795/99p0169w/0?frame=noframe&userID=984e7348@soton.ac.uk/01cce4405a00501b741a7&dpi=3&config=jstor [Accessed: 8/12/06].

Sen, A. (1979) Utilitarianism and welfarism, *Journal of Philosophy*, 76(9), 463–89. http://www.jstor.org/view/0022362x/di973159/97p0167c/0 [Accessed: 4/3/06].

Sen, A. (1980) Equality of what, in: S. McMurrin (Ed.) *The Tanner Lectures on Human Value* (Salt Lake City, Utah, University of Utah Press).

Sen, A. (1983) Liberty and social choice, *The Journal of Philosophy*, 80(1), 5–28.

Sen, A. (1988) *On Ethics and Economics* (Oxford, Blackwell).

Schagen, S. & Schagen, I. (2002) Faith schools and specialist schools – the way to raise standards? *Education Journal*, 62, 30–2.

Shokraii, N.H. & Youseff, S.E. (1998) *School Choice Programs: What's Happening in the States* (Washington, DC, The Heritage Foundation).

Shokraii Rees, N. (2000) *School Choice 2000: What's Happening in the States* (Washington, DC, The Heritage Foundation).

Smith, P. (1995) Performance indicators and control in the public sector, in: A. Berry, J. Broadbent & D. Otley (Eds) *Management Control: Theories, Issues and Practices* (London, Macmillan).

Smithers, A. (2001) Education policy, in: A. Seldon (Ed.) *The Blair Effect* (London, Little Brown).

Stevens, M. (1999) Human capital theory and UK vocational training policy, *Oxford Review of Economic Policy*, 15(1), 16–32.

Stewart, F. (2001) Women and human development: the capabilities approach by Martha C. Nussbaum, *Journal of International Development*, 13(8), 1191–2.

Stillman, A. (1990) Legislating for choice, in M. Flude and M. Hammer (Eds) *The Education Reform Act, 1988* (London, Falmer Press).

Taylor, C. (1979) What's wrong with negative liberty, in: A. Ryan (Ed.) *The Idea of Freedom* (Oxford, Oxford University Press).

Teddlie, C. & Reynolds, D. (2000) *The International Handbook of School Effectiveness Research* (London, Falmer Press).

Tymms, P. (1995) The long-term impact of schooling, *Evaluation and Research in Education*, 9(2), 99–108.

Valins, O., Kosmin, B. & Goldberg, J. (2001) *The Future of Jewish Schooling in the United Kingdom* (London, Institute for Jewish Policy Research).

Van Damme, J., De Fraine, B., Van Landeghem, G., Opdenakker, M.C., & Onghena, P. (2002) A new study on educational effectiveness in secondary schools in Flanders: an introduction, *School Effectiveness and School Improvement*, 13(4), 383–97.

Vickers, J. (1995) Concepts of competition, *Oxford Economic Papers*, 47(1), 1–23. http://oep.oxfordjournals.org/cgi/reprint/47/1/1?ck=nck [Accessed: 19/5/06].

Walford, G. (1995) *Educational Politics: Pressure Groups and Faith-Based Schools* (Aldershot, Avebury).

—— (Ed.) (1996) School choice and the quasi-market, *Oxford Studies in Comparative Education*, 6(1), 49–62.

Wallace, M. (1998) A counter-policy to subvert education reform? Collaboration among schools and colleges in a competitive climate, *British Educational Research Journal*, 24(2), 195–215.

Waters, M. (1995) *Globalization* (London, Routledge).

Webster, D. & Parsons, K. (1999) British Labour Party policy on educational selection 1996–8: a sociological analysis, *Journal of Education Policy*, 14(5), 547–59.

West, A. (1994) Choosing schools – the consumer's perspectives, in: M.J. Halstead (Ed.) *Parental Choice and Education: Principles, Policy and Practice* (London, Kegan Paul).

West, A. & Pennell, H. (1997) Educational reform and school choice in England and Wales, *Education Economics*, 5(3), 285–306.

Whitty, G., Edwards, T. & Gewirtz, S. (1993) *Specialisation and Choice in Urban Education: The City Technology College Experiment* (London, Routledge).

Witte, J. (2000) *The Market Approach to Education* (Princeton, NJ, Princeton University Press).

Woods, P. (1993) Responding to the consumer: parental choice and school effectiveness, *School Effectiveness and School Improvement*, 4(3), 205–29.

Woods, P.A. (2000) Varieties and themes in producer engagement: structure and agency in the schools public-market, *British Journal of Sociology of Education*, 21(2), 219–42.

Woods, P.A. & Bagley, C. (1996) Market elements in a public service: an analytical model for studying educational policy, *Journal of Education Policy*, 11(6), 641–53.

Zanzig, B.R. (1997) Measuring the impact of competition in local government education markets on the cognitive achievements of students, *Economics of Education Review*, 16(4), 431–41.

Index

accountability, 12, 58, 60, 73, 77,
    86, 98
achievement (of pupils and schools),
    see attainment
added value, 102, 103, 117
admissions, 17, 20, 28, 31, 33–6, 110,
    129, 132
    adjudication on / disputes about,
        33–4, 131
    and banding (by local authorities
        and schools), 36
    to boarding schools, 33
    and ceilings on numbers, 125,
        129, 130
    Codes of Practice on (UK), 33, 131
    criteria used for, 33, 125,
        131, 132
    and the curriculum, 114
    and examinations, 104
    to faith schools, 33
    and funding, 119, 131
    and headteachers, 129
    information on, 33
    and interviewing, 33–4
    and marketisation, 101
    open, 8, 100, 111, 130, 174
    and religion, 31
    and school closures, 124
    and school income, 75
    and selection by mortgage, 28, 110,
        130, 132
    of siblings, 34
    and surplus places, 123, 125
    and transport, 125
    and transition, 125
    for volatile intakes, 124
advantage
    evaluation of, 167–9
    as a freedom, 148
    and opportunity, 147, 167
    and well-being, 147–8
African-American, 13, 30, 46
Afro-Caribbean (in UK), 17

agency, 56–65
    societal, 139
    of state towards employers, 137
    of teachers, 78
agenda,
    global, 53, 55
    of business in schools, 85
    choice, 47
    cultural, 78
    of leadership, 77
aggregation
    and evaluation, 163–9
    of rankings, 166
ancillary services, 55
appearance and demeanour
    (of pupils), 43, 51
apprenticeships, 67
Arrow Impossibility theorem, 164–6
asset-mapping, 170–8
Assisted Places Scheme (UK), 7,
    26, 60
attainment, 66, 100, 106, 107, 133,
    156, 157, 168, 174 (*see also
    under* pupils)
    and admissions, 34
    in Charter schools, 20
    and commodity characteristics, 155
    and competition, 102, 112, 113
    and Education Reform Act (1988)
        (UK), 107–9
    and functionings, 149
    and social class, 28, 113
    system-wide, 113, 172
    and targets, 117
    and teacher effort, 21
    and quasi-markets, 112
    and utility, 146
    and well-being, 147
Australia, 71, 103, (and GATS) 81

benchmarking, 104, 122
boarding schools, *see under* schools
bullying, 44, 47, 48, 50, 160

Canada, 11, 40–1, 88, 116
    Catholic schools in, 15, 88
    Charter schools in, 88
    faith schools in, 17, 88
    home schooling in, 88
    middle class in, 26
    private schools in, 17, 88
capability, 144, 150–1, 168, 169, 156,
        170–2, 178
    and agency, 175
    choice and non-choice factors
        in, 156
    and commodity, 148–51
    in communities, 176–7
    and enabling assets, 170, 171
    and freedom, 150–1, (positive and
        negative freedoms) 173
    inputs, 171
    and well-being, 143–51
capacity inventory, 170
Capita, 62
capital
    activated, 24
    economic / financial, 23, 39,
        (international) 72
    cultural, 23, 25, 26, (of middle
        class) 39, 70, 78, 85, 90, 137
    social, 23, 26, 37, 39, 85, 88
    symbolic, 78
capitalism, 6, 53, 54, 58, 59, 69, 82
catchment areas, 12, 26, 29, 49, 120,
        128, 130, 148, 171
    and admissions, 34
    and competitive arenas / spaces, 44,
        93–4
    freedom to go outside, 151, 168
    hierarchy within, 93
    and house prices, 128
    in the Netherlands, 37
    and risk, 92
    and working class, 37, 92
Catholic, *see under* faith schools
changing schools, *see* transition
Charter schools, 3–4, 5, 7, 20, 45,
        99, 125
    in Canada, 88
    and citizenship, 32
    and class size, 20
    and low-income families, 26

China (and GATS), 81
choice function, 152
citizenship
    and Catholic schools, 32
    and public schools (in USA), 32
    and sovereignty, 164
City Technology Colleges (UK), 83
class size, 20
    in Canada, 41
    in the Netherlands, 38
co-curricular, *see* extra-curricular
        activities
commodification (of education),
        see under education
commodities, 146, 155, 156, 160
    and capability, 148
    characteristics of, 155
    command of, 149, 161, 167
    as entitlements, 156
communitarianism, 63, 68–70
communities, 171
    assessment of, 175–8
    capability of, 176–7
    failing, 171
    low income, 170, 174–5
    regeneration of, 171–2, 174, 175–8
    teacher turnover in, 177
competition, 4, 5, 14, 31, 39, 41, 57,
        58, 59, 60, 62, 63, 77, 85, 89,
        93–4, 98, 101, 118, 120, 122,
        123, 172
    acting first in, 102
    arenas / spaces, 44, 93–4
    avoiding, 44
    in Canada, 88
    and collegiality, 112
    constructive, 111
    and cooperation, 100–5
    and curriculum diversity, 114–17
    and diversity, 120, 122, 136
    dynamics of, 111–12
    and efficiency, 101, 102, 113
    and employers, 134
    and failing schools, 98
    geographical nature of, 93
    and individualism, 59
    in Ireland, 95
    and markets, 56, 101
    and middle-class families, 87

in New Zealand, 103
and private schools, 20, 39, 76
public support for, 95
and pupil attainment, 102, 113
and school fees, 133
and school improvement, 104, 119
and schools as organisations, 118–22
and segregation, 133
self-reporting of, 101
and social class, 93
and teacher professionalism, 78
and transition to secondary school, 47
understanding, 104
Competition Act (1998) (UK), 103
competitive arenas / spaces, 93–4
completeness, 151, 157, 158–9, 166, 168
complete ordering, *see* completeness
compliance, 4, 5, 6, 7
culture of, 74
of workers, 138
Comprehensive schools, *see under* schools
Confederation of British Industry (CBI), 135
Conservative Party (UK), 4, 5, 59–62, 65, 83–5
consumers, 9, 10, 11, 13, 41, 45, 55, 56, 62, 71, 87, 101, 103, 105, 111, 112, 116, 138
analyses of, 161
children as, 70
and citizenship, 91
freedom of, 166
and middle-class families, 87
satisfaction of, 174
consumerism, *see* consumers
control (demarchical), 68–70
cooperation, 101, 172
and collusion, 103, 112
and competition, 100–5
of secondary schools with feeder primary schools, 103, 104
and league tables, 101
coopetition, 100, 104
coupling, 121

cultural capital, 11–12, 23–5, 70, 78, 137
culture, 8, 71, 104
of compliance, 74
and diversity, 75
and educational change, 57
and leadership, 76
and pressure on teachers, 121
professional, 76, 77
and school improvement, 73
and setting of schools, 72–3
uniformity of, 9
curriculum, 6, 7, 11, 56, 61, 73, 116, 120
14–19 (UK), 66
in Australia, 71
collusion about, 44
and competition, 114–17
diversity and conformity of, 20, 114–17
entrepreneurial, 62
as a factor in choice, 36
and falling rolls, 129
freedom of, 8
innovation in, 116
leisure, 70–1
National (UK), 60, 66, 75, 115
and opportunity, 148
options within, 23
and risk, 116
and markets, 114
specialist, 3, 15
study of religion within, 41
vocationally oriented, 115
customers, *see* consumers

data, *see* information
deficiency assessment, 176–8
demarchical control, 68–70
democracy, 53, 54, 62, 63, 64, 70, 98, 143
features of, 144
majority rule, 165
under threat, 72
denominational schools, see faith schools
deprivation, *see* underprivilege
desire fulfilment, 146, 152
desiredness, *see* desire fulfilment

developing countries (and GATS), 81
developmentalism, 59, 65
disadvantaged, *see* underprivilege
discipline (within schools), 23, 25, 43,
        48, 51, 129, 168
    as factor in school choice, 36, 37,
        (in the Netherlands) 38
diversity, 60, 63, 65, 75, 118, 119,
        120, 122, 136, 158, (parents
        avoiding) 172
dominance, 157

Edison, 62, 99
education,
    14–19 (UK), *see under* curriculum
    and change, 75–8
    commercial sector involvement
        in, 56
    commodification of, 55, 79, 85, 93,
        143, 155
    desirable properties of, 55, 148,
        155, 158
    discourse on, 57, 90, 125, 136
    and employers, 134–9
    expansion of (Further and
        Higher), 136
    and functionings, 156
    funding of, *see* funding
    and headship, 125
    learning from business, 136
    market command of, 155
    marketisation of, 93
    reconstruction of, 78
    and social democracy, 135
    state intervention in, 56, 58
    trade in, 55
    and training, 60, 61, 65, 66, 75,
        134, 134, 137, 138
    transnational, 81
    and triage, 122–3
    types of, 155
    values and aims of, 55, 62, 67, 71,
        75, 102, 104, 126, 135–6
    vocational, *see* training
    workplace training, 134, 136–8
Education Act (1944) (UK), 130
Education Act (2002) (UK), 85
Education Action Zones (UK), 61, 84,
        100, 123

Education Reform Act (1980) (UK), 7
Education Reform Act (1988) (UK), 7,
        29, 36, (and pupil
        achievement) 107–9, 128, 129,
        130, 131
Education Reform Act (1993) (UK),
        8, 124
eleven-plus examination (UK), 130
employers, 5, 60, 72, 75, 139
    accountability of, 134
    and compliance of workers, 138
    using Further Education
        colleges, 138
    and low skilled jobs, 137
    and marketisation of schools,
        134–9
    motivation of, 134
    and risk, 135
    and supply of skilled jobs, 135
    targets for, 137
    and vocational education, 134
employment, *see* jobs
empowering assessment, 176–8
enrolment, *see* admissions
enterprise, 93
    agenda and schools, 85
    and headteachers, 126, 127, 128
    social, 176
    state-induced, 83
entrepreneur, *see* entrepreneurialism
entrepreneurialism, 58, 62, 64, 73,
        (and headship) 76
entrepreneurship, *see* enterprise
ethnicity, 9, 10, 11, 14, 19, 30
    in Canada, 43
    and competition, 30
    and markets, 30
    in the Netherlands, 29, 37
    in Spain, 31
    and transition to secondary
        school, 46
    and voucher schemes, 30
European Union, 53, 77, (and free
        trade) 90
evaluation
    and aggregation, 163–9
    elementary, 168–9
    elementary capability, 168–9
    of well-being, 158–9, 163

examinations, 6, 8, 14, 36, 60, 75, 92, 104, 123, 129, 134
  in Australia, 71
  boards (UK), 106
  and boys, 50
  and curriculum, 115
  and effectiveness, 106
  and enrolment, 104
  GCSE (UK), 107–9
  and movement of pupils, 93
  and social deprivation, 73
Excellence in Cities (UK), 85, 100, 123
Excellence in Schools (White Paper, 1997) (UK), 84
expectations (of schools), 14, (of teachers) 45
expenditure, *see* funding
expert systems, 24, 25
extra-curricular activities, 70–1, 129

faith schools, 7, 10, 13–17, 93, 94, 130
  admissions to, 33
  in Canada, 41
  Catholic, 10, 15, 15, 32, 105, 105
  Islamic (in the Netherlands), 16, 27, 29, 30, 39
  in the Netherlands, 16, 37, 39
  in New Zealand, 16
  Protestant (in the Netherlands), 16
  and pupil attainment, 113
  and secularism, 15
  and transport (in UK), 27
families, 8, 10, 12, 42, 69, 174
  benevolent heads of, 161
  divisions within, 160–1
  extended, 19
  and generational decline, 90
  income of, 19
  and links to school and admissions, 34–5
  out of catchment, 131
  and risk, 86–9
  and support for funding of education, 95
  as units of consumption, 160
Finland, 6
fragmentation, *see* segregation
France, 10

Free School Meals (UK), 64, 109, 110, 113
free trade, 53, 79
  and financial capital, 72
  and European Union, 90
  and growth, 68
friends (in school), 42, 47, 50–1, 86, 122
functionings, 149–50, 155–8, 164, 168, 169, 172, 173, 178
  assessment of, 162, 164
  ranking of, 151
  and utility, 152–62
  valuing, 156–7, 158, 163
  variation in, 162
  and well-being, 155, 158, 163
funding (of education and schools), 11, 13, 14, 16, 60, 62, 73, 95, 96–9, 129, 171
  of Charter schools (USA), 99
  curriculum, 114, 116
  devolved to schools, 115, 116
  and diversity, 122
  and enrolment, 119, 131
  of faith schools in the Netherlands, 29
  for Specialist schools (UK), 61
  subsidies from government, 99, 102
Further Education colleges, *see under* schools
futures, 169

gender, 57, (and transition) 49–52
General Agreement on Trade in Services (GATS), *see under* trade agreements
General Agreement on Trade and Tariffs (GATT), *see under* trade agreements
General Teaching Council (UK), 61
geographical location, *see* catchment areas
Germany, 10, 126
Global Education Management Systems, 62
globalisation, 53–78, 81, 82
  and change, 73–8
  characteristics of, 53
  and colonisation, 71

globalisation, (*continued*)
  cosmopolitan, 63, 68
  effect on nation states, 68
  and leadership, 74
  local moderation of, 77
  and implications for children, 70
  pressures on emerging nations, 73
  sceptics, 56
  and school effectiveness, 72
  and school improvement, 71–3
  and teacher professionalism, 73–8
  trends, 71
Greenwich Judgement, 131
Gross Domestic Product (GDP), 144
Gross National Product (GNP), 144

habitus, 23, 24, 25, 87, 93
happiness, 146, 150, 173
heads, *see* headteachers
headship, *see* headteachers
headteachers, 8, 21, 40, 44, 66, 73,
      75, 105, 113, 121, 128–9
  as apparatchiks, 75
  and collegiality, 112
  and competition, 112–14
  and curriculum, 116
  and enterprise, 127–8
  externally imposed, 170–1
  and feeder schools, 129
  and globalisation, 78
  and informal networks, 117
  market-based models of, 74
  and markets, 125–8
  and New Labour (UK), 76
  professionalism of, 102, 112
  qualifications of, 61, 76
  types of, 125–6
  utility of, 21–2
  values of, 113
Herfindahl Index, 113
Holland, *see* Netherlands, the
home schooling, 15, 24, (in Canada) 88
homework, 51–2, 61
Hong Kong, (single parenthood in) 19
Human Development Index (HDI), 144

immigrant communities and choice,
      24, 29, 39, 68, 172
impossibility of the Paretian, 166

Improving the Quality of Education
      for All (IQEA), 172
independence of irrelevant
      alternatives, 164–5
information, 40–1, 86, 91, 92,
      119, 121
  and Arrow Impossibility, 166
  about assets, 177
  centres (in schools), 27
  ceremonial / symbolic, 121
  for choice, 9, 11, 19
  complete, 151
  from friends, 122
  hot and cold, 88, 158
  market purchase data,
      159–61
  questionnaire data, 159–61
  from school inspections, 171
  and self-selection among
      pupils, 134
  about transition to secondary
      school, 47
  and utility, 163–4
International Bank for Reconstruction
      and Development, *see* World
      Bank
International Monetary Fund (IMF),
      53, 79
internationalisation, see globalisation
internet, 70–1
invisible hand, 145
Ireland, 95
  gender and transition in, 49
  marketisation in, 95
  private schools in, 95
Islamic, *see under* faith schools

Japan (and GATS), 81
jobs, 54, 65, 72
  flexible, 75
  leaving school for, 66
  high-skilled, 54, 66, 75, (and
      employers) 135
  low-skilled, 54, 68, 137
  low-wage, 54, 72

K12 Inc., 99
knowledge society, 56
Knowledge Universe, 99

labour, free movement of, 68
Labour Party (UK), 4, 5, 33, 59–62, 65,
    66–8, 83–5, 131, (and school
    leadership) 76
leadership, 75 (*see also* headteachers)
  collaborative, 76
  commercial, 74
  and followership, 76
  limits to, 75
  under New Labour (UK), 76
  patristic, 76
  political context to, 77
  transactional, 74
  transformational, 73–7
league tables, 8, 34, 41, 60, 64, 75,
    84, 94, 100, 104, 122, 146,
    158, 172
  and cooperation, 101
  and curriculum, 114, 116
  and targets, 101
Learning and Skills Councils
    (UK), 136
legitimation, 57–8
liberalism
  and communitarianism, 63
  nineteenth century, 59
  social, 59
literacy, 13, 60, 70, 71, 76, 161
low-income (families), *see* working
    class

Manpower Services Commission
    (UK), 83
marginalised, *see* underprivileged
marketisation, 12, 26, 56, 58, 92,
    93–5, 118, 122
  and consumerism, 101
  and curriculum conformity, 114
  and disadvantage, 31
  and diversity, 119, 120
  and Education Reform Act (1988)
    (UK), 110
  and the middle class, 90
  and open enrolment, 101
  public support for, 95
  and pupil attainment, 105–11
  and resources, 105
  and school choice, 79–99
  and segregation, 30

markets, 8, 10–12, 20–5, 39, 40, 41,
    44, 58, 59, 68, 70, 72, 119
  characteristics of, 93
  and class reproduction strategies, 86
  and competition, 56, 62, 101
  creating, 6, 7
  culture of, 95
  discipline of, 95
  efficiency within, 98
  factions within, 102
  failure of, 59, 59
  fee-charging within, 133
  free, 60, 64, 68–71
  global, 53
  hierarchies within, 101, 114
  and headship, 125
  incentives within, 102
  and individualism, 122
  integrated, 68
  internal, 75
  local, 93–5, 101, 102, 104, 111–12,
    113, 114, 115, 117, 118, 122, 131
  mechanisms of, 58
  networked, 117
  neutral, 118
  niche, 112, 120
  number of providers in, 112, 113, 114
  oligopolistic, 111
  ontology of, 91
  and pupil attainment, 112
  purchase data from, 159–61
  and private schools, 113
  quasi-, 28, 44, 58, 60, 62, 100–5,
    112, 125
  reputation within, 117
  resistance to, 14
  responsiveness of, 76
  with restricted exit / entry, 111
  and risk, 89
  and school admissions, 33, 34
  and school improvement, 109
  school types in, 94
  and segregation, 129
  and self-regulation, 68
  skilled at choosing in, 37
  social consequences of, 60
  supply and demand in, 118, 125
  systems of, 91
  and triage, 122–3

mathematics, *see* numeracy
media (for pupils), 71
meritocracy, 57, 59
middle class, the, 4, 25, 28, 37, 39,
    40, 44, 70
  and competitive selection, 87
  concerns of, 168
  and curriculum, 116
  and expansion of education, 136
  formation and reproduction of, 23
  guilt of, 93
  and higher education, 28
  and hot information, 88
  and markets, 86–91
  norms of, 50
  professional class, 26
  and risk, 26, 87–90
  and segregation fears, 29
  social networks of, 41, 92
  sources available to, 40
  in Spain, 30
  and stress, 87
  and transition to secondary
    school, 45
  and triage, 123
mixed schools, *see under* schools
mobility (of student welfare and
    support), 70–1, 81
monotonicity, 164
Multilevel Agreement on Investment
    (MAI), 80
multinational companies, 69, 74, 75
Muslim schools, *see under* faith
    schools

nation states, *see* states
neo-capitalism, *see* capitalism
neo-conservatism, *see* neo-liberalism
neo-liberalism, 3–8, 58, 59, 62, 63, 64,
    65, 68, 73, 78, 86, 91,
    105, 166
  in Ireland, 95
  and risk, 90
Netherlands, the, 5, 10
  ethnic composition in, 37
  faith schools in, 16, 37
  Muslims in, 16, 39
  parental preference in, 37–8
  segregation in, 29, 37

  social class in, 37
  transport and convenience in, 27
New Labour Party (UK), *see* Labour
    Party (UK)
New Zealand, 6, 86
  competition between schools in, 103
  faith schools in, 16
  and GATS, 81
  selection by postcode in, 29
  Targeted Individual Entitlement
    Scheme in, 26
No Child Left Behind programme
    (USA), 27, 174
non-dictatorship, 164–5
non-imposition, 164
Nord Anglia, 62, 95
North American Free Trade
    Association (NAFTA), 53
numeracy, 13, 60, 71, 76, 161

Office of Fair Trading (OFT) (UK), 103
Office for Standards in Education
    (Ofsted) (UK), 75
opportunity, 5, 8, 169, 172
  and advantage, 147, 167
  and curriculum, 148
  observable features of, 144
opulence, 155, 167, (and market
    purchase data) 160–1
Organisation for Economic
    Cooperation and Development
    (OECD), 53, 66, 77

Parental and School Choice
    Interaction Study (PASCI), 100
parents, 6, 8–12, 13, 15, 36–45, 60,
    84, 94, 106, 110, 113, 114,
    115, 118, 124
  acting selfishly, 40
  agency of, 23
  anxieties / stress of, 47, 89
  avoiding diversity, 172
  and careers, 86
  and collusion, 112
  consulting with children, 41, 44, 50
  and consumerism, 100
  and criteria for choosing, 134
  and curriculum, 115–16
  as customers, 143

education of, 18, 19, 24, 25, 39
frustration (at reforms) of, 18
and funding of schools, 96–9
high-achieving, 24
involvement (in learning) of, 19, 24
involvement (in schools) of, 4, 20,
	21, 23, 39
networks of, 40
and open enrolment, 101
partial ordering by, 151
'particular' expectations of, 45
as rational fools, 147
rights of, 39
and risk, 86
satisfaction of, 32, 39, 42–3
seeking information, 40
and self-selection, 133–4
single (in Hong Kong) 19, (and
	voucher schemes) 26, (in the
	Netherlands) 29
and social class, 25
step-, 19
and support for marketisation, 95
and uncertainty, 167
and understanding competition,
	104
utility of, 21–2
values of, 40, 41, 42, 45, 46
Parents Charter (1991) (UK), 8
Pareto principle, 165–6
partial ordering, 151, 157, 158–9,
	163–4, 166, 168
participation rate (USA), 18
peer group, 132–3
performativity, 65–8
physical condition neglect, 154
pluralism, *see* democracy
position dependency, 158
postcodes (selection by), 12, 28, 29
premature fixity, 157
principals, *see* headteachers
principal-agent problem, 20–1, 102
private education, *see* private schools
private schools, 5, 7, 10–14, 18, 20, 39,
	40, 41, 61, 62, 64, 66, 94, 102,
	103, 108, 130, 132, 160, 168
abolition of, 96–7
and aspiration, 92
and boys, 50

in Canada, 17, 41, 88
and comparison with public
	schools, 108
competition between, 41
competition within, 76
and culture, 93
and disadvantage, 26
gender mix in, 50
and information, 40–1
in Ireland, 95
in local markets, 113
and middle class, 28
overseas branding of, 81
and protection from uncertainty,
	92, 168
and public mission, 98
and risk, 92
satisfaction with, 42–3
shared values in, 42
and social class / reproduction, 92
in Spain, 30
teachers in, 76
in USA, 128
vocational courses and, 67
work ethic within, 92
privatisation (of education), 8, 9, 54,
	55, 62, 97–9, 105
as threat to academic freedom, 81
of public services and GATS, 79
of risk, 92
professional class, *see* middle class
protectionism, 68
public-private partnerships, 59, 61,
	62, 65, 82–5, 95–8, 127–8, 136
public services
definition in GATS, 80
ethic, 98, 105, 112, 113
and headship, 126–7
pupil teacher ratio, 20
pupils, 8, 10, 15, 48, 113, 114, 118
absenteeism of, 19
attainment of, 3, 11, 13, 17, 18, 19,
	(and competition) 102, (and
	markets) 105–12, 113,
	(Education Reform Act, 1988)
	107–9
ambition of, 18, 154, 174
appearance and demeanour of,
	43, 51

pupils, (*continued*)
  assessment of, 75
  and careers, 86, 173
  conduct of, 122
  confidence of, 42, 45
  as customers, 143
  distribution of, 19
  enthusiasm of, 19
  expectations of, 104, 154,
    156, 160
  failing, 122
  and friends, 42, 47, 50–1
  happiness of, 173
  and the internet, 70–1
  media for, 71
  motivation of, 160, 168
  movement of, 93, 125, 168
  and open enrolment, 101
  and peers, 50, 132, 167, 173
  and relationship to teachers, 74
  retention of, 66–7
  in rural areas, 19, 26, 27
  and school income, 75
  segregation of, 105
  selection of, 9, 28, 122, 129–30
  selflessness of, 147
  self-interest achievement of, 149
  self-selection of, 14, 132–4
  and social class (in the
    Netherlands), 38–9
  social relationships of, 173
  streaming / grouping of, 23, 73
  stress in transition of, 49–50
  support for selection on ability
    of, 97
  targeting by schools of, 44, 94,
    110, 116
  and transition to secondary school,
    45–9
  triage of, 123
  well-being of, 149, 153
  and welfarist headship, 126
  in urban areas, 19, 26, 27, 30

qualifications, 26, 67, 82, 85, 106,
  108, 135
  and employers, 137
  and skills, 135, 137–8
questionnaire data, 159–61

race, *see* ethnicity
ranking, 151, 153–4, 158–9
  of commodity sets, 160
  and complete ordering, *see*
    completeness
  and completeness, 151, 157, 158–9,
    166, 168
  and dominance, 157
  and partial ordering, 151, 157,
    158–9, 163–4,
    166, 168
  and position dependency, 158
  and social preference, 165
rational choice, 8, 40, 87, 118,
  119, 121
rational fools, 147
reading, *see* literacy
religion, *see* faith schools
residential segregation,
  see postcodes
responsiveness (of schools), *see under*
  schools
risk, 24, 86–7, 135
  awareness of, 86
  calculus of, 85–93
  commodification of, 92
  cultivating, 89
  and curriculum, 116
  and employers, 135
  and involvement of commercial
    companies in schools, 99
  and markets, 59, 89
  and middle class, 26, 87–91
  and private schools, 92, 168
  and social class / reproduction, 90,
    91, 92
  society, 86
  and tradition, 93
  during transition to secondary
    school, 45, 47
  and teachers, 127
Roman Catholic, *see under* faith
  schools

satisfaction (and utility), 146
School Inspections Act (1996)
  (UK), 124
School Standards and Framework Act
  (1998) (UK), 33, 131

schools, 11, 40, 41, 44, 56, 63, 64, 66, 67, 69, 70, 73, 94, 113
    academic integrity of, 55
    Academy (UK), 61
    adding value in, 102, 103, 117
    Beacon (UK), 85, 100
    boarding, 33, 102
    built environment of, 43
    business agenda in, 85
    Charter, *see under* Charter schools
    closure of, 124–5, 169
    collusion between, 44
    commercial activities in, 55, 61
    comparison of, 37, 59, 105, 177
    and competition, 89, 93–4, 100, 120
    Comprehensive (UK), 12, 29, 64, 91, 106, 130
    and conformity, 119, 121
    cosmetic changes in, 120
    and the curriculum, 115–17
    and culture, 71
    dealing with transition, 46, 50–2
    discipline within, 129
    drop-out rates from, 58
    effectiveness of, 66, 72, 77, 84
    efficiency of, 119, 121
    and employers, 138
    establishing new (in the Netherlands), 37
    ethos of, 38, 129, 160, 168
    and external help, 171
    facing challenging circumstances, 170, 176
    failing, 120, 61, 98, 120, 122, 170, 171, 176, 177
    faith, *see* faith schools
    fee paying, *see* private schools
    feeder, 125, 129
    freedom and agency in, 172–5
    Further Education colleges, 67, 83
    funding of, *see* funding
    goals of, 21, 83
    Grammar (UK), 67, 106
    hierarchy of, 93–5
    improvement of, 39, 41, 71–3, 95, 104, 107, 117–19, 127, 128, 170, 175–8
    individualism in, 172
    inspection of, 75–7, 175–8
    international comparisons of, 72
    isomorphic, 119, 120
    leadership of and within, *see* leadership
    local, *see* neighbourhood
    local management of, 60, 129
    mixed, 49–50
    neighbourhood, 4, 6, 8, 12, 21, 24, 25, 27, 29, 41, 49, 50
    networks of, 117, 125
    organisation of (and choice), 118–22
    partnerships, 123
    popularity of, 103, 104, 106, 132
    private, *see* private schools
    pupil attainment in, *see under* pupils
    and pupil intake, 89
    recruiting, 31
    re-culturing, 78
    regeneration of, 171
    rejecting, 43
    reputation of, 36, 38, 41–2, 43, 44, 89, 119
    residual, 123
    responsiveness of, 3, 4, 11, 13, 39, 100, 118, (symbolic) 120
    selective, 31, 94, 131
    single sex, 50, 113
    sixth form colleges, 67
    social and ethnic mix in, 89
    spare capacity in, 113
    in special measures (UK), 124
    Specialist (UK), (admissions to) 33–5, 61, 85, 89, 100, 104, 111, 148
    spiral of decline of, 32
    sponsorship of, 61
    structure and norms within, 119
    targeting of pupils by, 44, 110
    testing within, 60, 66
    and triage, 122–3
    in urban areas, 94, 104
    William Tyndale, 57
    and working-class pupils, 48
secularism, *see under* faith schools

segregation, 28–32, 39, 132
  by ability, 132–3
  and eleven-plus examination
    (UK), 130
  in the Netherlands, 37
  residential, 130
  and school admissions, 129–32
selection (*see also* admissions), 60,
    65, 73
  academic, 35
  by mortgage, 28, 110
  for Specialist schools (UK), 35, 61
self-interest, 144, 147–9
  rationality of, 145
  and utility, 146
  and well-being, 147
separation (of church and state), 7
single peaked preference, 165
single-sex schools, *see under* schools
sixth form colleges, *see under* schools
skills, 60–1, 67, 69, 71, 75, 76, 134–5,
    137, 138
  context-based, 137
  future demand for, 135, 136
social benefits, 54
social capability, 55
social capital, 63, 65, 88, 96, 151
social choice theory, 143–6
social class, 10, 12, 19, 23, 37, 39, 44,
    57, 63, 90, 113, 132
  asset-based approach to, 25
  and attitude to education, 25
  and competition, 93
  and culture, 25
  in the Netherlands, 37
  and risk, 23–6, 92
  and self-selection, 134
  and educational triage, 123
  and transition to secondary
    school, 46
social cohesion, 57
social contract, 83
social democracy, 59, 60, 62, 63, 64,
    65, 76
social demotion, 26
social deprivation, 144, 148
social dilemmas, 146
social division, *see* social segregation
social entrepreneurship, 176

social guilt (of the middle class), 93
social inclusion, 59, 67, 136
social inequality, (and risk) 10
social legitimacy, 119, 120
social liberalism, 59
social mobility, 9, 25, 26, 105
social polarisation, *see* social
    segregation
social position, (and risk) 86
social preference ordering, 165
social purposes, 56
social regulation, 68
social relationships, 170, 173
social reproduction, 86, 90, 91, 92
social security, 138
social segregation, 4, 10, 12–14, 28–30
social status, 23
social stratification, *see* social
    segregation
social well-being, 54
society, (knowledge) 56, 67, 119,
    164–5
  and employers, 139
South Africa, 49
Spain, 10, 30
spatial mobility, 28
special educational needs, 20, 23,
    (and admissions) 36
special measures (UK), *see under*
    schools
Specialist schools (UK), *see under*
    schools
spending, *see* funding
states, 53, 56, 63, 64, 69
  agency of, 56–65, 69
  agentic, 56, 61–2
  capitalist, 58
  decline of, 72, 74, 78
  developing, 57
  effects of globalisation on, 68
  intervention by, 58, 59
  and legitimation, 57
  and markets, 82–5
  partnerships with markets, *see*
    public-private partnerships
  regulation by, 68–71, 72, 73
  types of, 82
  welfare, 58, 63, 64, 66, 82, 84, 91
  well-being of, 82

streaming, 23
Structural Adjustment Programmes, 79
Sweden, (private education in) 56

targets, 74, 84
taxes, 57, 58, 72, 74, 75, 97–8
teachers, 4, 7, 40, 43, 50, 170–1
    agency of, 78
    classroom preparation by, 20
    and competition, 76
    cultural pressures on, 121
    and entrepreneurship, 127
    'general' expectations of, 45
    and globalisation, 77
    incentives for, 172
    and opposition to marketisation,
        95, 97
    pay and conditions of, 66
    performance related pay for,
        21, 76
    professionalism of, 73–8, 101, 102,
        103, 112, 121
    re-culturing of, 127
    and relationship to pupils, 74
    and risk-taking, 127
    and school closures, 125
    shortages of, 58, 59, 61
    training of, 121
    and transition, 47, 48
    turnover in poor communities
        of, 177
    utility of, 22–3
    working effort and hours, 20,
        21–3
tests, *see* examinations
Thailand, 81
trade agreements
    and their effects on education, 53–6
    General Agreement on Trade in
        Services (GATS), 54–5,
        79–81, 90
    General Agreement on Trade and
        Tariffs (GATT), 54
    Trade-Related Intellectual Property
        Rights (TRIPS), 80
trade unions, 138
training, *see under* education
transferring, *see* transition
transformationalists, 56

transition (from primary to secondary
        school), 18, 43
    and admissions, 125
    cost of, 21–2
    and ethnicity, 46
    and gender, 49–52
    and hierarchy of selection, 48
    in Ireland, 49
    psychodynamic of, 45–9
    risks and dangers of, 45
transitivity, 165
transnationals, *see* multinationals
transport, 8, 11, 18, 41, 49, 125, 151,
        173, 174–5
    and admissions, 35
    cost of, 51
    to extra-curricular activities 70–1
    funding own, 44
    in Massachucetts, 27
    in Minnesota, 27
    in the Netherlands, 27
    in New York, 27
    and poor pupils, 27
    and rural pupils, 26
    in United Kingdom, 27
    and urban pupils, 27
    and working-class pupils, 49
triage, 122–3
Tyndale, William (school), 57

uncertainty, 167–9
underprivileged (pupils), 5, 8, 9, 10,
        11, 54, 61, 63, 72 (*see also*
        working class)
    and educational achievement, 73
    and open enrolment, 111
    and marketisation, 31
United Kingdom, 4, 5, 7, 8, 9, 12, 14,
        19, 57, 59, 61, 62, 65, 71, 82,
        89, 92, 95, 98, 113, 148,
        174, 175
    Afro-Caribbean pupils in, 17
    Assisted Places Scheme, 7, 26
    Black Africans in, 17
    catchment areas in, 26
    community regeneration in, 172
    curriculum in, 18, 114–15
    enrolment in, 105, 125, 130
    examination boards in, 106

United Kingdom, (*continued*)
  and GATS, 81
  gender and transition in, 49
  higher education policies in, 149
  localised markets in, 100–1
  private schools in, 103
  public-private partnerships in, 128
  retention of pupils in, 66
  role of schools in, 124
  secularism in, 15
  socialism in, 60
  school closures in, 124
  school effectiveness research in, 72
  school leadership in, 74–5
  school transport in, 27
  single sex schools in, 50
United Nations (UN), 53, (Financial
    and Economic Conference) 79
United States of America, 3, 6–8, 10,
    12, 13, 15, 20, 62, 113, 115,
    128, 138, 175, 176
  African-American values in, 46
  bus routes in, 174
  Charter schools in, 99, 125
  childcare in, 174
  commercial involvement in schools
    in, 99
  community regeneration in, 172, 174
  ethnic communities in, 93
  Euro-American values in, 46
  and GATS, 81
  local incentives in, 93
  No Child Left Behind, 27
  participation rates in, 18
  private schools in, 128
  religion in schools in, 15
  school effectiveness research in, 72
  states and cities within
    Arizona, 20
    California, 19
    Cleveland, 7
    Dayton, 13
    Detroit, 30, 93
    Florida, 7
    Massachusetts, 18, 27
    Michigan, 20
    Milwaukee, 7
    Minnesota, 18, 27, 128
    New York, 7, 27
    North Carolina, 7, 13
    Texas, 20
    Washington DC, 7, 13
    Wisconsin, 7
  supreme court (Zelman v.
    Simmons-Harris), 7
  transition to secondary school
    in, 46
  voucher schemes in, 83, 92, 125
  Welfare to Work schemes, 65
utilisation functions, 149, 156
utility, 67, 95, 146–7
  approaches to, 152–5
  as desire fulfilment, 146, 152–3,
    163, 167
  and functionings, 152–62
  of headteachers, 21–2
  information on, 163
  interpersonal comparisons of,
    163, 167
  and market purchase data,
    159–61
  maximising, 40
  of parents, 21–2, 122
  real-valued approach to, 152
  as satisfaction / happiness, 146,
    152–3, 163, 167
  of teachers, 22–3
  and well-being, 146
universality, 165
unrestricted domain, 164–5

valuation function, 163, 166
valuation neglect, 154
value-added, *see* added value
vested interests (in education), 4
vocational training, *see under*
    education
voucher programmes, 7, 14, 83, 97,
    98, 125, 133
  and ethnicity (USA), 26, 30
  in Sweden, 56

wealth, 57, 63, (distribution of)
    68, 82 (*see also* capital,
    financial), 170
welfare function, 164–5
Welfare to Work schemes, 65
welfarism, 77

well-being, 69, 82, 172–3, 178
  and achievement, 167
  and advantage, 147–8, 169
  aggregation of, 163–4
  and capability, 143–51
  as choice, 153
  as evaluation, 150
  and functionings, 149, 157, 158
  as index of functionings, 155
  influences on, 144
  interpersonal variation in, 159
  measurement of, 159–62
  as opulence, 155
  self-assessment of, 161
  and self-interest, 147
  and utility, 146, 154, 157
  valuing, 158–9, 166
'white flight'
  in the Netherlands, 29
  in USA and UK, 43
William Tyndale (school), 57
work, *see* jobs
work-based learning, *see*
    apprenticeships
work effort, 21–1
workforce, 66, 67, 75
working class, the, 5, 6, 7, 10, 17, 18,
    25, 26, 93

  and disconnected parents, 37
  in Canada, 17
  and cold information, 88
  and concerns about
    teachers, 44
  cost of travel for, 51
  and enrolment, 124
  and family ties, 49
  and fatalism, 87–8
  and the geographical convenience
    of schools, 38
  girls from, 50–2
  and homework, 51–2
  and local schools, 49
  and self-selection, 134
  social activities of, 52
  social networks of, 50
  and transition to secondary school,
    46, 48
  and triage, 123
World Bank, 53, 56, 79
World Trade Organisation
    (WTO), 79

Youth Training Schemes (UK), 83

Zelman v. Simmons-Harris
    (US supreme court), 7